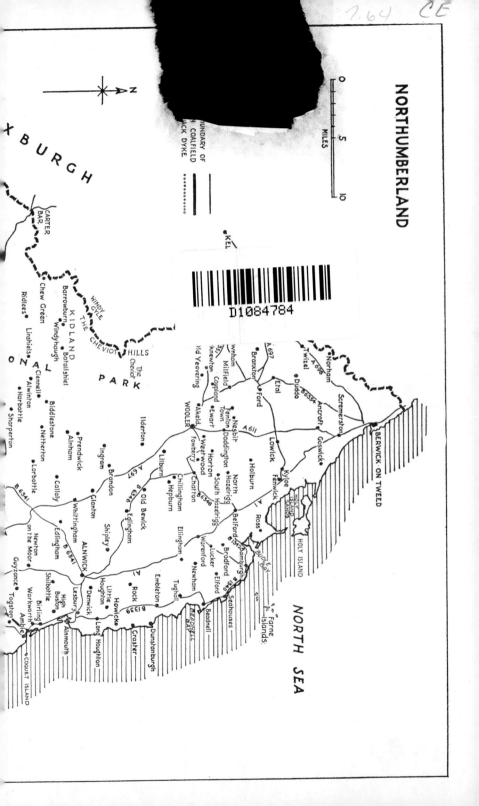

NORTHUMBERLAND

NORTH SEA

THE MAKING OF THE ENGLISH
LANDSCAPE

THE NORTHUMBERLAND LANDSCAPE

THE MAKING OF THE ENGLISH LANDSCAPE
Edited by W. G. Hoskins

The Making of the English Landscape, W. G. Hoskins
West Riding of Yorkshire, Arthur Raistrick
Dorset, Christopher Taylor

Forthcoming Volumes
The Shropshire Landscape, Trevor Rowley
The Oxfordshire Landscape, Frank Emery
The Suffolk Landscape, Norman Scarfe

THE MAKING OF THE ENGLISH LANDSCAPE

The Northumberland Landscape

by

ROBERT NEWTON

HODDER AND STOUGHTON

LONDON   SYDNEY   AUCKLAND   TORONTO

Universitas
BIBLIOTHECA
ttav ensis

DA
670
.N8N4
1972

Copyright © 1972 by Robert Newton. First printed 1972. ISBN 0 340 02885 8. All rights reserved. No part of this publication may be reproduced or transmitted in any form or by any means, electronic or mechanical, including photocopying, recording, or any information storage and retrieval system, without permission in writing from the publisher. Printed in Great Britain for Hodder and Stoughton Limited, St. Paul's House, Warwick Lane, London, EC4P 4AH by The Camelot Press Limited, London and Southampton

To

JILL

For her share of rigs, drove roads and sea-frets

Author's Acknowledgments

I SHOULD LIKE, above all, to express my appreciation of the invariable kindness and courtesy of the farmers, farm workers and shepherds of my native county which my wife and I experienced during the making of this book.

I am grateful to His Grace the Duke of Northumberland for facilities to examine the Percy Estate maps in Alnwick Castle, and for permission to make the photographic copies from which Figures 8, 14 and 16 have been reproduced; and to Mr David Graham, of Alnwick Castle Estate Office, for his advice and help. My thanks are due to Mr John Hope, Senior Warden of the Northumberland National Park, for putting his local knowledge so readily at my disposal, and particularly for his assistance in the exploration of Border tracks and the plotting of the position of ridge-and-furrow and cultivation terraces shown at Figure 5.

I have received much advice and guidance from Mr Robin Gard and his staff of the Northumberland County Record Office; from Professor G. W. S. Barrow, Dr Constance Fraser, the late Mr Percy Hedley, Mr George Jobey, Mr Edward Miller, Mr Douglas Percy, Mr Godfrey Watson and Mr A. J. Woodcock. I am much indebted to Mr Robert Cowper for putting his extensive knowledge of Northumbrian drove roads at my disposal. To all these I am grateful and I wish to express my thanks particularly to Mr Roland Herdman, of Hexham, for the patience and skill which he devoted to the many photographs he has provided for the book and for the photograph of Shillmoor reproduced on the cover.

The debt owed to the contributors to the *Northumberland County History* and to *Archaeologia Aeliana* will be apparent but is none the less gratefully acknowledged. For reasons of history the details of the formation of the Northumbrian landscape, until the relatively recent past, are still little known, though knowledge is now being accumulated by modern archaeological methods. In consequence the author must take responsibility for statements based on reasonable probability rather than on demonstrated fact.

Contents

List of Plates

ACKNOWLEDGMENTS

The author wishes to thank the following for permission to
use their photographs:
Philipson Studios, Newcastle: Plates 1, 3, 4, 7, 10, 11, 14,
15, 17, 22, 25, 30, 34, 36, 38
Northumberland County Council: Plates 2, 19, 23, 31, 32, 33
Roland Herdman: Plates 5, 6, 8, 9, 12, 16, 18, 20, 24, 26,
27, 28, 35
V. Blankenburgs: Plates 13, 37
John Dewar Studios: Plate 21
Blyth Harbour Commission: Plate 29 (copyright reserved)

List of maps and plans

Editor's Introduction

SOME SIXTEEN YEARS ago I wrote: "Despite the multitude of books about English landscape and scenery, and the flood of topographical books in general, there is not one book which deals with the historical evolution of the landscape as we know it. At the most we may be told that the English landscape is the man-made creation of the seventeenth and eighteenth centuries, which is not even a quarter-truth, for it refers only to country houses and their parks and to the parliamentary enclosures that gave us a good deal of our modern pattern of fields, hedges, and by-roads. It ignores the fact that more than a half of England never underwent this kind of enclosure, but evolved in an entirely different way, and that in some regions the landscape had been virtually completed by the eve of the Black Death. No book exists to describe the manner in which the various landscapes of this country came to assume the shape and appearance they now have, why the hedgebanks and lanes of Devon should be so totally different from those of the Midlands, why there are so many ruined churches in Norfolk or so many lost villages in Lincolnshire, or what history lies behind the winding ditches of the Somerset marshlands, the remote granite farmsteads of Cornwall, and the lonely pastures of upland Northamptonshire.

"There are indeed some good books on the geology that lies behind the English landscape, and these represent perhaps the best kind of writing on the subject we have yet had, for they deal with facts and are not given to the sentimental and formless slush which afflicts so many books concerned only with superficial appearances. But the geologist, good though he may be, is concerned with only one aspect of the subject, and beyond a certain point he is obliged to leave the historian and geographer to continue and complete it. He explains to us the bones of the landscape, the fundamental structure that gives form and colour to the scene and produces a certain kind of topography and natural vegetation. But the flesh that covers the bones, and the details of the features, are the concern of the historical geographer, whose task it is to show how man has clothed the geological skeleton during the comparatively recent past—most within the last fifteen centuries, though in some regions much longer than this."

In 1955 I published *The Making of the English Landscape*. There I claimed that it was a pioneer study, and if only for that reason it could not supply the answer to every question. Four books, in a series published between 1954 and 1957, filled in more detail for the counties of Cornwall, Lancashire, Gloucestershire, and Leicestershire.

Much has been achieved since I wrote the words I have quoted. Landscape-history is now taught in some universities, and has been studied for many parts of England and Wales in university theses. Numerous articles have been written and a few books published, such as Alan Harris's *The Rural Landscape of the East Riding 1700–1850* (1961) and more recently Dorothy Sylvester's *The Rural Landscape of the Welsh Borderland* (1969).

Special mention should perhaps be made of a number of landscape-studies in the series of Occasional Papers published by the Department of English Local History at the University of Leicester. Above all in this series one might draw attention to *Laughton: a study in the Evolution of the Wealden Landscape* (1965) as a good example of a microscopic scrutiny of a single parish, and Margaret Spufford's *A Cambridgeshire Community (Chippenham)* published in the same year. Another masterly study of a single parish which should be cited particularly is Harry Thorpe's monograph entitled *The Lord and the Landscape*, dealing with the Warwickshire Parish of Wormleighton, which also appeared in

1965.[1] Geographers were quicker off the mark than historians in this new field, for it lies on the frontiers of both disciplines. And now botany has been recruited into the field, with the recent development of theories about the dating of hedges from an analysis of their vegetation.

But a vast amount still remains to be discovered about the man-made landscape. Some questions are answered, but new questions continually arise which can only be answered by a microscopic examination of small areas even within a county. My own perspective has enlarged greatly since I published my first book on the subject. I now believe that some features in our landscape today owe their origin to a much more distant past than I had formerly thought possible. I think it highly likely that in some favoured parts of England farming has gone on in an unbroken continuity since the Iron Age, perhaps even since the Bronze Age; and that many of our villages were first settled at the same time. In other words, that underneath our old villages, and underneath the older parts of these villages, there may well be evidence of habitation going back for some two or three thousand years. Conquests only meant in most places a change of landlord for better or for worse, but the farming life went on unbroken, for even conquerors would have starved without its continuous activity. We have so far failed to find this continuity of habitation because sites have been built upon over and over again and have never been wholly cleared and examined by trained archaeologists.

At the other end of the time-scale the field of industrial archaeology has come into being in the last few years, though I touched upon it years ago under the heading of Industrial Landscapes. Still, a vast amount more could now be said about this kind of landscape.

Purists might say that the county is not the proper unit for the study of landscape-history. They would say perhaps that we ought to choose individual and unified regions for

---

[1] *Transactions of the Birmingham Archaeological Society*, Vol. 80, 1965.

such an exercise; but since all counties, however small, contain a wonderful diversity of landscape, each with its own special history, we get, I am sure, a far more appealing book than if we adopted the geographical region as our basis.

The authors of these books are concerned with the ways in which men have cleared the natural woodlands, reclaimed marshland, fen, and moor, created fields out of a wilderness, made lanes, roads, and footpaths, laid out towns, built villages, hamlets, farmhouses and cottages, created country houses and their parks, dug mines and made canals and railways, in short with everything that has altered the natural landscape. One cannot understand the English landscape and enjoy it to the full, apprehend all its wonderful variety from region to region (often within the space of a few miles), without going back to the history that lies behind it. A commonplace ditch may be the thousand-year-old boundary of a royal manor; a certain hedge-bank may be even more ancient, the boundary of a Celtic estate; a certain deep and winding lane may be the work of twelfth-century peasants, some of whose names may be made known to us if we search diligently enough. To discover these things, we have to go to the documents that are the historian's raw material, and find out what happened to produce these results and when, and precisely how they came about.

But it is not only the documents that are the historian's guide. One cannot write books like these by reading someone else's books, or even by studying records in a muniment room. The English landscape itself, to those who know how to read it aright, is the richest historical record we possess. There are discoveries to be made in it for which no written documents exist, or have ever existed. To write the history of the English landscape requires a combination of documentary research and of fieldwork, of laborious scrambling on foot wherever the trail may lead. The result is a new kind of history which it is hoped will appeal to all those who like to travel intelligently, to get away from the guide-book show-pieces now and then, and to know the reasons behind what they are looking at. There is no part of England, however unpromising it may appear at first sight, that is not full of questions for those who have a sense of the past. So much of England is still unknown and unexplored. Fuller enjoined us nearly three centuries ago

"Know most of the rooms of thy native country
before thou goest over the threshold thereof.
Especially seeing England presents thee with
so many observables."

These books on The Making of the English Landscape are concerned with the observables of England, and the secret history that lies behind them.

Exeter, 1970   W. G. HOSKINS

1. The Northumbrian scene

A LAND OF SPACE, contrast and diversity, swept by winds off the moorlands and the sea, Northumberland "is the land of far horizons, where the piled and drifted shapes of gathered vapour are for ever moving along the farthest ridges of the hills, like the succession of long primeval ages, that is written in tribal mounds and Roman camps and Border towers".[1]

It is the shipyards of Wallsend and the collieries of Ashington and Lynemouth. It is the Cheviot plateau, where the cloudberry grows among the moss-hags. It is the dour Walker road and the long ridges of Redesdale; the treeless hedges of the coastal plain and the wooded banks of the Coquet. It is the arable farms of Tweedside, and the wet fells where grouse and golden plover call among the debris of lead-mining on the high roof of the Pennines. It is Whitley Bay; and the Holy Island of St Aidan and St Cuthbert, once the hearthstone of Christianity in the North.

By nature, and in historical origins, the land between the Tyne and the Firth of Forth is one. The Border is a political boundary marking the limits of the power of medieval kings. The Tyne is a frontier, as the Tweed is not. The traveller from the South, crossing the windy uplands of Tow Law or the high Alston Moors, looks across the Tyne to a landscape which is different in form and character from the Pennine Fells. Even today, Newcastle seen from Gateshead appears dramatically as a frontier gate.

The modern county, fifth among the English counties in area, second only to Yorkshire in the number of its sheep, was the last to acquire its modern administrative form. It was not till 1844 that County Durham surrendered the ancient patrimony of St Cuthbert: Islandshire, comprising

[1] G. M. Trevelyan, 'The Middle Marches', *Clio, A Muse* (1930), p. 19.

Holy Island and the chapelries of Lowick, Kyloe, Ancroft and Tweedmouth; Bedlingtonshire; and Norhamshire. Until the end of the fifteenth century Tynedale and Redesdale formed an independent franchise; in the reign of Elizabeth I a section of Dere Street could still be regarded as the boundary between Northumberland and Redesdale. The archbishops of York exercised somewhat ineffectual power over the regality of Hexhamshire until 1572.

In shape Northumberland is a rough triangle. Its base is the Tyne, with a projection into the Pennines to the point where three counties meet on Killhope Law at a height of over 2000 feet above Allendale Common. Here, in good conditions, the view takes in the whole of the north borderland of England, mile after mile across the long ridges to Cheviot and the Solway.

At the apex of the triangle the western boundary begins north of Berwick, following the Tweed to a point west of Carham, then turning south-east to cross the Bowmont and to climb to a height of 2400 feet on Cheviot. From Cheviot the boundary follows the ridge which forms the watershed between the Tweed and the Northumbrian rivers, Coquet, Rede and Tyne. At Scots Knowe, where the new forest of Kielder sweeps over the smooth slopes of the Border fells and flows down into Liddesdale, the line turns south. It makes for the Irthing, passing through moorlands which were for centuries a debatable land, the wildest, wettest and most trackless area of the Border. Bending eastwards, to leave Gilsland in Cumberland, the boundary crosses the gap where the Roman Wall, the road and the railway converge on the way to Carlisle. Thence it climbs the northern bastions of the Pennines up through the wide fell pastures, through the cotton grass, heather and blaeberry, handed from one height to another of the fells between the South Tyne and the Eden.

The eastern boundary is the coast, a succession of stretches of sand and links broken by rocky headlands, and guarded at either end by the fortresses of Berwick and Tynemouth. Offshore in the north, Holy Island curves across the front of the wide flats of mud and sand which form the coast from Goswick to Budle Bay. South lie the Farnes. Off the mouth of the Coquet, St Mary's Island, more hospitable to human settlement, stands up from the sea opposite Amble.

The whole county is tilted towards the North Sea. Along the western boundary the general level is well over 1000 feet, and much of it over 2000. The continuous belt of high fell and moorland from the Border to Cross Fell is broken only by the Tyne Gap between Haltwhistle and Gilsland, a pass of immemorial age through which the glaciers once carried rock from the Lake District. The foothills of the Cheviots form a relatively narrow belt of land between 400 and 500 feet.

South of the Coquet the intermediate zone widens to form the central highland belt of Northumberland, a wide grazing country for cattle and sheep extending diagonally from near Longhorsley to Thirlwall Common across the North Tyne.

The coastal plain lies below the 200-foot contour, approximately the line of the Great North Road through Morpeth, Alnwick and Belford. It is widest in the south, between Newcastle and Morpeth; and in the north, where it is carried westwards by the Tweed, and south from Tweedside into Glendale. In the centre, south of Alnwick, it is reduced to a narrow strip little more than a mile wide.

The tidy pattern of descending heights from west to east is broken by the Fell Sandstone ridge, which curves north-east and north, from its junction with the highlands near Elsdon, to form the heather moorland and crags of Rothbury Forest, Chillingham and Kyloe, a barrier pierced by the Aln and the Coquet (Fig. 1).

The climate is bracing; the bitter north-east winds in March and April delay the spring. Snow lasts long on the

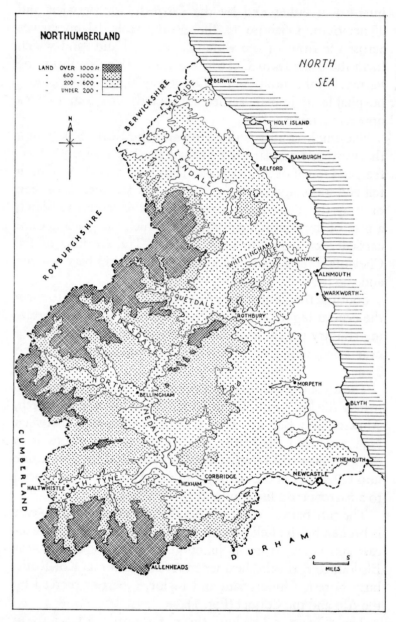

Fig. 1. Relief.

hills at an altitude of over 800 feet and can persist until June on Cheviot in the deep northward-facing chasm known as the Henhole. Snowstorms in May are not unusual and can cause heavy losses among flocks. The rainfall declines with the general slope from west to east, from an average of sixty inches along the Border hills and the Pennines of the south-west to twenty-five inches along the coast. With a light rainfall wheat grows well on the heavy soils of the Boulder Clay; arable farming has long been concentrated along the coastal plain on Tweedside and in Glendale. Over the greater part of the county the annual rainfall does not normally exceed thirty-five inches; deep peat bogs, the 'flows' and 'mosses' of the North, are relatively few in number and small in area. There are bogs in the Cheviots, as on the plateau summit of Cheviot itself, among the Pennines of the south-west, and especially along the upper reaches of the Irthing.

Rural Northumberland is pastoral country, as it has been since before the Romans (Fig. 2). In 1966 the county contained over 1,100,000 sheep and over 241,000 cattle. Over 307,000 acres are under permanent grass, and over 434,000 acres are rough grazings. In 1966, 144,000 acres were under corn, principally barley. Over eighty per cent of the population is concentrated in the south-eastern corner of the county; and Newcastle for centuries has been the only town of any significance, even by medieval standards. Berwick did not pass finally into English hands until 1482, its prosperity wrecked by war.

The creation of the modern landscape by man has necessarily evolved within the geological framework. The Cheviots emerged some 350 million years ago. Earthquakes and volcanic eruptions threw up lava and rocks, which were swept down to form in due course the rounded, grassy hills spread out like a fan around Cheviot itself; the hills behind Wooler, Ingram, Alnham and Alwinton. The harder granitic rocks remained to form the higher fell tops, with

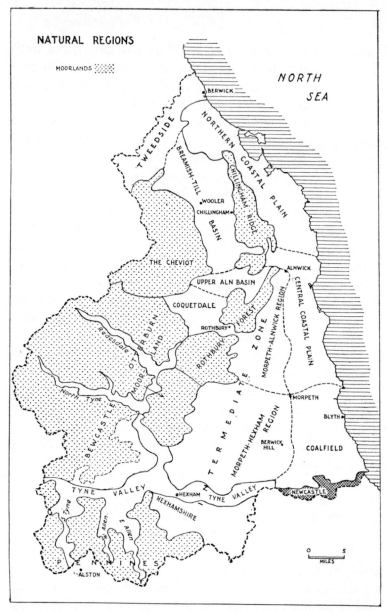

Fig. 2. Land use of natural regions. The large areas of moorland and hill pasture include the predominantly grass-covered Cheviots and Otterburn moorlands, the wet heather and cotton grass of the Pennines and, on the east the Fell Sandstone heather moorlands of the Chillingham Ridge and Rothbury Forest. All are very sparsely inhabited. The Intermediate Zone is primarily grazing country, though the Morpeth–Hexham region contains a high proportion of deserted medieval village sites (see Fig. 11) and ancient ploughlands. There is 'dale type' dairy farming in the Allendales. Tweedside and the north of the Breamish–Till basin (Glendale) is the main arable area. The bulk of Northumberland's population is concentrated in the area marked coalfield.

their sour soil favoured by blaeberry, cloudberry and the purple moor-grass, as on Cheviot and Hedgehope.

A primordial river flowing from the north washed down enormous quantities of sand which, under pressure through the aeons, formed the Fell Sandstone, the raw material of the heather moorlands of Rothbury, Chillingham and Kyloe with their characteristic crags. This sandstone composed the ridge which forced the rivers of Glendale to run north to the Tweed, thus influencing medieval strategy and the siting of famous castles. It provided the well-known building stone of Doddington.

Mud and sand eroded from the Cheviots, and combining, in later epochs of clear warm seas, with the lime of marine organisms, formed the Cementstones, an easily eroded rock which is the foundation of the low hills of Whittingham Vale and was sufficiently soft to enable the Aln to cut its way east to the sea.

During a later warm and damp period the luxuriant vegetation of tropical Northumberland became the coal of the Scremerston group of rocks in a mixture of sandstone, shale and limestone. This provided the thin coal seams of Redesdale and North Tynedale worked in small pits such as Plashetts and Lewisburn, which influenced the promotion of the Border Counties railway. The main coal measures were laid down in a later and longer warm period. Except in the Cheviots, sandstones and limestones are the prevailing rocks of Northumberland. South of the Tyne they include the easily split Yoredale slates of the Pennines, which provide roofing material.

At the end of the Carboniferous period, some 200 million years ago, new upheavals in the depths forced molten lava to the surface. This spread outwards on the older rocks to form the Whin Sill, Northumberland's best-known geological feature. It appears as the Nine Nicks of Thirlwall, and carries the Roman Wall triumphantly above Crag Lough. It forms the castle rocks of Bamburgh and

Dunstanburgh, and emerges from the sea as the Farne Islands, with their characteristic basalt columns, the Pinnacles, providing breeding sites for kittiwakes, razorbills and guillemots.

The last stage in the creation of the landscape before man was the Ice Age, a series of cold phases ending some 25,000 years ago. Ice covered the whole land except perhaps the higher Cheviots. The glaciers moved down from Scotland and eastwards from the Lake District. The hills were scraped, gouged and planed down. Their debris formed the Boulder Clay, which covered most of Northumberland and lay heaviest on the coastal plain.

The growth of the forests and the beginning of continuous human settlement began with the improvement of the climate and the retreat of the ice. Small groups of Mesolithic people, hunters and fishermen, reached Northumberland about the time the climate had become warm and wet, and the peat deposits were being formed, from approximately 3000 to 2000 B.C. The early prehistoric inhabitants left no enduring mark on the countryside until about 2000 B.C., when the last ripples of the migration of the Beaker-folk from the Continent, precursors of the Bronze Age, arrived. These left their strange inscribed stones, such as those on the Doddington Moors, in the heather of Lordenshaws, and at Roughting Linn; their standing stones and circles, and the barrows over their dead.

When the Romans crossed the Tyne, in A.D. 70–80, Northumberland was inhabited by Celts of the Iron Age. As the Votadini they are the first inhabitants of the county to appear in written history; a race of "Celtic cowboys, footloose and unpredictable, moving with their animals and herds over rough pastures and moorland".[2] The Celts reached Northumberland about 600 B.C. Their early settlements were formed of small groups of timber huts and

[2] I. A. Richmond, *Roman and Native in North Britain* (1958), p. 25.

palisades. Later they constructed the hill forts defended by stone ramparts, as on Yeavering Bell, which remain as sometimes imposing features of the Northumbrian landscape today. During the Roman period their buildings were constructed of stone, and their small homesteads and settlements were rectangular in shape. Northumberland formed the southern fringe of Votadini territory, and their largest stronghold was on Taprain Law, in Lothian. In culture and achievements they were markedly inferior to their contemporaries of the South of England; but their use of timber for building, and the grazing of their herds, made the first significant impression on the Northumbrian forests. They inhabited Northumberland at a time when the climate had become cool and damp, with mild winters, and the peat deposits were again forming.

The Roman sentries gazing northwards from the parapet on the Wall would have seen a landscape which can still be evoked today, despite the conifers on Haughton Common. There were wide moorlands and extensive bogs; but much of the higher ground was covered with scrub birch, hazel, alder and rowan and hawthorn. It must have been sufficiently open for cavalry operations, since the major forts of the Wall, Wallsend, Benwell, Rudchester, Halton and Chesters, were all designed for cavalry. There was heavy forest on the lower ground, including much oak, which the pastoral Celts had neither the means nor the inclination to clear, and thick fringing forest, especially alder, along the burns and rivers. There are still places today where patches of alder, hazel and birch have survived sufficiently to give some suggestion of these forests, as along the steep sides of the Black Burn in North Tynedale, and the thin cover of oak and alder above the lower reaches of the Grasslees Burn between Elsdon and Hepple (Plate 1).

The Roman failure to consolidate the conquest of Scotland, in A.D. 81, confirmed the position of Northumberland as a frontier province. Their direct military influence on the

North lasted 300 years. At the end of the fourth century the Wall was abandoned and the defence of the northern frontier of Britain was left to the small Celtic kingdoms. In the South, Britain was being subjected to increasing raids from across the seas. In about A.D. 430 Cunedda, king of the Votadini, was moved with most of his fighting men to hold North Wales against the Irish invaders and to found the kingdom of Gwynedd. Northumberland must have become even more thinly populated, though it could not have been completely deserted. The Anglian invaders were held on the coast for more than a generation by the opposition of Celtic kingdoms based on south-west Scotland and north-west England; there are numerous Celtic place-names in Northumberland, and a basically Celtic form of society survived in North Tynedale and Redesdale until the end of the sixteenth century.

The Anglians were one element of the Anglo-Saxon peoples from the lands between the lower Rhine and the Baltic who first raided, and then conquered, the former Roman province of Britain. The Angles themselves came from what is now Slesvig. In the year A.D. 547 their chieftain, Ida, seized the great rock of Bamburgh and made it a fortified base, a pirate stronghold which became the capital of Northumbria. A generation later Aethelfrith of Bamburgh broke the Celtic resistance and won control of Scotland as far north as the Forth. In his reign Northumbria was born out of the always precarious unity of two Anglian kingdoms, Bernicia, with its capital at Bamburgh, and Deira, with its capital at York. Both are names of Celtic origin.[3] Northumbria was a territorial name for the lands of the mixed population dwelling north of the Humber, the *provinciae omnes Northymbryorum,* extending for a time from the Humber to the Forth. It was not till after the Northumbrians were defeated by the Scots, at Carham on Tweed in

[3] P. Hunter Blair, *Roman Britain and Early England* (1963), p. 186, and for the point made below.

1018, that the name was applied to the smaller area between Tyne and Tweed which became Northumberland.

The Anglians laid the foundations of an Anglo-Celtic society which comprised enduring differences of organisation, customs and settlement. After the Norman Conquest the inhabitants of both sides of the Border were ruled by an Anglo-Norman aristocracy. The Border Ballads of Northumberland and Scotland are also identical in form and language.

Before the Anglian invasions the herds of the pastoral Celts must have done much to modify the primeval landscape, and would have checked regeneration of the primeval forests, especially if there was much burning of scrub and heather to improve grazing. The needs of the Roman garrison, for building material, fuel and metal working over a period of some 300 years, would have made further inroads on the forests, especially along the line of the Wall. But it was the Anglian farmers, clearing the heavier soils for the plough, who did most to eradicate the original tree-cover, and to set in motion a process which ended in the denuded landscape of the early eighteenth century.

The rapid Anglian expansion into Northumberland and Lothian, within forty years of the seizure of Bamburgh, suggests the collapse of native opposition. A conquest so rapid and extensive is unlikely to have involved a war of extermination. The royal palace of Edwin (583–633), at Old Yeavering, was already in existence by the end of the sixth century, indicating that the Anglians had overrun Glendale and secured the Cheviots. Celtic place-names abound. They include Yeavering itself, and the rivers such as Aln, Blyth, Breamish, Till, Tweed, Wansbeck and Coquet.[4] Cambois is a Celtic word, meaning 'estuary', its local pronunciation, *kamus*, is close to the Welsh and Irish. Ross, meaning 'promontory', is Celtic. So are Kielder, Troughend in

4 For the derivation and meaning of place-names see E. Ekwall, *The Concise Oxford Dictionary of Place-Names,* 4th ed. (1960).

Redesdale, Amble at the mouth of the Coquet; and Glendue, 'the black glen', under the fells of Hartleyburn above the South Tyne. The word *carr* used for offshore rocks along the coast is also Celtic in origin. It is similar to, but distinct from, the Scandinavian *ker* or *carr*, meaning 'a marsh', which forms an element in the Northumbrian place-names Walker and Prestwick Carr.

Of the earliest form of Anglo-Saxon place-names common in the south and east of England, there is only one example, Birling, now a small village near Warkworth. The *-ingaham* names, which also indicate an early form of settlement, include Ovingham in the Tyne valley, Bellingham in North Tynedale, and Chillingham, Edlingham and Eglingham north of the Coquet.[5] They were followed by the *hams, tons, wicks* and *leys* of the second phase of settlement based on the original centres, and later, during the Middle Ages, by the new towns, *shields* and *biggins*. In general, the eastern half of the county is the area of nucleated villages, while settlement in the west forms a pattern of farms and scattered hamlets suggesting, especially in Redesdale and North Tynedale, the survival of Celtic settlement on land which was not sufficiently attractive to the Anglian farmers. Boundaries of this nature are not clear-cut and the wider dales took the Anglians deep into the hills as at Bellingham, the capital of North Tynedale. Nevertheless, there is a perceptible frontier of settlement patterns extending from Mindrum, below the northern foothills of the Cheviots, to Ingram and Alwinton, down the Coquet to its junction with the Grasslees Burn near Hepple, and east of the Rede and the North Tyne to Warden.

The final conversion of Northumbria to Christianity by Celtic monks, and the strong government of outstanding Northumbrian kings, provided the soil for the flowering of an Anglo-Celtic culture of European importance; but in the

---

[5] Chillingham is pronounced as spelt. The termination of the others is pronounced as in jam—Bellingjam.

eighth century the history of Northumberland became a sombre record of bloodshed and violence. The ruin of the Anglian kingdom was completed by the Danes, who destroyed Lindisfarne in 793.

Danish influence on Northumberland was largely destructive. There is only a handful of Danish place-names, such as Byker and Walker near Newcastle, and Lucker near Belford. There are no place-names ending in *by, thorp* and *thwaite,* so common in Yorkshire and Cumberland. A number of words used for topographical features, however, passed into the local dialect, such as *fell, flow, haugh, cleugh, sike* and *knowe*; and also *stell,* the round dry-stone sheep-fold of the hills (Plate 2).

In the eleventh century Northumberland enjoyed comparative peace under the earls of Northumbria and there was some restoration of churches. The towers of the churches of Warden, Bywell St Andrew and Bolam are substantially of this period. But the Norman Conquest at first initiated a further period of disorder caused by opposition to the Conquest itself, the ambitions of the new Norman aristocracy and the policy of Scottish kings. It was not till some sixty years after the Conquest that Northumberland settled down.

The Norman conquerors were few. It has been suggested that 100 years after the Conquest "the total foreign element need not have reached 400 individuals".[6] Place-names of French derivation are rare. They include Blanchland, from Blanche-Lande in Normandy, and Bolbec, the name of the moorland above Blanchland. Bolbec is derived from the name of the French village near the mouth of the Seine which gave its name to the barony of Bolbec, whose lord founded the Premonstratensian monastery of Blanchland. Guyzance is derived from Guisnes, near Calais. Beaufront, near Corbridge, is a French descriptive name.

The Norman feudal system was imposed incompletely on

[6] W. Percy Hedley, *Northumberland Families* (1968), Vol. I, p. 18.

a countryside whose inhabitants owed military and personal service to their overlords but did not to any great extent work on the lord's demesne. Celtic services, such as *drengage*, and the Saxon tenure of *thegnage,* long survived. The county was very thinly populated, with an estimated density of 5·4 persons to the square mile in 1086, as compared with 27·1 in Dorset and 31·5 in Lincolnshire.[7]

Norman rule was consolidated in time for Northumberland to share in the economic development and colonisation of the waste which were features of European history as a whole during the thirteenth century. Monasteries were founded and churches rebuilt. The flocks of the monks of Newminster grazed in the heart of the Border hills. Boroughs and new towns were founded.

This relatively golden age ended with the death of Alexander III of Scotland, in 1285. Edward I's attempt to enforce his overlordship of Scotland was followed by 300 years of wars and raiding. Outside the walls of Newcastle the development of Northumberland was checked and thrown back. Manor houses were converted into castles. An archaic military society was perpetuated, organised to produce armed men.

> In the long northern evenings about Lammastide moormen win their hay with axes in their belts and bows piled in the corner of the field, and customary tenants are bound by their copies to provide horse and armour, and to ride in person or in proxy. No wonder that while elsewhere landlords pore over their accounts of wool and timber, in Northumberland they should measure their wealth by the men whom they can bring out as the summons goes, and insist on feudal obligations with a vigour unknown to the South . . . A holding means not only a piece of land that grows wheat and feeds sheep, but a horseman in harness.[8]

[7] J. C. Russell, *British Medieval Population* (1948), pp. 53–4, 313.
[8] R. H. Tawney, *The Agrarian Problem in the Sixteenth Century* (1912), p. 190.

In Tudor Northumberland the clan chieftains of Redesdale and North Tynedale ruled a society resembling that of the Scottish Highlands. Far from the Tweed and the Deadwater, the townships of the coastal plain kept watch on the fords of Seaton Burn, and the people of Hexhamshire guarded the crossings of the North Tyne.

In Northumberland, as in Scotland, later peace and economic development rendered unnecessary the maintenance of large numbers of men to follow the banners of chieftain and feudal magnate. Even in the sixteenth century farm holdings were being consolidated in few hands and men were being evicted to enable arable land to be converted to pasture. In the eighteenth century the great landowners, the successors to those who had reckoned their wealth in terms of armed men, turned their immense authority, traditional and legal, to the management of their estates. The landscape of Northumberland is pre-eminently a landlord-created landscape, the creation of the Hanoverian peace. The landlords used their power to build, enclose, hedge, drain and plant—and to evict. They transformed a generally desolate and neglected countryside. With their large estates and their ownership of many villages, and the new wealth derived from coal or lead, they could impose a pattern of regular fields and large hill pastures throughout nearly all Northumberland. The typical Northumbrian hamlet with single-storey labourer's cottages subordinate to castle or hall is the product of this period.

It is a relatively empty landscape even today, as William Cobbett saw it in the early nineteenth century when riding from Morpeth to Alnwick: "the farms enormously extensive; only two churches, I think, in the whole twenty miles, and not a single dwelling house having the appearance of a labourer's cottage".[9]

History and geology alike have divided Northumberland into distinct regions, with marked characteristics of their

9 W. Cobbett, *Rural Rides* (1908 ed.), Vol. II, p. 387.

own, so that no general description is adequate for the whole county. The south-west corner is an extension of the Pennine Dales, a land of cotton grass, heather and bog, where the stone walls climb the high fells and form a regular pattern of small enclosures in the valleys. The small villages with their austere chapels are the legacy of mining, of lead and coal. Farms are few, the older buildings with massive stone roofs under the sheltering sycamores.

The North Tyne and the Rede have their sources on the Border line itself. The North Tyne begins under Peel Fell, 1975 feet high, where the view, given the right conditions, comprises the whole Border country from the North Sea to the Solway. The burns forming the headwaters of the Rede descend from the fells which form an arc between Carter Fell and Hungry Law. Here the modern A68 crosses into Scotland at the Carter Bar, a *swire,* or neck of land, connecting Catcleugh Shin and Arks Edge, once called the Redeswire. Both rivers flow at first on parallel courses south-easterly, the Rede, looping through the alluvium of a wider valley, eventually turning south-west below Otterburn to join the North Tyne below Redesmouth. Their combined waters reach the South Tyne through the narrow gap in the hills where the Romans bridged the river and the Anglians made their settlement under the Celtic hill fort of Warden, the *weard-dun* or 'watch hill'.

Though providing easy routes for man and beast into the heart of Northumberland, the two dales formed a distinct world of their own throughout the Middle Ages and as late as the seventeenth century. On the east they were enclosed by the moorland ridges. On the west the mosses and flows formed far more difficult obstacles for all but moss troopers. Their inhabitants shared with their kindred, the Scottish borderers, customs and social organisation, and particularly a dislike of authority imposed by wardens of the Marches on both sides of the Border.

For centuries Bellingham was the only nucleated village

in North Tynedale. Simonburn was a post-Conquest settlement, Simon's *burb*, probably named after Simon of Senlis,
grandson of Waltheof, the last Anglo-Danish earl. Wark, the
Old English word for fort or stronghold, seems to have
been applied to the Norman castle. North Tynedale and
Redesdale have remained a land of scattered farms since at
least Roman times. Here the term 'township', relevant to the
compact Anglian village amid its common fields, has been
used for groups of widely-dispersed farms, such as the
townships of Wark's Burn, Smalesmouth and Wellhaugh.
By Tudor times law and order in these dales had reached
their lowest level since Bannockburn in 1314.[10] The
chieftains of the Northumbrian clans, or 'surnames', lived
in their small strongholds, Hesleyside, Troughend, Girsonfield and Monkridge. The clansmen, members of a kinship
group, had their 'known' lands. Their inheritance system
was Celtic. They plundered the tents and stole the horses
of the English at Flodden. When the muster was taken for
the defence of the Border in 1538 a note was made of 'the
Tyndell theiffs' numbering 350, all with horse and armour.
There were 185 'foot thieves' in Redesdale.[11]

Today the old pattern of settlement in these dales has
been obscured, though not eradicated, by sheep farming
and eighteenth-century enclosures, by improved communications and tourism, which led to the growth of
Otterburn, and, in recent years, by the activities of the
Forestry Commission. But it still remains distinct from the
pattern of Anglian Northumberland east of the Coquet and
the North Tyne.

The Coquet, perhaps the loveliest of Northumbrian

[10] Tudor reports and despatches contain much information on conditions
on the Border; e.g. the survey by Sir Robert Bowes and Sir Ralph Ellerker
of 1542, printed in J. Hodgson, *History of Northumberland*, Part II, Vol. i,
and, in the reign of James I, the *Survey of the Debateable and Border Lands,* of
1604, ed. R. P. Sanderson (1891).

[11] *Musters of Northumberland in 1538*, summary and copy made by J.
Hodgson in 1842; Library of the Society of Antiquaries of Newcastle upon
Tyne.

rivers, rises close to the Border below the Roman camps of
Chew Green. Its upper reaches form a well-defined geological boundary. South are the long ridges of Redesdale.
To the north the hills are steep and rounded, concealing in
their narrow clefts the burns descending from the Border
ridge. This area, to the casual glance trackless, has in fact for
centuries been traversed by tracks between Northumberland
and Scotland (Fig. 19). Many of them must have linked the
Northumbrian outposts of the Votadini with the main
tribal area north of the Tweed. It is a bare land, a landscape
created by sheep, drawing its life from the moving cloud
shadows and the wind in the grass. An occasional rowan
among the scree survives to suggest the original hill forest.
Modern sheep farms and cottages, Shillmoor, Linshiels,
Batailshiel and Fairhaugh, represent eighteenth-century
resettlement of an area first colonised during the thirteenth-
century peace.

At Alwinton the Coquet breaks from the hills to turn
south between the crags and heather of the Fell Sandstone
moors above Harbottle and the Cementstone country of
hawthorn hedges and nucleated villages. Here the river
forms a frontier of settlement, the point at which the
exploring Anglian farmers came up against the western
fells. West of the river are no *tons* or *hams*. East were 'the
ten towns of Coquetdale' organised in pre-Conquest times
to give military service to Harbottle. The Border tracks
cross the Coquet by the many fords between Hepple and
Rothbury; cattle have left their deep hollow ways in the
heather where they climbed the Simonside moors. At
Rothbury the river has cut its path through the Fell Sandstone, flowing east to the sea under the woods of Brinkburn, passing the wide haugh of Brainshaugh, and forming
a series of deep loops in its dene from Guyzance to Warkworth.

Whittingham Vale (Plate 3), north of the Coquet, was
described by a usually peevish observer of the North-

umbrian scene in the late eighteenth century as "an extensive, rich, cultivated country, where every object is highly pleasing . . . [and] the fields are well fenced with quicksets".[12] From the escarpment of the Rimside Moors, between Rothbury and Alnwick, the vale is spread out below the heather, bounded to the north by the green slopes of the Cheviot foothills. In June it is white with hawthorn blossom. Like Coquetdale, Whittingham Vale has been traversed by ancient trackways from the hills. Whittingham itself, with its two fords, was one of the earliest of the Anglian settlements and is situated close to the junction of two Roman roads in a gentle and fertile landscape.

North of Whittingham the modern road, and the older turnpike, cross the narrow ridge which separates Whittingham Vale from Glendale. Glendale is named from the Glen, which begins under the northern slopes of the Cheviots as the Bowmont. The Bowmont flows past Yetholm and then turns from the Border to round the Cheviots between Kirknewton and Yeavering Bell as the Glen, and to join the Till in the flat gravel and alluvial plain which was once the great lake of Milfield. The Till itself begins as the Breamish, a Celtic name, descending from the heart of the Cheviots to emerge from the hills under the ancient church and wide haughs of Ingram.

The hill slopes which define Glendale, and the lower Doddington Moors in the centre of the plain, were one of the main centres of pre-Roman settlement in Northumberland. The hills are sculpted with the ramparts of hill forts, such as Yeavering Bell, and Ross Castle in the heather above Chillingham. Along the upper courses of the Breamish settlement extended far into the hills, to the stone walls of Greaves Ash in the bracken above Linhope. There are fine prehistoric inscribed stones near Roughting Linn. Glendale provides an easy route into Scotland. The Devil's Causeway was driven through it, through Lowick to

[12] W. Hutchinson, *A View of Northumberland* (1778), Vol. I, p. 230.

Berwick. Between the plain and the hill crests an ancient track sought the crossings of the Tweed at Carham and Kelso, through the narrow gateway formed by the Bowmont under Housedon Hill.

Glendale, like Tweedside, is a country of farm hamlets, with a handful of nucleated villages such as Doddington and Chatton. Chillingham was one of the earliest Anglian settlements. Wooler is a small market town undistinguished in history but an early centre of the woollen industry, and so in the thirteenth century one of the richest townships in Northumberland. Drawn by its position into the centre of Border warfare, it was not till the eighteenth century that Glendale laid the foundations of its high reputation for arable farming.

Tweedside north and south of the river is a country of castles and great estates with carefully tended woodlands. The farms, on the generally heavy soil with its patches of alluvium, are large, many between 500 and 1000 acres, with wide fields between neat hawthorn hedges. Villages are small and the characteristic settlement is the farming hamlet. The countryside is the creation of the era of improved farming and enclosures, which began in the eighteenth century and made Tweedside one of the great wheat-producing areas of England. The Tweed itself forms a line of communications which link Glendale with the valleys reaching far into the Scottish hills. The natural port for the whole area is Berwick.

Berwick is the northern termination of some eighty miles of coast which begins at the cliff fortress of Tynemouth in the south. North of Bamburgh, to within a short distance of the Tweed, the coast has its own special characteristics. The tides slide swiftly over the sands and mudflats where the geese fly in winter and the wild swans come down from the north; a wide flat landscape with clear light and soft colours; a landscape of haunting beauty where the Farne Islands stand high from the sea facing Bamburgh on its

Plate 1 Birch woodland, North Tynedale
After the end of the Ice Age, birch, hazel and rowan became the dominant trees of the Northumbrian highlands and covered most of the county. They were destroyed by clearance and grazing and only small vestiges survive. Light woodland of this kind enabled the Romans to use cavalry based on forts along the Wall.

Plate 2 A Cheviot *stell*
Northumberland was little influenced by Scandinavian settlement but a number of words of Scandinavian origin are still in use. *Stell* is derived from the Norse *stallr* or 'stall', and these shelters are a characteristic feature of the Border landscape.

Plate 3   Whittingham Vale

The photograph looks north from the Fell Sandstone escarpment of Simonside. It shows easily-eroded Cementstone country, most of it long famed for its fertility, which brought Anglian settlement to the foot of the higher moorlands. It is a landscape of eighteenth-century enclosure. The hedges 'of long-standing' were remarked upon by a visitor in the 1770s.

Plate 4 The Roman Wall

The Roman military presence north of the Tyne lasted some 300 years. It had little permanent effect beyond its strategic road system. The photograph shows the Wall, constructed about A.D. 122–6 along the lines of the Whin Sill. The escarpment faces north, looking towards a countryside sparsely inhabited by a pastoral Celtic society in Roman times.

Plate 5 The Black Dyke, Muckle Moss

The Black Dyke is a Dark Age earthwork, with a ditch on the western side shown in the photograph between the wall on the left and the mound of the dyke under the firs on the right. It demarcated a boundary and was not a continuous line but filled gaps between natural obstacles such as bogs, crags and forest. It was probably a frontier between the Anglian settlers in the east and the Celtic kingdoms in the west.

basalt crag, and the sandhills and links of Holy Island curve on the horizon. The Lindisfarne of the Saxons, renamed Holy Island in the eleventh century, is, like Iona, a place of pilgrimage, for here the Celtic monks Aidan and Cuthbert kindled a torch of learning and culture which shone throughout Europe.

From Bamburgh southwards the coast is formed of long stretches of sand and links alternating with stretches of rock and cliffs. There are no good natural harbours between the Tweed and Tyne. The small fishing villages, now depending predominantly on tourists, such as Beadnell, Craster, Newton, Bulmer and Cullercoats, depend on the local shelter provided by the headlands, and by the protection of the offshore reefs. Some of these small havens were improved, in the eighteenth and nineteenth centuries, to develop fishing and for the coastal trade in salt, lime and coal, as at Beadnell, Craster and Seahouses. Alnmouth acquired a brief importance in the late eighteenth century for the export of corn, when landowners promoted the construction of the 'Alemouth Road', or 'Corn Road', across Northumberland from Hexham. The coal ports of Amble and Blyth were the creations of the nineteenth century. Until the construction of these coal ports the natural facilities offered by the Tyne were unrivalled, affording access deep into Northumberland and, since the Middle Ages, water transport for the coal mined near the river banks.

The coastal plain is divided into two parts by an eastward projection of the 200-foot contour which brings the hills close to the sea between the mouths of the Coquet and the Aln. Strategically the keys of this narrow gap were held by Warkworth and Alnwick. The lower reaches of the Coquet form the northern boundary of the north-eastern coalfield; and also between the predominantly farm hamlet area of the north and the nucleated villages which were the characteristic settlements between the Coquet and the Tyne until the end of the eighteenth century. North of the Coquet the soil is generally a heavy loam. The Boulder Clay covering the coal measures provides a cold and more difficult soil for arable farming. It is a stark land between the sea and the hills, where the rivers have cut their denes through the clay and so have provided some shelter for the trees along their banks. Almost uninhabited before the Anglian settlement, so far as is known, the coastal plain remained a poor and generally unimportant part of the county until technical advance made the deep mining of coal possible in the eighteenth century and the colliery railways were constructed to the staithes on the Tyne and the coast.

Notwithstanding the great concentration of population, the slagheaps and colliery towns and villages, the power-lines and pylons, this corner of Northumberland still provides a clear picture of Anglian settlement in its simplest form. Villages such as Earsdon, Backworth and Widdrington retain much of their original compact form, though changed in detail, on the ridges and knolls which rise out of the Boulder Clay (Fig. 3). They stand above their wide and treeless fields, the streams which provided the hay meadows, ringed by the encroaching built-up areas of the twentieth century, the new towns and roads. Despite widespread impressions to the contrary, the south-eastern corner of Northumberland has not been one gigantic coal heap or a vast brick-built colliery town. There was room for pits and pitmen within a rural setting, of which the suburbanisation of the twentieth century has been the prime destroyer.

Modern developments are but the latest chapter of a tale, not yet ended, that began when the barrows and earthworks of ancient settlement first arose on the Northumbrian hills, when the sheep and cattle of pastoral tribesmen first grazed and trampled the young trees. Much of this tale is hard to read. Few possessions have been left by the ancient societies of the north for the information of later archaeologists. No Old English land-charters exist. There was no Domesday Book. "Anyone wishing to plot the pre-Domesday land-

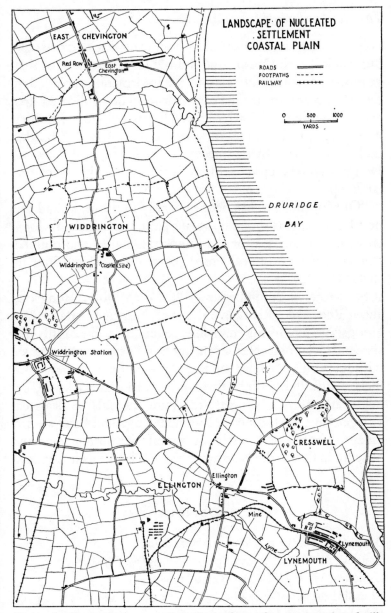

Fig. 3. Anglian settlement usually took the form of compact nucleated villages surrounded by wide expanses of common fields and waste. On the Boulder Clay of the coastal plain the settlements were usually on small hills, as at
Widdrington. Within the area covered by the map the villages of Red Row,
East Chevington, Lynemouth, Ellington and Widdrington Station are almost entirely the creations of the nineteenth century or later. Early nineteenth-century maps of the plain between the Tyne and the Wansbeck show a
similar pattern of settlement.

holdings of northern England is confronted with a frustrating blank."[13] Not until 1296 did the tax assessment of that year provide something akin to the information recorded in Domesday 200 eventful years before. Then followed 300 years of raiding and war, followed by an epilogue of Border insecurity in the time of the Commonwealth. Border Ballads and the battle pieces of Froissart, old tales of Douglas and Percy, contribute little to the history of the landscape.

"Our journey . . . has been generally in the dark; and the best light that has shone upon our path, has lasted only long enough to let us see for the moment a mailed and plumed chieftain, with hosts of armed myrmidons around him in shadowy array."[14]

So wrote Northumberland's historian, John Hodgson, about Redesdale. Redesdale is not all Northumberland, but Hodgson's comment remains generally valid until the sixteenth century, and even then villages could vanish without written record of their going. Some other light flickers fitfully, the light thrown by ford and trackway, by field patterns and lynchets, the faint mounds of deserted village sites and long abandoned ridge-and-furrow, by village, church and castle. It reveals in outline, leaving obscure in detail, the Northumbrian landscape as it is today.

SELECT BIBLIOGRAPHY

Bates, C. J. *History of Northumberland* (1895).
Bradley, A. G. *The Romance of Northumberland* (1908).
Cameron, W. *English Place Names* (1961).
Ekwall, E. *Concise Oxford Dictionary of English Place-Names* (1960).
H.M.S.O. *National Forest Parks Guides,* 'The Border' (1962).
H.M.S.O. *National Park Guide No. 7,* 'Northumberland' (1969).

13 R. Cramp, *Northern History* (1970), Vol. V, p. 223.
14 J. Hodgson, *History of Northumberland,* Part II, Vol. I, p. 67.

Hodgson, J. *History of Northumberland in Three Parts,* 7 volumes (1820–58).

Honeyman, H. L. *Northumberland* (1949).

Northumberland County History Committee, *A History of Northumberland* (*N.C.H.*), 15 volumes (1893–1940).

Pawson, H. C. *A Survey of the Agriculture of Northumberland* (1961).

Ridley, N. *Northumbrian Heritage* (1968).

Robson, D. A. *A Guide to the Geology of Northumberland and the Borders* (1965).

Sharp, T. *Northumberland: A Shell Guide* (1969).

Stamp, L. D. *The Land of Britain,* Part 52, 'Northumberland' (1945)

2. The countryside

Before the Anglian settlement

THE ROMAN ARMIES reached the Tyne in A.D. 79, in the course of their advance into Scotland, and at once constructed the important lateral road between Corbridge and Carlisle. With the construction of the bridge and fort of *Pons Aelius,* in the reign of the emperor Hadrian (A.D. 117–138), the sites of the future Newcastle and Carlisle became the keys to the control of the North by any ruler from either side of the Border.

The Romans found a country sparsely inhabited by a pastoral people living on the southern fringes of a tribal territory of which the centre lay north of the Tweed. They lived in hill forts and scattered settlements, especially along the eastern fringes of the Cheviots, from the Bowmont near Yetholm to Alwinton in Whittingham Vale, and in North Tynedale and Redesdale. The Iron Age culture had reached southern England some 400 years before the Romans and had produced the huge stronghold of Maiden Castle in Dorset and the Colchester of Cunobelinus (*c.* A.D. 5–43). The Celts of Northumberland still lived in what was a Bronze Age culture, far poorer in material possessions, and more primitive, than the culture of the south. Their major stronghold, or *oppidum,* occupied the summit of Yeavering Bell, above Glendale. Here, where the tumbled grey stones of pre-Roman ramparts emerge from the blaeberry and heather, a relatively large community occupied about 130 timber huts in an area of some seventeen acres. The summit of Yeavering Bell scans the whole course of Northumbrian history. Immediately below the steep slopes lie under the grass the remains of the royal manor of Anglian kings called by Bede *Ad Gefrin,* a name of Celtic origin. The coast is visible, from Berwick to the nineteenth-century coal port of Amble; and the castles of Holy Island, Bamburgh and Dunstanburgh, Etal and Ford. East and north-east are the broad fields of Glendale and Tweedside, the creation of eighteenth-century enclosure.

The ancient earthworks which scarp the hills of Northumberland, or exist as mounds amid the bent and heather, are diverse in form; and few are likely to be much older than a century or so before the Roman occupation. Besides Yeavering Bell they include smaller, though impressive, strongholds such as Great Hetha, on the crest of the ridge above the College Burn, and Humbleton above Wooler, both in areas where the hills are terraced by later medieval ploughing. They include Old Bewick, high above the Till south of Chillingham; and Warden, commanding the junction of the North and South Tyne. Many of these hill forts are associated with ancient trackways through the hills, as at Castle Hill and High Knowe above the Salter's Road at Alnham. At Alwinton a hill fort is situated on the ridge between the Housedon Burn and the Alwin, where Clennell Street begins its climb through Kidland to the Border. Across the Alwin there is a stronghold on Camp Knowe above Clennell.

All were inhabited by primitive people, the majority with few material possessions, whose lives can have made little impact on the natural landscape. Accurate dating so far has been impossible. Some may well have been reoccupied in the Dark Ages.

Under Roman rule some of the old hill forts were reoccupied by people who used stone instead of timber, as at Yeavering Bell, and Castle Hill above Alnham. The main areas of native settlement in Roman times were, however, concentrated along the lines of the Roman strategic road system, Dere Street and the Devil's Causeway, linked by the lateral road from Redesdale to Whittingham. It is always possible that the coastal plain was more thickly populated in Roman times than the number of sites identifiable today might suggest, and that the existence of such sites has been obscured by the plough and urban development.

The settlements of Roman times were small, family homesteads consisting of a handful of stone-built huts within an enclosure, and often with a cobbled stockyard, as at Riding Wood above Bellingham. Settlements such as these were numerous on the hills above the North Tyne, as at Carry House, below the modern farm of Birtley Shields, which contained five huts within the enclosure. Here were found numerous fragments of Roman pottery and also quernstones.[1]

At Huckhoe, near Bolam, at an altitude of 500 feet and close to the line of the Devil's Causeway where it descends to the crossing of the Wansbeck, the enclosures of a pre-Roman settlement were reoccupied by the early second century; occupation of this site was continued almost to the eve of the Anglian seizure of Bamburgh. The pastures on these hills above the Wansbeck must therefore have evolved gradually from the waste over a continuous period of some 600 years, from the first century A.D. to the late fifth or early sixth century, a slow process unaffected by the swaying fortunes of military history north of the Wall. Huckhoe in these years was occupied by a pastoral community which also used coal from local outcrops in Roman times and, in view of the number of querns discovered, must also have grown some corn.[2]

At Witchy Neuk above the Coquet near Hepple, where a still impressive rampart surges out of the heather above the steep drop to the river haughs, there was also evidence of occupation in Roman times; and the circular enclosure of Lordenshaws, on the northern slopes of Simonside near

[1] *N.C.H.*, Vol. XV, pp. 27–31.
[2] G. Jobey, 'Excavations at the Native Settlement at Huckhoe, Northumberland', *Archaeologia Aeliana* 4th series, Vol. XXXVII, (1959), pp. 217 78.

Rothbury, was certainly occupied by a pastoral community during the same period.

The Roman Wall remains today as one of the most imposing monuments of antiquity anywhere in the world, despite its use as a convenient quarry from the Anglian settlement until the early nineteenth century. It still conveys a moving impression of imperial power and purpose on the frontiers of the civilised world where it strides along the crest of the Whin Sill poised between the Pennine fells and the wide expanses of the Northumbrian moorlands (Plate 4). A similar impression is conveyed by the inflexible advance of Dere Street across Redesdale and the camps above the source of the Coquet.

These works of Rome were purely military. The 'North-West Frontier of Rome'[3] could provide no environment suitable for the estates and villas of Romanised local magnates such as existed in the south. The garrison town and supply base of Corbridge were Northumberland's sole example of urbanisation. Small settlements for retired legionaries and traders made a brief appearance. By the fourth century Housesteads had become a small frontier settlement with shops and markets. Civilian villages grew up under the protection of the forts at Wallsend, Halton, Chesters and Carrawburgh. But when, at the end of the fourth century, the Wall was abandoned and the defence of the frontiers was left to the petty kings between the Tyne and the Forth, urban life in the shadow of the Wall dwindled and vanished.

In the fifth century the scant population of Northumberland reverted to their ancient ways and pastoral life, which in this frontier area are unlikely to have been permanently affected by the military occupation. The roads remained, unrepaired but in use, throughout the Middle Ages. And, since the Anglian invaders at first experienced determined opposition, it is reasonable to assume that some inhabitants

[3] The title of David Divine's interesting study of Hadrian's Wall (1969).

of Northumberland remained on, or near, the settlements of the Roman period. Excavations at Ollerchesters, close to the line of Dere Street in the heart of Redesdale, have revealed one shadowy link between Roman and medieval Northumberland.[4] On Troughend Common a low mound and a few grey stones are visible among the rushes of a moorland pasture. Here traces of a wooden building and a small pond were found enclosed within a bank of earth and stones. Fragments of pottery have been ascribed to the Dark Ages, as well as to the thirteenth and fourteenth centuries. These offer a fascinating suggestion, it can be no more, of continuity of settlement from a remote past.

The small and scattered homesteads of the Roman period appear today as no more than low mounds and scattered stones. But many of them are found in a landscape which is still a pattern of dispersed hamlets and farms (Fig. 4), and which was originally remote from the main areas of Anglian settlement. Since these abandoned sites knew the patrols and tax-collectors of Rome, the creation of the modern landscape by human agency has been a continuous process, unbroken though not unchecked. Where they existed, the Tudor officials of the sixteenth century described in the same areas the life of the Celtic fringe of Northumberland. Somewhere among them must lie the elusive traces of continuity of settlement through the Dark Ages, of which Ollerchesters has given some glimpse, the dwellings in the wilderness of the men who held the North after the Roman withdrawal and managed for some forty years to confine the Anglian invaders to their foothold on the coast. Their flocks and herds continued the long erosion of the forests and scrub. They extended the grazing grounds which became the great hill pastures of Northumberland and laid the foundations of the pastoral life of the county which was sufficiently marked by the time of St Cuthbert

4 N.C.H., Vol. XV, p. 36.

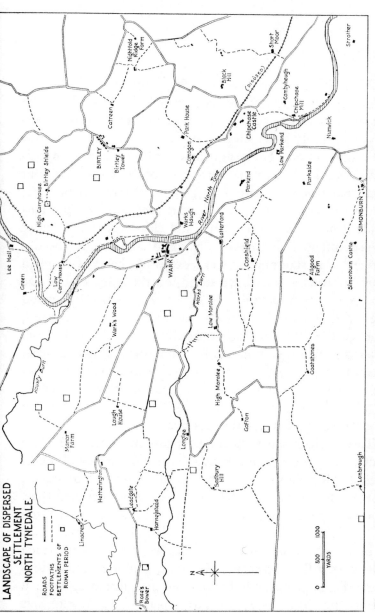

LANDSCAPE OF DISPERSED SETTLEMENT NORTH TYNEDALE.

ROADS ———
FOOTPATHS - - - -
SETTLEMENTS OF ROMAN PERIOD ▢

Fig. 4. Western Northumberland is primarily an area of scattered farms and hamlets, as in North Tynedale. In the area covered by the map Wark and Simonburn (Simon's *burh*) are post-Conquest. During the disorderly sixteenth century this area was controlled by two of the Northumbrian surnames or clans, the Ridleys and the Charltons. Government was represented by the Keeper of Tynedale, an officer exposed to murder or kidnapping, based on Chipchase. Names such as Parkend and Parkside recall the medieval deer park of Wark. Sites of Celtic homesteads contemporary with the Roman occupation are marked ▢.

(d. 687) for the Cheviots to be noted for their sheep nearly
1300 years ago.[5]

The Anglian settlement

After the first forty years of the Anglian occupation of
Bamburgh and Lindisfarne (later called the Holy Island) the
Anglians overran the Scottish lowlands and Northumberland so rapidly as to suggest that henceforward there was
little opposition. The Anglians established complete political domination and the supremacy of their language. But
there was room to spare, and, to use the terms of biology,
the two races occupied a different ecological niche. This
made it possible to establish a still clearly defined frontier
of settlement. It is revealed by sharp contrasts to the observer today standing, as some exploring band of Anglian
warrior-farmers must have stood, on the ridge east of the
Coquet above Wreighill or Sharperton. Westwards, beyond
the river, rise the heather-clad outcrops of the moorland,
whence the Roman road from Redesdale descends from
what is now a countryside of sheepfarms and pele towers.
Eastwards is a softer landscape of farm hamlets and nucleated villages, tree-shaded roads and the hawthorn hedges
of eighteenth-century enclosure. Between the two lies
Harbottle, guardian of the frontier.

The Anglians settled in compact communities, each in the
centre of a wide area of potential farmland, forest and waste,
with ample room for the creation of daughter settlements.
The great majority of their villages were of nucleated type.
The sites chosen were below the higher ground favoured
by the Celtic herdsmen, sufficiently close to a stream or river
to be assured of well-watered meadows, yet out of the reach
of floods. All the earlier settlements, Chillingham, Ovingham, Edlingham and Bellingham for instance, have a
similar situation. The Anglian royal palace of Yeavering was

[5] I. A. Richmond, *Roman and Native in North Britain* (1958), p. 27.

constructed close to the Glen, not on the site of the Celtic stronghold on the summit of Yeavering Bell.

On the coastal plain of the south-east the sites were similarly stereotyped. Here, where the first settlers had to contend with the harsh and ill-drained Boulder Clay, their villages were constructed at the points where rock outcrops rose to the surface, as at Earsdon, Backworth and Widdrington. A similar site was chosen for Thockrington on its Whin Sill outcrop in the central highlands.

Bamburgh itself, traditionally the first Anglian settlement, was designed for defence. Its Anglian occupants had to face strong opposition and they depended on their communication by sea. Birling, north of Warkworth, means 'Baerla's people' and is Northumberland's sole example of a very early form of Anglo-Saxon place-name. The village has had an undistinguished history. Today it is no more than a handful of stone cottages in the valley where the road descends to the crossing of the Coquet at Warkworth; but the features which would have made the site attractive to the original settlers are still apparent (Plate 22). It is only a mile from the slack which was once the mouth of the Coquet, and which would have afforded a protected anchorage to the Anglian long-boats; water would have been provided by the small stream. But Birling later became supplanted by Warkworth, a settlement better sited strategically at the crossing of the Coquet, within easy reach of the sea and defended on three sides by the river. In the Middle Ages part of the lands of Birling were taken as the site for Warkworth New Town; part were incorporated in the deer park of the lord of the manor.

The so-called *-ingaham* names are also folk-names compounded with *ham*, meaning homestead or village. They belong to an early stage of the Anglian settlement. Whittingham means 'the village of the people or followers of Hwita'. Chillingham was founded by the followers of Ceofel or Ceofa. All the villages belonging to this group have

eschewed the higher ground preferred by the Celts. Edlingham, some five miles from Alnwick, occupies a typical site
above the burn under the Fell Sandstone moorlands. Once
one of the villages given to Lindisfarne, it is now a small
grey hamlet. Its early Norman church, the ruins of the
fourteenth-century castle, and the now disused railway
viaduct, together record human aspirations throughout the
centuries. The village fields slope down to the Edlingham
Burn, where the fringing alder thickets recall some shadow
of the ancient landscape. On the slopes, the ridges of old
ploughing are visible to picnickers on the modern road
between Alnwick and Rothbury.

Chillingham lies under the steep slopes of heather
moorlands, where the position of Celtic Ross Castle at the
edge of the escarpment contrasts with the site of the castle
and its dependent cottages at the edge of the relatively well-
drained slopes between the escarpment and the Till.
Whittingham lies among the smooth contours of the Cementstone country at the point where two fords cross the Aln.
Well-watered, with a fertile soil, the village has been for centuries an important track-junction. Its fords are close to the
point at which the Devil's Causeway, the Roman road to
Berwick, is joined by the lateral Roman road from Redesdale. That the Anglians were not interested in the advantages of the Roman road system is suggested, however, by
the fact that their settlement was not sited on the road itself.
The village, the centre of a large parish, prospered sufficiently to enjoy the possession of a large Anglian church
with a tower, though little of this escaped the alterations of
the 1840s.

The filling-in of the Northumbrian countryside proceeded
rapidly and the framework of rural settlement, as it exists
today, is likely to have been completed by the end of the
seventh century, about the time when the Northumbrian
king Oswy (d. 641) established his supremacy in Britain.
The final details had to await the population expansion of

the twelfth and thirteenth centuries. It is possible to form some impression of the process on the great royal estates, such as Rothbury, where land was brought into cultivation by means of grants to individuals who, at Hepple and Snitter, held their property by means of a form of personal service, Celtic in origin, known as *drengage*.

As population grew, and Anglian rule became more effective, small groups and individuals with their personal households moved out into the wilderness to establish their own *hams*, *tons*, *wicks* and *leys*. The family and followers of Dodda founded their *ton*, the modern Doddington in Glendale, around the springs under the hills which were once an important area of Celtic and pre-Celtic settlement. The site was a typical one chosen by the Anglian farmers. Sheltered from the east by the Doddington moors, to which easy access was provided by a gap in the moorland ridge, westwards potentially good arable land sloped almost imperceptibly down to the Till.

More adventurous spirits moved into the heart of the Celtic hills. Elsdon probably means 'Elli's dene' or valley. In appearance it is a fine example of a 'green village' surrounded by late eighteenth- and early nineteenth-century houses, and by later additions. The lordship of Kidland, in Upper Coquetdale, was 'Cydda's land'; and the isolated farm of Buteland, high above the North Tyne, was 'Bota's land'. But in these remote places the Anglians can have done little to influence the habits and way of life of the original inhabitants, many of whom must have survived on their ancestral holdings. Elsdon, as late as the sixteenth century, was the centre of a society which had little in common with Anglian Northumberland and can have been scarcely affected by the construction of the castle, or the thirteenth-century grant of a market, by the Umfraville lords of Redesdale. Relatively large-scale colonisation, such as led to the settlement of Bellingham, was required to give a distinctive Anglian pattern to life in the hills.

Alnham, Alwinton and Ingram are all situated on the western frontier of this type of settlement, at points where the ancient trackways descend from the hills onto the lower ground under the promontory forts of the earlier inhabitants.

Alwinton, the *ton* on the Alwin, is now a hamlet of stone cottages at the point where the ancient track known as Clennell Street, from the Border crossing above Outer Cocklaw, descends the ridge between the Alwin and the Housedon Burn (Fig. 5). The original settlement was probably at Low Alwinton, the site of a deserted medieval settlement, near the point where the interesting old church, dedicated to St Michael, stands alone east of the river midway between the fords across the Alwin and the Coquet. Alwinton was situated at the important junction of drove roads and Border tracks, and since Anglian times was the most important of the 'ten towns of Coquetdale'. Ingram was founded at the point where the Breamish emerges from its narrow valley which, like the valley of the Coquet, gave access deep into the Border hills. The name is derived from the Old English word *angr*, meaning 'grassland', indicating that its grassy hills above the river were distinctive features some twelve hundred years ago. Similarly Alwinton church looks west over Angry Haugh, 'the grassy level', beside the Coquet.

Some of the *wicks*, or farms, cleared from the forest and marshes, have become famous in history, Berwick, 'the corn farm', or grange, by the mouth of the Tweed; Alnwick, 'the farm on the Aln'. Alnwick for centuries was included in the ecclesiastical parish of Lesbury, the original settlement near the mouth of the Aln. Other *wicks* have remained as the farm hamlets of the original settlement: Fenwick, 'the farm by the fen' under the Kyloe Hills, and also above the marshy valley of the Pont near Stamfordham; Goswick, 'the goose farm', at the edge of the long sands and salt marshes north of Holy Island where the wild geese still fly in winter; Old Bewick, 'the bee farm', the place where the people of near-by

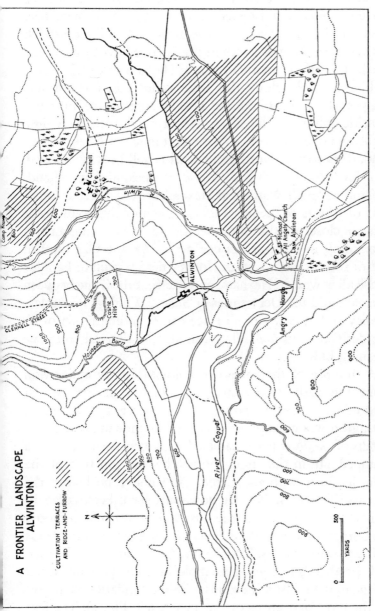

Fig. 5. Alwinton, the Anglian *ton* on the Alwin, was strategically sited at the point where the Coquet and the ancient trackway known as Clennell Street emerge from the hills. The original site of the village was near the church, at Low Alwinton. The township was prosperous during the thirteenth century and was assessed at a higher figure than Morpeth for the Lay Subsidy of 1296. The shaded areas mark the position of the ridge-and-furrow and cultivation terraces of the medieval farmers. The cultivation terraces are on the steeper slopes, such as below Camp Knowe and west of Alwinton.

Eglingham took their bees in summer to the heather-covered hills. An isolated farm which must have been founded later, judging by the name, is Willimontswick, 'the farm of Wilmot', with its fine fortified gatehouse above the haughs of the South Tyne near Haydon Bridge.

In the south, along the Tyne valley and the northern fringes of the Pennines, the heavily forested country was considerably more difficult to clear than the relatively light scrub and open forest dominant over much of Northumberland. This part of Northumberland is still heavily wooded. Horsley Wood near Wylam and the beautiful woodlands along the Devil's Water near Hexham are the direct descendants of forests of medieval times. Much of this countryside was not closely settled until the Middle Ages but it is an area abounding in place-names ending in -*ley*, the Old English *leah* or forest clearing, from Horsley near Wylam to Langley and Ridley west of Hexham, and south of the Tyne between Hexham and the Derwent as at Slaley, Whitley, Broomley, Ordley and others. Not all place-names ending in -*ley* or -*ly* are derived from *leah*. They can also be derived from *law* meaning hill.

A glimpse of the spread of colonisation by emigration from the early settlements, and of the factors which determined township boundaries, is given by Ovington. Ovington was a daughter village of Ovingham, one of the group of -*ingaham* place-names. Ovingham is situated on a cramped site in the angle formed by the junction of the Whittle Burn with the Tyne. At some time before the Norman Conquest the decision must have been taken to form a new settlement to the west of the burn, and to choose the burn itself as a well-defined boundary between the fields of the two townships. Today Ovington, 'the *ton* of the men of Ovingham', is a good example of a compact nucleated village in the midst of its fields within boundaries which are for the most part burns or the Tyne itself (Fig. 6). The few buildings outside the village are almost exclusively post-

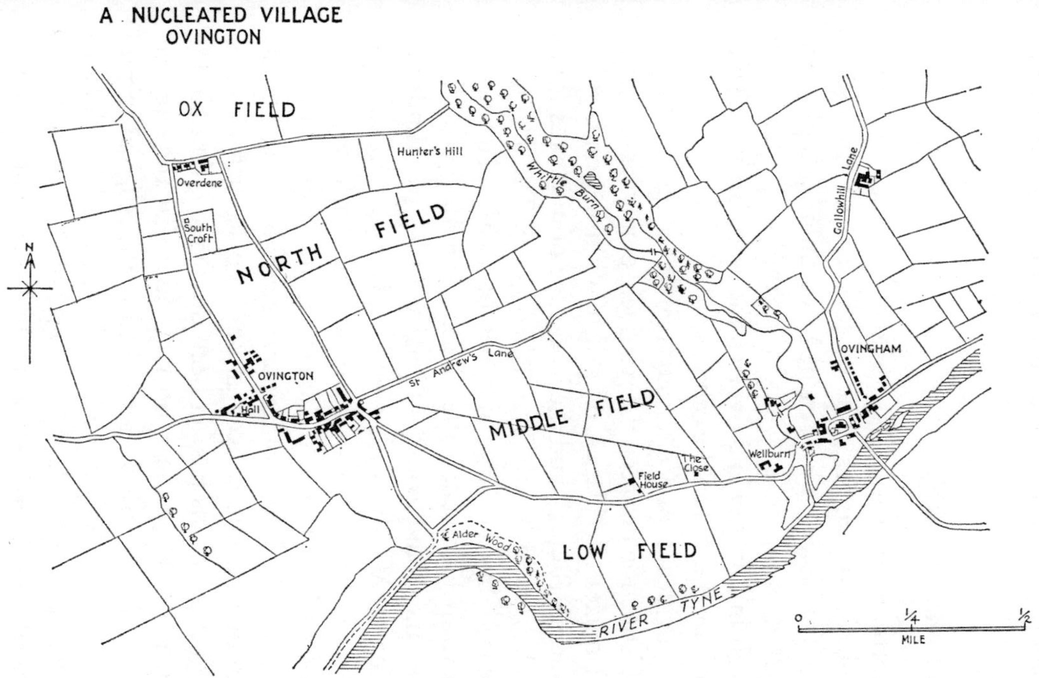

A NUCLEATED VILLAGE
OVINGTON

Fig. 6. Ovington was the daughter-settlement of Ovingham, one of the earliest of the Anglian settlements in Northumberland. It is still a compact village surrounded by what were originally the common fields divided by agreement in about 1680 and 1780. Except for Ovington Hall and Wellburn all isolated buildings are post-division. The approximate position of the original common fields has been indicated on the basis of information in the *Northumberland County History*.

enclosure in the eighteenth century. According to the tax assessment of 1296, Ovington became more prosperous than its parent; but Ovingham remained the parochial centre and its church is still renowned for its pre-Conquest tower.

Celtic survivals: a summary

The Northumbrian rural landscape of today has been formed by two peoples, the descendants of the Celtic-speaking tribesmen, who reached Northumberland some time after about 1000 B.C., and the Anglians, who seized Bamburgh in A.D. 547 and overran the lands between Tyne and Forth by the end of the century.[6]

Direct evidence of Celtic survival rests on the fundamental distinction between the relatively empty landscape of compact nucleated villages, of which Widdrington is still a good example (Fig. 3), and the landscape of dispersed farms and hamlets, as in North Tynedale (Fig. 4). The argument is supported by the large number of Celtic place-names ranging from Plenmeller, the Welsh *blaen Moelfre* or 'bare hill', the moorland south of Haltwhistle, to Mindrum, containing the Welsh words *mynydd* and *drum*, or 'mountain-ridge', on the north bank of the Bowmont. The landscape of dispersed settlement is also the land of the dispersed Celtic homesteads and hill forts of Roman times. No archaeological evidence of continuous occupation from Roman times to the Anglian invasions has yet been discovered, though discoveries at Huckhoe, near Bolam, show that the site was still occupied to a period shortly before the Anglian seizure of Bamburgh. Investigations at Ollerchesters have demonstrated that this site at least, so typical of the sites occupied in Redesdale and North Tynedale in Roman and medieval

[6] Aethelfrith of Bernicia defeated the Scots of Dalriada in 603 and for several hundred years "eliminated the Scots from the claimants to supremacy in northern Britain"; P. Hunter Blair, *An Introduction to Anglo-Saxon England* (1966), p. 44.

times, was also occupied in the Dark Ages. Full exploration
of the ancient earthworks of Northumberland is an immense task, and probably much archaeological evidence
lies beneath farms occupied today.

A study of Northumbrian institutions shows traces of
Celtic influences, but these are not reflected in the landscape. That an essentially Celtic society survived in the sixteenth century is demonstrated by contemporary reports.
The *Border Survey* of 1604[7] reported of "certain high lands
called summer grounds" above Elsdon that:

> The aforesaid grounds are used as summer and shieling
> grounds by the whole inhabitants of the Manor, wherein
> each man knoweth his shieling stead; and they shield
> together by surnames; not keeping cattle according to the
> proportion of the rent, but eating all in common without
> stint or number.

They sowed, reaped and mowed "each man his known
ground"; and "if a man have issue ten sons . . . and sits on a
holding but of 6s rent, every son shall have a piece of his
father's holding".[8] Accordingly Tynedale was "over-
charged with so great a number of people" that the land
could not support them. The young and active were therefore "constrained to steal or spoil either in England or
Scotland".[9]

This society was probably unique in sixteenth-century
England, though not in Scotland. *Shiels* or *shields* is derived
from a Norse word meaning 'summer hill pastures'. The
word was also applied to the temporary shelters of the
herdsmen, and then to temporary shelters of any kind, such
as the fishermen's huts on the Tyne called 'the north shields'.

[7] *Survey of the Debateable and Border Lands,* ed. R. P. Sanderson (1891),
pp. 85–104.

[8] *Calendar of Border Papers,* Vol. I, p. 23. Partible inheritance or *gavelkind*
long survived in Kent, but not as part of a social and economic complex such
as existed on the Border.

[9] Survey of Bowes and Ellerker of 1542, quoted in J. Hodgson, *History of
Northumberland,* Part III, Vol. II, p. 233.

Shieling was a common practice in sixteenth-century Northumberland; but in the Anglian areas it was based on the occupancy of a 'farm', one of the units into which the total area of the common fields was divided; and the number of animals allowed to be grazed by a farmer on the township grazing grounds depended on the number of farms, with grazing rights attached, which he might occupy. In Redesdale grazing rights depended on clan membership, a common surname, and was not otherwise restricted. Arable land in the Anglian common fields was usually divided into strips distributed among three or more fields. In Celtic Northumberland each man had his own holding, his 'known ground'.

The clan heads of this society lived in their isolated strongholds, now primarily eighteenth-century buildings incorporating or replacing an older tower, as at Hesleyside, Troughend, Girsonfield and Monkridge. All over the area are the pele towers, the fortified farmsteads of the later Middle Ages, such as the group near Raw, north of the Grasslees Burn; above the Rede between West Woodburn and Redesmouth; in the old fastnesses of Tarsetdale and Tarret Burn. Some show little more than the original site, such as the mound of the pele at Whitlees near Elsdon; others are almost complete, like Raw pele, or Hole pele above the lower reaches of the Rede.

In the Elsdon area there are numerous traces of small enclosures formed by the remains of turf dykes, or traces of stone walls, but these are difficult to interpret and none can be attributed with any certainty to a definite period. Older field systems have been ironed out and refashioned by the extensive enclosures of the eighteenth century and later, when landlords, requiring sheep rather than men, formed the wide sheep farms of the modern landscape. It was a process which began almost immediately after the succession of James I, when landlords and government alike viewed with disfavour the old Border tenure, by which tenants held

their land on easy terms subject to the provision of an armed
and mounted man at the summons of the Wardens of the
Marches.

Earthworks

Apart from the earthworks of pre-Roman and Roman times,
and the mounds covering deserted villages and manor
houses, there are numerous linear earthworks in Northumberland. The longest, and the best known, is the Black
Dyke, romantically and inaccurately marked on some
eighteenth-century maps in a manner which roused the
scorn of Captain Armstrong, who himself made an excellent
map in 1769. "What is laid down on some maps," wrote
Armstrong, "and called the Scots Dyke, running across the
Map like a great Bar, never existed but in the Brain of some
dreaming Antiquarian."[10] Armstrong's scorn for the
representation of the Black Dyke on some eighteenth-century
maps was justified. But he dismissed it too easily. It exists
today, a compelling subject of study for the walker through
some of the most unpeopled country in Northumberland,[11]
and some of the finest country to walk through, though in
recent years its exploration has been made more difficult by
the activities of the Forestry Commission.

The Black Dyke is a bank with a ditch on its western side
which can be followed intermittently from a point on the
Tyne below Bardon Mill to the junction of the High Carri-
teth Burn and the North Tyne opposite Tarset Haugh, a
distance of thirteen miles as the crow flies but considerably
more for the pedestrian struggling over fell and bog. The
clearest section, and the easiest to approach, is the descent
from a height of 760 feet above Muckle Moss to the Stane-

[10] *Companion to Capt. Armstrong's Map of Northumberland* (1769), p. 10.
[11] Col. G. R. P. Spain made a detailed survey of the Black Dyke, with
excellent maps, published as 'The Black Dyke of Northumberland' in *A.A.*,
3rd series, Vol. XIX (1922).

gate and Grindon Lough below the Wall (Plate 5). There is a good section north of the Wall, below Sewingshields Crag, where it forms the eastern boundary of a block of the forestry plantation on Haughton Common. It can also be identified, with more difficulty, north of the Watch Crags, in an area where it forms the boundary between Bellingham and Falstone. In recent years much of the line has been obscured by the modern Wark Forest.

The Black Dyke of Northumberland, like the altogether more ambitious and better-known Offa's Dyke, was never a continuous line. It was a boundary bank, as was Offa's Dyke, filling in gaps between natural features such as bogs, forest and crags. It has been suggested that the similar Catrail, of Roxburghshire, was "the line on which the Anglian colonists, pushing up the Teviot from Bernicia, temporarily established their position";[12] and it is probable that the Black Dyke was also a boundary between the early Anglian settlers who reached Bellingham, and the Celtic kingdoms of Rheged or Strathclyde.

Short lengths of earthworks, known as cross-dykes, abound in the vicinity of the modern Border. They are most numerous on the Scottish side. Their purpose was to block or delay passage along the ancient tracks. Tweedside was relatively more important to Scotland economically than rural Northumberland was to England, and suffered at least as severely from raids from the south as Northumberland did from the north. Despite their proximity to hill forts and settlements, it is probable that most of the cross-dykes were medieval works to check raiding parties encumbered with sheep or cattle. One such dyke extends across the Border line itself, high above Catcleugh, to block the narrow ridge giving access to Redesdale. There are two more close to the Border on Black Braes; these span the old trackway, and later drove road, known as The Street, which

[12] Royal Commission on the Ancient Monuments of Scotland, *Roxburghshire*, Vol. II, p. 483; also Vol. I, pp. 51–3.

climbs from the Coquet to the Border by means of the ridge between the Rowhope and Carlcroft burns. Another spans the ridge, between the junction of the Buckham Walls Burn and the Coquet, and is crossed by the drove road up Eald Rigg. Yet another, west of Holystone, lies across the ridge between the Dovecrag and Holystone burns and was apparently constructed to block the old Roman road from Redesdale.

None of these earthworks can be dated; nor can it be assumed that they all belong to the same historical period. It is clear that they were intended as obstacles across trackways. For this purpose they were constructed across ridges so that each end of the earthwork could be based on a steep, and originally scrub-covered, hillside, and thus slow down, though not entirely prevent, the progress of light horsemen driving cattle. The majority, such as the earthwork near Holystone, were probably constructed in the sixteenth century to check the northward return of raiding parties. In 1561 an order was made for 'great trenches and ditches'[13] to be dug on commons or wastes where quickset or stone were not available.

Villages

The original Anglian settlements were formed by groups of farmers who lived for defensive purposes behind a hedge or stockade. Their open fields, at first two in number, were cleared out of the waste. The village meadow, for the all-important provision of hay, was situated at the edge of a nearby burn or river. Beyond the cleared fields, woodland provided forest products, building materials and firewood. Large areas of waste, forest and moorland, provided ample room for new settlements when the population increased. The settlements were generally compact, enclosing a space where the livestock could be driven for safety from men or

[13] J. Raine, *The History and Antiquities of North Durham* (1852), p. 32.

wolves. This space became the village green with many variations in shape. Street-villages, where the green took the form of a long rectangle between the houses, are rare in Northumberland. Most of the apparent street-villages existing today appear to be modifications of compact, green-villages, as at Norham.

Today the original village green is often obscured by later developments or has even disappeared. Kirkwhelpington is an interesting nucleated village of the central highlands of Northumberland. Once an outpost of the arable landscape, it is situated in a strong position on a ridge above the Wansbeck, which encloses two sides of the village. A third side is bounded by the stream in the Whiteridge Sike. Kirkwhelpington had a large, circular village green until 1795, when the green was divided into allotments for the villagers, who were tenants of the Duke of Somerset.

Earsdon, near Whitley Bay, is primarily a Georgian village with later additions, but in form it remains a fine example of a nucleated village of the Anglian settlement, on a rocky knoll above the Boulder Clay, and was constructed round a green. Described in 1888 as a "pleasant rustic village of one street, with a little grove of white poplars in the middle of it",[14] Earsdon's original village green was on the site of the crossroads formed by the modern road system to the east of the gaunt church. At Wallsend the village green still survives in the heart of industrial Tyneside, having been saved for posterity by the vigorous opposition offered by the villagers to encroachment in the 1840s. Here the ghost of ancient Anglian settlement at the end of the Wall still survives. On the eastern slopes of the Cheviots, under Humbleton Hill, the village green of Humbleton remains as a patch of long grass, nettles, rushes and whin where piles of stone and crumbling walls on the steep hillside still mark the position of the old village situated by the

[14] W. W. Tomlinson, *Comprehensive Guide to Northumberland* (1968 ed.), pp. 58–9.

side of a track, now a by-road, which leads from Glendale into the heart of the hills.

One of the finest examples of a surviving village green is at Stamfordham, a village which remains a harmonious picture of eighteenth-century architecture surrounding the green with its lock-up and well. At Elsdon, once the central meeting place for the men of Redesdale and North Tynedale, the large green, popular with summer visitors, is composed of a loose ring of eighteenth-century houses under the vicar's pele, and the motte of the small Norman stronghold.

Norham, famous for its castle by the Tweed, and once the *'North Ham'* of the monks of Lindisfarne, consists today of a wide street which connects the castle on the east with the church and village green on the west. But Norham had associations with the missionary monks of Iona long before the Norman castle was built. The lay-out of the village today strongly suggests that Norham was originally a nucleated settlement centred on the church and green, and that this was later developed as a borough along the line of a single street between the church and the castle, as at Warkworth.

In the early twelfth century Norham's overlord, the bishop of Durham, made Norham a borough, with "all the liberties and customs as freely as any borough north of the Tees, and as Newcastle had them".[15] The experiment failed. Norham later acquired a traditional reputation as the most dangerous place in England. Burghal life was unlikely to flourish in a Border outpost. But the modern village still retains the traces of medieval planning and is essentially laid out as a precise rectangle bounded on the north by North Lane and on the south by South Lane, the latter now transformed by modern houses, such as the inevitably named 'Marmion View'.

Harbottle too, though at first sight a street-village, retains faint indications of another form. According to the *Border*

[15] Victoria County History, *A History of Durham,* Vol. I, p. 308.

Survey of 1604, "the town of Harbottle was sometimes a market town, and the tenants there inhabiting claim to be free burghers".[16] The shape of the modern village, with the remnants of the long crofts extending down the slope to the Drakestone Burn, suggests the formal plan of a medieval borough. But Harbottle throughout most of the Middle Ages provided hardly more security for the development of town life than did Norham.

Felton is an example of medieval ribbon development along the line of the Great North Road. Bedlington similarly developed along the line of the ridge-road above the Blyth. Acklington is a street-village. The name does not appear in historical records until 1176, one of the many examples of the lack of early records in Northumberland, but in origin it is Old English and the village must therefore have existed before 1066. Now a neat village of grey cottages and fine sycamores, Acklington was constituted a parish in 1859. The map drawn for the earl of Northumberland in the early seventeenth century shows that the village then was substantially larger than it is today and that it was aligned along the track, now the modern road, between its north and south fields. In the Middle Ages the village was a settlement of small farmers, each with a croft and eighteen acres of land. Like Long Houghton, Acklington has been changed in recent years by the requirements of the R.A.F. The modern airfield, recently closed, occupies practically the whole of the former south and east fields of the medieval village; but the small gardens behind the cottages on the north of the road still occupy the sites of the garths of the seventeenth-century villagers.

Long Houghton, between Alnmouth and Alnwick, appears as a street-village in the map made for its owner, the ninth earl of Northumberland, in 1619. The name, Houghton, is derived from the Old English word meaning 'the ton on the hill'. The descriptive Magna was attached

---

[16] *Survey of the Debateable and Border Lands,* p. 91.

after the Conquest, probably to distinguish the village from its daughter-village of Little Houghton. Through Long Houghton passed an important coastal route between Alnmouth and Bamburgh, and development along the roadside gave the village its later form; but the original settlement seems to have been based on a green near the church.

Similarly Longbenton, now part of the great conurbation of Tyneside, was originally centred on a crossing formed by the intersection of the track to Bedlington across Killingworth Moor and over Seaton Burn, with the track leading to the coast from Gosforth over the Shire Moor. The name first appears, in the twelfth-century records, as *Bentune*. By the middle of the following century it is recorded as *Magna Beneton,* and the village was thus distinguished from *Parva Bentona*, the Little Benton of today. The original meaning is uncertain. It could be either 'the ton in the bent' or 'the bean farm'. Bent is the widespread moorland grass *Agrostis tenuis,* which would have been a feature of the ridge of relatively high ground above the 200-foot contour which links Gosforth with the Shire Moor; and it is probable that Long Benton in origin was not, as its later appearance and name might imply, a street-village, but a small settlement on a moorland crossroad.

Hamlets

The naturalist Pennant, after crossing over into Northumberland from Cornhill in 1772, commented that the countryside was "miserably depopulated, a few great farm-houses and hamlets, appear rarely scattered over vast tracts".[17] A visitor describing Northumberland in about 1800 wrote:

> The farm-houses or onsteads as they are usually called are scattered over the face of the country at a distance frequently of two or three miles from each other, and

[17] T. Pennant, *A Tour in Scotland* (1776), Vol. II, p. 279.

from the other villages and towns. In these onsteads the farmers reside like the feudal barons of old, surrounded by their vassals and dependents.[18]

The farm hamlet with its massive farmhouse and dependent cottages, often incorporating the remains of a medieval stronghold in a nineteenth-century building, is a characteristic feature of the Northumbrian countryside. The great majority are the descendants of Anglian or medieval estates, where the concentration of land in the hands of a single owner necessitated in the eighteenth century special provision for labourers' accommodation in a relatively empty countryside.

It was pointed out, in a paper contributed to the Royal Agricultural Society in 1840,[19] that it was the absence of villages, and the consequential difficulty in obtaining seasonal labour, which forced the big Northumbrian farms to become self-contained communities in which, by the so-called bondage system, each labourer had to provide a member of his family, boy or woman, to work at a stipulated rate. Examples of this type of farm hamlet are found all over the county, especially in the north, as at Akeld, Coupland, Lanton and Fenton Town in Glendale. Akeld, with its massive fifteenth-century fortified house above the burn under the Cheviots has in particular retained much of the atmosphere of its early origins and recalls the isolated settlement, with its hall and dependent buildings, of a medieval landowner. Fenton Town, a group of nineteenth-century brick and slate buildings, represents a migration to the fields by the Till from the older tower of Fenton, itself a more usual site of early settlement under the Doddington Moors; but even Fenton Town tells an old story in more modern language.

[18] E. Mackenzie, *An Historical, Topographical and Descriptive View of the County of Northumberland* (1811 ed.), Vol. II, p. 61.
[19] J. Grey, 'View of the past and present state of Agriculture in Northumberland', *Trans. Royal Agric. Soc.* (1840), p. 184.

Farm hamlets are numerous in Bamburghshire. Elford is an imposing example of the type adapted to the needs of modern large-scale farming. Others are Burton, communicating with Bamburgh in the Middle Ages by a now overgrown lane where brambles and nettles provide nesting sites for whitethroats and yellowhammers; Bradford, the ford across the Waren Burn; Old Mousen near Belford, a building of weathered stone accompanied by a small row of single storey cottages, once the site of a larger village.

Many of the farm-hamlets of Bamburghshire must have come into existence as grants to the followers of the Anglian kings who brought land into cultivation by this means and exacted services in return. Mousen and Beadnell were both held by the ancient tenure of *drengage*; the occupiers of these estates, long after the Conquest, were responsible for the conveyance of fuel and timber to Bamburgh Castle. The hamlet of Fowberry, in the damp fields above the upper reaches of the Ingram Burn, was once a horse-pasture. The name means 'the burg where foals are kept'. There was probably no permanent dwelling here until the pasture was given to the chantry chapel of St Aidan at Bamburgh in the fourteenth century.

The majority of the numerous hamlets of Northumberland are derived from a late stage in the Anglian colonisation. Most were settlements grouped round the wooden house of a landowner, or a later medieval stronghold. Some record the expansion of farming, probably after the Conquest, by emigration from earlier settlements. They have retained much of their original characteristics as compact, self-contained settlements. The wide valley between the Kyloe Hills and the Doddington Moors, where the Devil's Causeway runs north to Lowick, has five basic place-names: Holburn, 'the hollow stream', and its offshoot Holburn Grange; Old Hazelrigg, 'the hazel ridge', with North and South Hazelrigg; Old Lyham, 'the farm by a clearing', with North, South and East Lyham; Hetton, 'the *ton* on the heath, with its offshoots Hetton Law, Hetton Steads and Hetton North Farm; East and West Horton, 'the ton on the muddy land', twin hamlets on either side of the Horton Burn where there was once a manor house in the thirteenth century. Old Hazelrigg is now no more than the site of a tower, which held twenty men at the time of Flodden, on a good defensive position on the high ground under the escarpment of the Kyloe Hills. North and South Hazelrigg are situated on more level ground near the Hetton Burn and suggest a migration from the original stronghold onto land more suitable for farming. Similarly Old Lyham, now no more than a row of cottages, was situated in a strong but relatively cramped position under the Kyloe Hills, at the point where the hedges of the lower fields are replaced by the stone walls of the hills.

These place-names are all Old English in origin and the original settlements must have existed, therefore, before the Conquest. When their offshoots were founded is unknown. The Lay Subsidy Roll of 1296 merely assesses each township, at a reasonably high figure for rural Northumberland of the thirteenth century.

Village fields

Northumberland today is pre-eminently a county of wide and regular fields enclosed by stone walls or hawthorn hedges. An important exception is the landscape of small enclosures in the lead-mining country of the Allendales (Fig. 7). Smallholdings in the Allendales were encouraged by the mine proprietors in the nineteenth century; but immigrant labour was brought to the mines of the Northern Pennines in the Middle Ages. It is probable that a pattern of farming distinct from that of the normal Northumbrian township developed in this area long before the nineteenth century.

The details of the field systems of the Anglo-Saxons are

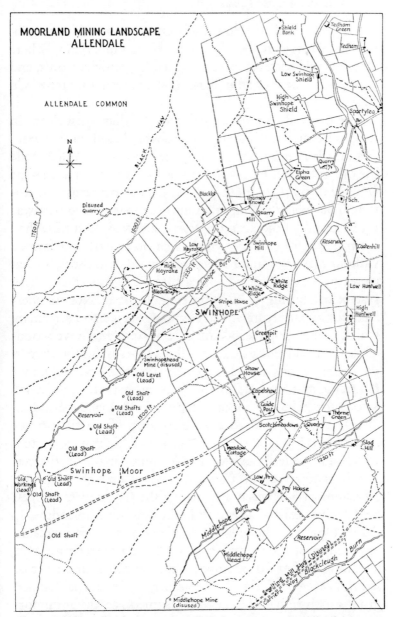

Fig. 7. Between about 1700 and 1896 lead-mining on the Allendale moors created a distinctive landscape of small cottages and cabins, chapels and small stone-walled allotments forming a narrow ribbon on the lower slopes of the fells. Many of the enclosures shown on the map are derived from the consolidation of stints after enclosure.

still "a topic full of hazards, controversies and uncertainties".[20] This is markedly so in Northumberland, where Anglian field systems were modified by Celtic customs, and where huge areas of an under-populated land long remained waste.

The original primitive system of Anglian agriculture in much of Northumberland was probably based on two areas of arable land in each township, one of these was tilled while the other was left fallow. North of the Border, as late as the eighteenth century, the *infield* was kept in perpetual cultivation. The *outfield* was divided into two parts. One part was given an initial manuring by cattle and was then ploughed for oats for four or five years. The other part was farmed without manuring until it was exhausted, and then allowed to revert to waste or rough pasture. This was essentially a system of shifting cultivation suitable, as in Northumberland, for a sparsely inhabited country.[21] It is also a system by which a small population could very rapidly remove woodlands over wide areas. The holdings of each farmer were in the forms of long raised ridges, or rigs; and because, under the Celtic system, holdings were being perpetually divided among co-heirs, it became necessary to make periodical distributions of land to ensure equality of distribution of land of varying quality. This was the Celtic run-rig system which undoubtedly existed in Northumberland in the sixteenth century, as at Cowpen, now a suburb of Blyth. Northumberland was not an area of the classic form of open field such as existed above all in the English Midlands.

In addition to the areas of arable farming each township required waste for grazing grounds and forest products, including timber for building, and meadows near a river or stream. Many of the Northumbrian townships formed groups with rights of grazing on, sometimes, distant moorlands. The Shire Moor of Tynemouthshire, a large area

---

[20] P. Hunter Blair, *An Introduction to Anglo-Saxon England* (1966), p. 257.
[21] H. L. Gray, *English Field Systems* (1959), pp. 162, 226.

which once reached from Murton, 'the moor town', to North Gosforth, was the common grazing ground of all the townships which came to form part of the medieval Liberty of Tynemouth. Eleven townships, including Ovingham and Ovington, Halton, Bywell and East Matfen, shared Shildon Common, south of the Wall above Corbridge; and in the seventeenth century the people of Shilbottle drove their cattle in summer to the shielings on the Rimside Moors.

By the end of the Middle Ages, after close on 1000 years of farming, the open-field system had become more sophisticated. Villages often had three or more arable fields. The waste was becoming the township common, an area of broom, gorse and heather, where the freeholders had rights of stinted grazing for their stock according to the number of their farms.[22] The arable fields and the individual farms were usually unfenced, though permanent fences enclosed the small crofts and garths of the villagers. Rough tracks formed the boundaries between the fields and crossed the commons into neighbouring townships. Many of these tracks were the predecessors of the footpaths and roads of today. The main outlines of villages and fields, as they existed in the transitional period in the late sixteenth century, are still visible.

Shilbottle is situated on a high ridge in sight of the coast. The second element of the name is derived from the Old English *botl* meaning 'dwelling or building'. The first element *Shil*, which appears as *Sipli* in its thirteenth-century form, is derived from the Old English word meaning 'the people of Shipley'. The village therefore was a late settlement, though still pre-Conquest in origin, founded from the neighbourhood of the Shipley Burn, in Eglingham parish. The church was built in the later eleventh century. The pele next door to the church appears in the list of Border strongholds of 1415. It is inhabited by the vicar

[22] 'Farm' in this context means a unit of arable land to which certain rights, such as common grazing, were attached.

today but it does not appear to have been a genuine 'vicar's pele', At the close of the sixteenth century the township contained "a good and rich myne of coles very profitable to the countrey hereabouts".[23] Modern mining in recent years has led to the construction of a new village at Shilbottle Grange, once part of the demesne of the lord of the manor.

The map of Shilbottle drawn for the ninth earl of Northumberland, in 1624 (Fig. 8), shows how the existing pattern of the landscape was formed by late medieval agriculture. Tracks, the boundaries of fields and pastures, as they were in the early seventeenth century, had themselves evolved from the more primitive open-field system of Anglian Northumberland.

In the early seventeenth century the arable land of the township was divided into three open fields, "each tenant having his land lying on the field rig by rig to his neighbour according to the old division of lands in this country".[24] Four holdings north of the village were compact and enclosed by hedges, an arrangement which was noted as being more convenient to the tenants. The entire western half of the township was common land. This is the area traversed by the modern A1, itself following the line of the Great North Road. Patches of gorse and rough grazing near South Moor remain as vestiges of its ancient vegetation. By the time the moor was enclosed in 1759 only seven persons had grazing rights upon it. Of its 1509 acres, 1261 acres were awarded to three persons headed by the duke of Northumberland. This left a free hand for the construction of the large and regular fields, which are a feature of the area today, and for the reconstruction of roads on a more convenient alignment with the wide tree-shaded verges characteristic of enclosure roads.

Roads, lanes and footpaths, even field boundaries, reflect with accuracy today the basic patterns of the early seventeenth century. Thus the footpath marked by the modern

[23] *N.C.H.*, Vol. V, p. 431.   [24] Ibid., p. 424.

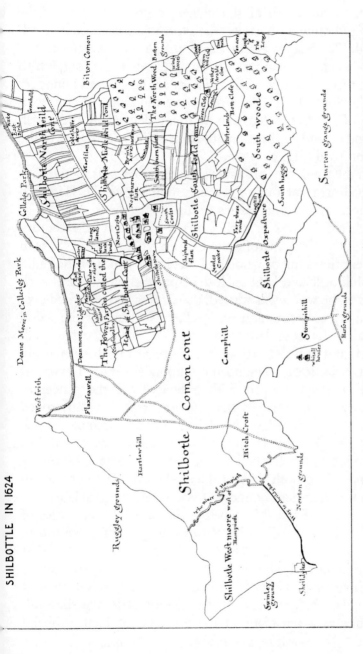

SHILBOTTLE IN 1624

Fig. 8. This map shows the ancient open-field system in its later stages. There were three arable fields, North, Middle and South. North-west of the village an area called the Four Farms had already been enclosed by the tenants. Half the area of the township was common, with the track which became the Great North Road running through the centre. Shilbotle West Moor formed a salient south-west of the Hampeth Burn and was acquired from the barony of Mitford in the Middle Ages. The Hitch Croft was meadow separated from the common by a boundary ditch on the line of the arc formed by modern lanes.

map, to the north of the village, follows the line of the former boundary between the North Crofts and the North Field. The lane to South East Farm, a farm which did not exist when the map was drawn, continued as a footpath to the Sturton Grange road, and formed the western boundary of the South Field. The position of the North Wood, then part of the lord's demesne, is today defined by the parish boundary and by the footpath from Shilbottle Grange to the Bilton road (Fig. 9).

In the south the earl's surveyor recorded a distinctive fan-shaped area cut out of the common above the Hampeth Bridge, which now carries a dual-carriageway. Marked as Hitchcroft in 1624, an earlier survey of the sixteenth century calls it the Hedge Croft, and explains that this area "was in ancient times full of wood and was in the hands of the bailiff of Shilbottle and kept enclosed from the tenants until such time as the wood was wasted, then it was laid open and ever since lay as a common pasture".[25] No trace of the wood remains. Its boundaries on two sides were the Hampeth Burn and a small tributary; these form the township boundaries today. The northern boundary was a mound or dyke, perhaps topped with a hedge; for the sixteenth-century survey records that Hedge Croft was "environed with one old dyke".[26] This dyke must have been on the line of the lane curving from south-east to south-west, and thus reproducing the distinctive shape of the seventeenth-century boundary, on both sides of the modern A1. It is not uncommon for an ancient boundary to become a modern lane.

It is clear from the map that the original boundaries of Shilbottle were primarily streams, as they still are today. The salient across the Hampeth Burn, known as the West Moor in the early sixteenth century, was an area given by the neighbouring baron of Mitford in the thirteenth century at some date before 1272. It was described in the sixteenth century as a tenement in the east end of Nether Sheild

[25] *N.C.H.*, Vol. V, p. 425.   [26] Ibid.

MODERN SHILBOTTLE

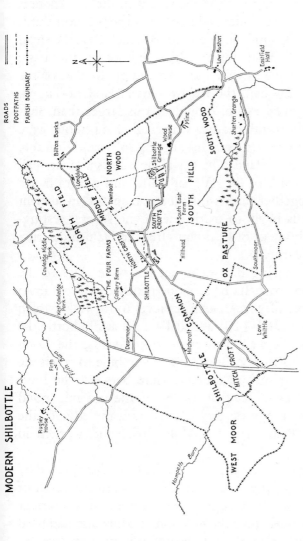

Fig. 9. This map should be compared with Fig. 8. The names of the main divisions of the township of 1624 have been added. For the sake of clarity modern field-boundaries are not shown. The modern landscape retains the pattern of the early seventeenth-century landscape, itself the product of previous centuries. Many ancient boundaries survive as modern roads, lanes and footpaths. The footpath running north from Shilbottle Grange was the western boundary of the demesne land of North Wood.

Dyke, given to the lord of Shilbottle, whose cattle, pastured on the Rimside Moors near Rothbury, were "brought to the said tenement for it was his hind's house during the time of the cattle pasturing in the said Rimside".[27] There is still a farm known as Shiel Dyke south of the Newton Burn.

Further north, a mile inland from Beadnell Bay, the small township of Tughall retains, like Shilbottle, the basic pattern of its fields as they had evolved at the end of the Middle Ages. Tughall, the flat or alluvial land of Tugga, was always a small estate, though it was larger than Shilbottle in the thirteenth century when eighteen persons were assessed at the very respectable sum of £46 19s. 4d. in 1296. There is now no village. The township consists of the hall on the north bank of the Tughall Burn and a farm half a mile away, together with the scant remains of an ancient chapel which is likely to mark one of the several resting-places of the body of St Cuthbert after the Danish destruction of Lindisfarne.

Tughall lies facing the sea under the wide skies of the Northumbrian coast. Its fields slope gently eastwards from a height of only fifty feet above sea level to the links which fringe the long sands of Beadnell Bay. As at Shilbottle the boundaries of Tughall were primarily streams, the Long Nanny and the Brunton Burn, which combine to reach the sea through a miniature estuary. Here between the links and the pastures of Tughall traces of the old mill pond survive among the gorse and hawthorn at the edge of the Long Nanny where Ivo the Miller lived and worked in 1296.

The ancient common fields of Tughall had disappeared by the early years of the seventeenth century. In the reign of Elizabeth I the lands of Tughall had been leased to a farmer who had previously held the position of bailiff and had used his position to reduce the number of tenants from twenty-three to eight.[28] When the estate was surveyed in the reign of

[27] *N.C.H.*, Vol. V, p. 424.   [28] Ibid., Vol. I, p. 350.

James I the field boundaries reflected a process of rational-
isation which had gone much further than at Shilbottle, but
even here boundaries remain basically as they were in the
seventeenth century and these in turn suggest the evolution
of the field systems after centuries of farming. The northern
boundary of the great field immediately to the east of the
Hall between the road and the salt marshes is represented by
the lane to the mill and its continuation, a long fence
through an area of ridge-and-furrow. In view of the tend-
ency for divisions between medieval fields to become lanes
or roads it is probable that this boundary was older than the
seventeenth century.

Tughall Common comprised almost half the area of the
seventeenth-century manor and included most of the land to
the west between the Brunton and Tughall burns and the
railway. Across the common ran the tracks connecting
Tughall with neighbouring townships. These are now
represented by foot-paths; the junction of paths marked on
the modern one-inch map represents an ancient crossroad
mapped by the seventeenth-century surveyor. The modern
road system did not then exist, even in rudimentary form.
Then, and for long afterwards, communications between the
coastal villages were maintained along the sands at low tide,
or by the track behind the links, such as the track which
exists today between Newton by the Sea and Beadnell.

The magnificent early seventeenth-century maps in
Alnwick Castle make it possible to demonstrate with some
precision how the ancient Anglian field systems of Northumberland formed the skeleton of the modern rural landscape. Maps of Long Houghton, Lesbury and Bilton,
tell the same story. No such surveys and no detailed terriers
were made in the Celtic areas where the stone walls and
enclosures of the eighteenth century created a new field
system.

In Pennine Northumberland, the south-western corner
of the county, East and West Allendale show a pattern of

tiny, stone-walled enclosures which contrast remarkably with the generally large fields typical of Northumberland as a whole. These small enclosures, above the rivers and below the long stone walls which define the edge of the moorlands, are reminiscent of the Norse pattern of settlement in the Yorkshire and Cumbrian dales, but the majority originate from the allotments given to the leadminers in the early nineteenth century (Plate 6).

Parishes and churches

Early Celtic Christianity was based on the monastery, the headquarters of missionary monks who wandered far and wide preaching and performing the ceremonies of the Church as required. St Aidan founded the monastery of Lindisfarne in about 635, and there is a tradition that he died leaning against the west wall of his wooden church at Bamburgh. Traces of a Celtic church, also constructed of wood, have been found on the site of King Edwin's palace under Yeavering Bell.[29] This church seems to have been contemporary with St Aidan. Stone churches appear in Northumberland in the latter half of the seventh century in the lifetime of St Wilfred (634–709). St Wilfred's church at Hexham was constructed of stone. Its remains today have been described as "perhaps the most moving monument of medieval Northumberland".[30]

Parish churches required an endowment to maintain the buildings and their priests, no easy matter in the poor and underpopulated countryside of Northumberland. In consequence only the kings and greater landowners could afford to build and endow a church. For this reason there is no Anglican church in old and substantial villages, such as Glanton, Great Whittington or Ovington. The traditional English picture of a village with its church and big

[29] *Medieval Archaeology*, Vol. I, (1957), pp. 148–9.
[30] N. Pevsner, *The Buildings of England: Northumberland* (1957), pp. 175–6.

house is not characteristic of Northumberland; where it is found it is often the creation of the eighteenth or nineteenth centuries, as at Etal or Matfen. The ancient ecclesiastical parishes of Northumberland were vast by southern standards. Bamburgh parish, a royal estate, once comprised twenty-one townships; Rothbury, another royal estate, comprised twenty-three. Simonburn parish, before the Conquest an estate of the earls of Northumbria stretched from the Border to the Roman Wall (Fig. 10). Woodhorn, where a church was built in the first half of the eighth century, included the whole coast from Cresswell to the mouth of the Wansbeck and was also an estate of the pre-Conquest earls.

The ancient parish of Warden included the much later settlement of Haydon Bridge and extended as far west as the Black Dyke, which was used as a convenient boundary between the parishes of Warden and Haltwhistle. In the north, the mainland estates of Lindisfarne constituted one parish, with its subordinate chapelries of Kyloe, Lowick, Ancrum, Tweedmouth and Ancroft formed after the lands of St Cuthbert were granted to Durham in 1082.

St Wilfred's church at Hexham was the centre of a parish extending from the Erring Burn, in the uplands north of the Wall, to the moorlands below Nenthead, in County Durham. It was not till the late eighteenth century that the parochial chapelry of Allendale was constituted a separate parish. Its boundary was then demarcated on the moors by a series of straight lines, in marked contrast to the boundaries of the ancient parishes, which were usually streams or other natural features. An early natural boundary was Hebburn Wood, near Chillingham, mentioned in 1293 as the boundary between Chillingham and Eglingham parishes, and still the boundary today.

An interesting parish is Kirknewton, which today comprises fifteen scattered farms or hamlets in Glendale. The attractive church under the Cheviots, close to the junction

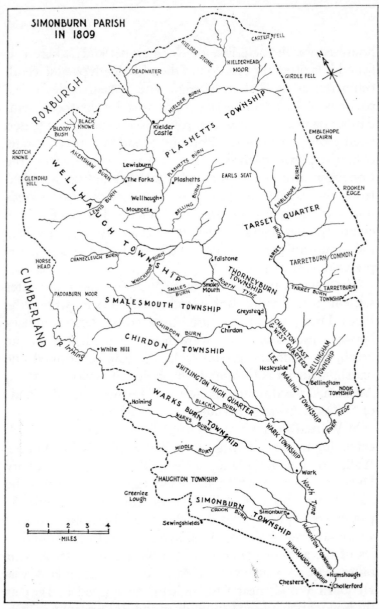

Fig. 10. (Based on the map by John Fryer and Sons.) The ancient parishes of Northumberland were for the most part exceptionally large in a sparsely inhabited countryside. Simonburn parish extended from the Border to the Roman Wall until it was divided into six parishes by Act of Parliament in 1811. The parish church was at Simonburn but there were also chapels, as at Bellingham, which became a parish church, at Bell's Burn on the Border, and at Falstone. Because parishes were so extensive the township, or more rarely the quarter, was the important administrative unit. The township could be a nucleated village such as Bellingham, or a number of dispersed farms as in Wellhaugh township.

of the College Burn and the Till, is largely a nineteenth-century building, though it contains "architecture of a very northern and primeval kind".[31] It is situated less than a mile from the site of King Edwin's palace under Yeavering Bell. The modern parish of Kirknewton has all the appearance of the remnant of a large royal estate once centred on the palace of Yeavering in Anglian times. This estate seems to have included the townships of Mindrum, Shotton, Elterburn and Thornington, included in a grant of twelve townships, on both sides of the later Border, to St Cuthbert in about the year 670. Shotton means 'the *ton* of the Scots'. Archaeological investigation has revealed that the royal palace of Old Yeavering was abandoned in the eighth century, and it is possible that it was succeeded by the new *ton* and church on a very similar site a short distance away.

By the early eleventh century Northumberland had recovered sufficiently from the destructive Danish invasions to embark on an extensive programme of church restoration. The well-known church towers of Bolam, Bywell St Andrews, Corbridge, Ovingham (Plate 7) and Warden all date from this period, the half century or so before the Norman Conquest, though at Bywell and Corbridge they incorporate work of an earlier period. The engaging simplicity of the little church at Warden must have been achieved at some date very close to the Conquest. The church of St Michael at Ingram is largely Norman, but there are indications that repairs of an earlier stone church were undertaken at some time in the early eleventh century, perhaps in the time of earl Siward, of Shakespeare's *Macbeth*. At Norham the discovery of old carved stones suggests that the existing church, also of Norman origin, replaced a pre-Conquest building.

The parishes received an enduring form under the Norman regime. Many new churches were built and the older buildings were reconstructed. The Bertram lords of Mitford

<hr />

[31] N. Pevsner, *Northumberland*, p. 201.

built their church below their castle by the Wansbeck shortly after the Conquest, though the present building is primarily a nineteenth-century reconstruction of a thirteenth-century church and little survives of the original Norman work. Alnwick, rising in importance as a major baronial head-quarters, was given its church of St Michael, technically a chapel in the parish of the older Anglian settlement of Lesbury. The original Norman churches were small and unassuming buildings, such as the little grey church of Thockrington on its Whin Sill outcrop in the grasslands (Plate 8). They included churches such as those at Alnham and Alwinton, both dedicated to St Michael, on the frontiers of arable farming under the hills. The majority were enlarged, or substantially rebuilt, in the thirteenth century, as were St Aidan's of Bamburgh and Holy Trinity of Embleton. The attractive little church of St John, at Edlingham, is a Norman church which was probably built on the site of an Anglian predecessor.

Bywell on Tyne has two parish churches, Bywell St Andrew and Bywell St Peter. There is now virtually no village, though in the sixteenth century Bywell was a large village inhabited by workers in iron. Bywell St Andrew is the older of the two and was probably the original parish church, built in the seventh century and with a fine tower completed about the year 1000. Much of Bywell St Peter's is also pre-Conquest. In origin it may have been a monastic church and it has been suggested that it may have been contemporary with St Wilfred's foundation at Hexham. After the Conquest, and the formation of the two baronies of Baliol and Bolbec, which met at Bywell, both churches became parish churches. Each is situated on the edge of its parish. They remain today amid their trees, forming part of the loveliest scenery of the Tyne, with stones handled by Roman soldier-masons and the men of Anglian Northum-bria.

In the large parishes, and with primitive communications,

86

people could not be expected to attend a remote parish church, even for the important festivals of the Church. Parish churches were therefore supplemented by chapels all over the countryside. In Eglingham parish, which comprised sixteen townships, there were at least four chapels built, or rebuilt in stone, soon after the Conquest. One is a romantic ruin withdrawn under the trees of West Lilburn. One, at Old Bewick under the Chillingham moors, stands alone by the Kirk Burn. Of Brandon chapel there is little to see save the foundations above the Breamish, the relics of a thirteenth-century reconstruction of a pre-Conquest building. Bolton chapel was extensively restored in the nineteenth century. At Tughall, in the ancient ecclesiastical parish of Bamburghshire, a few stones remain from the post-Conquest reconstruction of a chapel associated with St Cuthbert.

Many of these small chapels have vanished. There was a medieval chapel at Bell's Kirk, close to the Deadwater. At the time of the colonisation of the waste lands, in the thirteenth century, a chapel was built in the heart of Upper Coquetdale, near Quickening Cote on the Ridlees Burn. The founder of Newstead, a new settlement as its name implies, in the thirteenth century, also built a chapel, after satisfying the ecclesiastical authorities that he could maintain a chaplain and would not infringe the vested interests of the parish church at Bamburgh.

It was not till the reign of George III that steps were taken to recast the ancient parochial system. The vast parish of Simonburn was divided into the six parishes of Bellingham, Falstone, Greystead, Simonburn, Thorneyburn and Wark.[32] In the Middle Ages there had been chapels at Falstone, Wark and Haughton, as well as at Bellingham. Little is known about the history of the first three buildings, though the vanished chapel at Hawkhope, near Falstone, may have

[32] Greystead and Thorneyburn were held together after 1910. Humshaugh was a chapel of the new parish of Simonburn till 1832.

been associated with the remains of an ancient cross with a
runic inscription, "the oldest post-Roman inscription in
Northumberland".[33] and a tantalising survival from the
shadowy past of Tynedale. The stone-roofed chapel at
Bellingham became the new parish church. Small and seemly
churches were built by the Commissioners of Greenwich
Hospital at Wark, Greystead, Thorneyburn and Humshaugh,
and by subscription at Falstone. Essentially nineteenth-
century in conception, these unpretentious buildings fit
quietly into the Tynedale landscape.

The golden age of colonisation, 1150–1300

It has been estimated that at the time of Domesday Book,
Northumberland was one of the most thinly populated
areas of England. The population probably averaged 5·4
persons per square mile, as compared with 23·1 in Devon
and 42·5 in Norfolk.[34] It was long uncertain whether the
land between Tyne and Tweed would be ruled by England
or Scotland; not until Henry II had finally asserted the
power of the English crown, and had built the great stone
keeps necessary to maintain it, could Northumberland
settle down, in time to share in the economic expansion and
colonisation of the waste lands which took place all over
Europe in the high noon of the Middle Ages.

The small, but powerful and efficient, Norman military
aristocracy were active in the foundation of new towns and
and settlements. Leading barons granted land to the new
religious houses, with permission to build, dig and clear,
and to pasture their sheep. In this respect, as in many others,
the study of the landscape is sorely hampered by the lack
of a Domesday Book. Nevertheless, it seems that the
majority of the new *tons, hams, steads* and *biggins* of North-

33 *N.C.H.*, Vol. XV, p. 257.
34 J. C. Russell, *British Medieval Population*, (1948), p. 313.

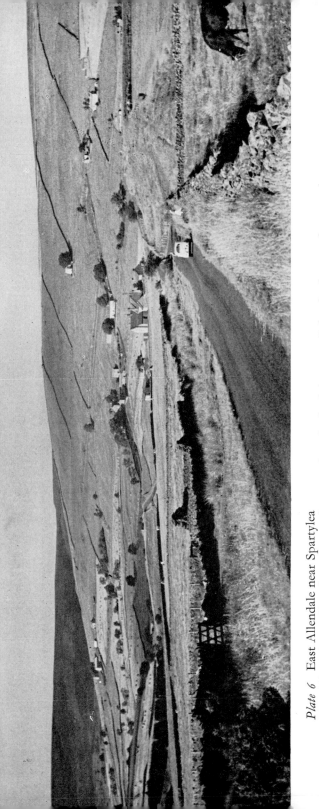

Plate 6 East Allendale near Sparrylea

The Allendales are Pennine country, for centuries a lead-mining area. It is a landscape of scattered cottages, many of them originally on the smallholdings of the lead-miners. Above them, under the high moorland ridges, are the stone walls of eighteenth and nineteenth-century enclosure.

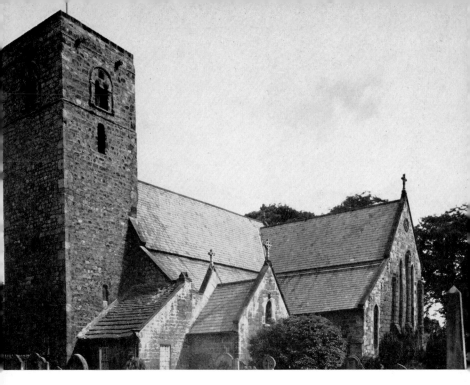

Plate 7   Ovingham church
Ovingham was one of the earlier Anglian settlements in Northumberland, becoming the centre of a large estate and later a parish including seventeen townships. The church tower is late Saxon and the church itself was remodelled in the peaceful thirteenth century.

Plate 8   Thockrington church
A lonely Norman church on an outcrop of the Whin Sill in wide grasslands, Thockrington is typical of the small, grey churches of the Norman countryside. The village is now reduced to a single farm though in the late thirteenth century it was a relatively populous and prosperous township.

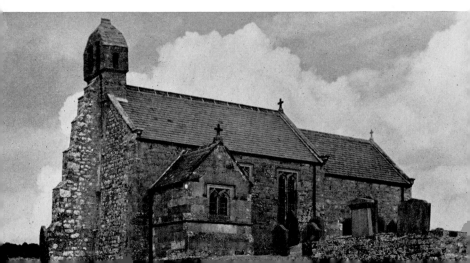

Plate 9 Cultivation terraces, Sandhoe
These medieval cultivation terraces were formed by the heavy ox-drawn plough introduced by the Anglian farmers. There are good examples elsewhere, as near Birtley, Alwinton, Ingram, Wooler and Hethpool. Since surviving terraces are found on steep slopes they are usually in close proximity to pre-Anglian settlements.

Plate 10 The keep, Newcastle upon Tyne
Henry II's stone keep succeeded the motte and bailey castle built by Robert, son of William the Conqueror, to guard the vital strategic crossing of the Tyne which the Romans had bridged. It is the work of the architect who was later responsible for Dover Castle. The keep and the medieval bridge below led to the rise of Newcastle.

umberland came into existence during the latter half of the twelfth century and the first half of the thirteenth.

On the eve of the war with Scotland, at the end of the thirteenth century, parts of Northumberland were more thickly settled than they were to be again till the mid-eighteenth century, or perhaps ever again. There was a medieval settlement among the Roman embankments of Chew Green, above the source of the Coquet. Medieval ploughs were at work by the Ridlees Burn, between Linshiels and Quickening Cote, in a countryside which might otherwise appear to have offered nothing but sheep pastures and uninhabited moorland since time immemorial. In this area there are mounds, which are probably remains of the medieval settlement of Aldenscheles. Here, even after Bannockburn, in 1317, land was dedicated in *mortmain* to maintain a chaplain.

New settlements were founded in the far corners of parishes or estates where there was land to spare. Newbiggin on Sea, one of several settlements called 'the new building', was founded, in the twelfth century, on the coastal moorlands which formed the southern extremity of the Anglian parish of Woodhorn. Newbiggin was granted a market and fair in 1203. Its church, dedicated to St Bartholomew, was erected on the prominent headland, but it remained for centuries a chapel of Woodhorn. Alnmouth, which was also named Newbiggin,[35] was similarly founded on the edge of a parish. It was founded, in the second half of the twelfth century, on the southern boundary of the South Field of Lesbury (Fig. 16). During the same period Newton on the Moor represents a colonisation of unoccupied land in the far western corner of the parish of Shilbottle; here some of the wide fields of the modern landscape still retain something of their former characteristics.

South of the Tyne the small barony of Dilston emerged after the Conquest by a series of grants of rights over forest

[35] J. Hodgson, *History of Northumberland,* Part II, Vol. I, p. 153.

land within the royal manor of Corbridge. Until the enclosures of the eighteenth century the inhabitants of Dilston shared with Corbridge rights of common on Corbridge Fell. In the thirteenth century it was the burgesses of Corbridge who granted to Thomas of Develstone twenty acres of waste and pasture on the fell "with liberty to enclose, dyke, hedge and empark" but not to put land under the plough.[36] The Park Wood of today was once part of the forest above the Devil's Water known as Dunstan Wood, which was granted to Dilston in 1297.

All over Northumberland, from the coastal plain to the Border fells, new settlements were being founded and virgin land was being cleared and ploughed. In about 1200 Hugh de Morwick received a grant of land east of Morpeth "to build a village upon in Pendmoor" between Morpeth and Ulgham.[37] A few years later Hugh de Baliol granted part of Whittonstall "to be assarted, cultivated, built upon and enclosed by a ditch and a hedge".[38] This grant was probably the origin of Newlands near Ebchester. Rothbury Newtown was founded between 1214 and 1240 on the well-watered slopes of Simonside above the Coquet. Above the farming area of the new settlement the boundaries of the lord's deer park were delineated by a wall, of which traces still remain in the bracken and heather. The moorlands and scrub of Rothbury Forest were also brought into some measure of cultivation during this period.

Peaceful conditions, increasing population, and the need for corn at a time when local communities had to be self-supporting, encouraged the growth of new farm settlements. Many of these have reverted to small farm hamlets, such as Chillingham Newtown astride the Devil's Causeway and separated from its parent village by the Till. Chillingham Newtown was a substantial village in the sixteenth century.

[36] *N.C.H.*, Vol. X, p. 70.

[37] Hodgson, op. cit., Part II, Vol. II, p. 158. Ulgham is pronounced 'Uffam'.

[38] *N.C.H.,* Vol. VI, p. 179.

It could supply eleven men equipped with horse and armour, and therefore prosperous farmers, to the muster of 1579, and also eight men unequipped.[39] Edlingham Newtown is now a single farm on the ridge above the village.

Settlements such as these resembled in situation and purpose the farms which began to fill some of the open spaces of the country in the eighteenth and nineteenth centuries. More ambitious attempts were made to found towns in the modern sense. The new town of Bamburgh is now Newtown Farm overlooking Budle Bay and lying among its fields below the rocky outcrops, gorse and heather of Bamburgh golf course and Newtown Hill. Below the farm the ground slopes to the sandhills and low cliffs of the bay, where a small beach lies below the New Town Caravan Park of modern visitors. Bamburgh Newtown was founded in about the year 1250 by Sir William Heron, constable of Bamburgh Castle, whose accounts of 1257 include an item in respect of the town of Warenmouth newly built by himself.[40] The name suggests that the new settlement might have been founded further to the west, where the Waren Burn emerges on to the muddy shore of the bay below the mill; but in 1293 it was reported that William Heron had "caused to be built a certain town called Warenmouth on the common pasture of the town of Bamburgh".[41] From the fourteenth century the settlement was usually known as Newtown.

Bamburgh Newtown was designed as a port, the most northerly port in England before Berwick was captured in 1296. It is not in an area suitable for arable farming since the rock lies close to the surface, though there are signs of the ridge-and-furrow of old ploughing in the hollows. The little bay, protected on the north-west and east by the low cliffs, would have provided some protection for the small

[39] *Calendar of Border Papers*, Vol. I, p. 15.   [40] *N.C.H.*, Vol. I, p. 194.
[41] Ibid.

medieval ships; access inland would have been provided along the line of the modern lane off the modern Bamburgh–Belford road.

Henry III granted to the burgesses of the new settlement all the rights and liberties of Newcastle upon Tyne, but the site was poor and the circumstances on the eve of 300 years of war were not propitious. Today Bamburgh Newtown is but a shadow where the winchats flit among the surrounding gorse and heather and the fulmars sweep in from the sea over Budle Point.

An equally unsuccessful settlement was the contemporary Warkworth Newtown, which was in existence by 1250. A survey made 300 years later, in 1567, explains that it was

> thought good for divers causes [that] those persons which should trade their traffic by sea as mariners or fishermen [owners of ships and merchants only excepted] should inhabit and dwell together, even so was set forth one parcel of ground for them to inhabit upon, as is this day called Newtown, [where the inhabitants] should always be near the haven and see their ships.[42]

The site selected was taken out of the arable fields of Birling and was astride the rough track which now gives access to the golf course and the big caravan park. To the east, where the golf course and the caravan park are now situated, there is a slack which is protected from the sea by a line of sandhills. This slack was once the mouth of the Coquet before the river changed course in the flood of 1765. The medieval settlement did not prosper. The fifty acres or so allotted to the site became an arable field attached to the burgage tenements of Warkworth and a nuisance to the people of Birling whose fields it divided (Plate 22).

A marked feature of Northumberland today is the extent to which the rigs, the ridge-and-furrow of ancient plough-

[42] *N.C.H.*, Vol. V, p. 149.

ing, can be seen over all the county, often at heights at which marginal land has been abandoned for centuries. Much land was ploughed, or reploughed, during the Napoleonic Wars, at a time when corn was grown on the high ground of Allendale; but much was farmed by medieval farmers, when many villages held larger populations than they do today, and some of which no longer exist. There are rigs on the high grasslands of Great Bavington and Ryal; among the hill pastures above Sweethope Loch, at an altitude of over seven hundred feet. Their bold curves sweep across the fields of East Trewick, between Whalton and Belsay.

Impressive examples of the work of early medieval farmers, and an indication of the extent to which all available land was used, are the lynchets, or cultivation terraces, such as those above the Elsdon Burn near Hethpool, seen to best advantage from the site of the pre-Roman settlement on the summit of Little Hetha. There is also a fine series near Wooler below the rampart of the imposing hill fort on Humbleton Hill. Others form prominent terraces on the hillside above the North Tyne, between Birtley and Birtley Shields; and also on the green hills above the Breamish, near Ingram.

Except at Sandhoe, near Corbridge (Plate 9), these terraces are found today in close association with ancient settlements of the pre-Roman and Roman periods; but on Ingram Hill at least they are medieval[43] and so, almost certainly, are the others. There are well-known lynchets above Clennell and Alwinton, a countryside which abounds with the ridge-and-furrow of medieval ploughing. At Clennell they are situated on the slopes below the earthwork on Camp Knowe above the Alwin. This settlement was occupied in pre-Roman times; but the terraces appear as extensions, on steeper ground, of the rigs still visible beside

[43] A. H. A. Hogg, 'Excavation in a Native Settlement at Ingram Hill', *A.A.*, 4th series, Vol. XX (1942), p. 111.

the track up the Alwin valley, and must be the work of the inhabitants of the lost medieval village of Clennell. In the Middle Ages the whole of this area supported a relatively large farming population, and the cultivation terraces on the hills represent the use of the plough on the higher and more difficult ground long since left to the sheep.[44]

Monasteries and the landscape

Soon after the Norman Conquest the new abbeys and monasteries took a leading part in the evolution of the landscape. Lindisfarne was refounded, as a Benedictine priory of Durham, towards the end of the eleventh century, and the priory church reached its final form by the middle of the twelfth. Its ruins today form part of one of the most haunting scenes in England against the wide background of sea and sky. At their feet the eider drakes, the birds of St Cuthbert, display their black and white plumage. The waves surge against the rocks of St Cuthbert's island, the Inner Farne. On the mainland the keep of Bamburgh Castle stands massively above the sands.

The estates of the priory were on the mainland, as at Fenham, north of Ross Links, where the monks owned a manor house, grange and mill on the land granted to them in 1082. By the early thirteenth century they were cutting peat, by leave of the lord of Holburn, in the moss on the Kyloe Hills, east of the present road from Holburn to Fenwick and Kyloe. They received grants of pasturage for the horses and oxen which drew their four-wheeled wagons, and grazing rights for their sheep.

There is still an area of dark and soggy peat known as Holburn Moss east of the escarpment above Holburn

[44] See A. Graham, 'Cultivation Terraces in South-Eastern Scotland', *Procs. of the Soc. of Antiquaries of Scotland*, Vol. LXXIII (1939), pp. 289–315, for a discussion of this problem which is relevant to similar conditions in Northumberland.

Grange. Now a landscape much changed by the planting of conifers among the heather, and in the past much traversed by eighteenth-century miners, the older tracks were still in part visible some thirty years ago. The monks were granted grazing rights over the whole of the moss, east of the medieval route from Holburn to Fenwick. In their business with Holburn they would have used the defiles in the escarpment, of which the most practical would have been the gap under Raven's Crag. On the eastern side of the hills their sheep and cattle were given pasturage among the scrub which then grew above Buckton Burn, and so continued the centuries-long clearance which preceded the wide modern fields.

Brinkburn, on the Coquet, its buildings magnificently restored in the nineteenth century, was founded in about 1135. In its setting and appearance it is the peer of Fountains and Tintern. The monks began to bring into cultivation the wastes on the high ground to the east of Rothbury, and were granted, by the lords of Mitford, rights of ditching and clearing along the road from Longframlington to Rothbury. This road cannot now be traced with any certainty, though topography suggests that it ran the length of Thorney Hill on the boundary between the townships of Debdon and Mount Healey.

In 1165 the Premonstratensian abbey of Blanchland was founded, in sparsely inhabited country by the Derwent, at the southern edge of the barony of Bolbec. The monks began the transformation of the river haugh into the trim fields of today and built a mill at what is now the north-east corner of the modern bridge.

Newminster Abbey, near Morpeth, was founded in 1157 as the eldest daughter of the great Cistercian house of Fountains. Within fifty years its sheep were taming the wild fells of Kidland and Upper Coquetdale.

New pressure on land for arable farming and grazing during this period required more precise definition of

95

boundaries. The stones known as the Golden Pots, on the high moors south of Thirlmoor close to Dere Street, were probably set up in the Middle Ages on the boundary between the parishes of Elsdon and Holystone. Towards the end of the thirteenth century the owners of four estates disputed an area at the edge of the Kyloe Hills near the point at which the Belford road climbs from Glendale onto the open moor. It was subsequently agreed that the disputed boundary should begin at the "standenstan at the head of Cockenheugh".[45] The big stone stands today at the edge of a small fir copse on the line of the parish boundary which runs north along the ridge above St Cuthbert's cave.

In the wilds of thirteenth-century Upper Coquetdale the western limits of the grazing grounds of Newminster were defined by a stone bank and ditch, which can still be seen. Beginning on the north bank of the river, opposite Windyhaugh, it ascends the grassy slope of Barrow Law, crosses the ridge between the junction of the Coquet and the Barrow Burn, and ends at the head of Barrow Cleugh. On the spine of the ridge, within sight of the Hanging Stone on Cheviot, a later drove road passes through the bank, through a gap marked by massive stones. This is sheep country of grass, bracken and scree. It was created by sheep close to the Border line.

The growing population and increasing wealth of the thirteenth century led to the rebuilding of the majority of the rural churches. Elsdon church, for instance, was rebuilt and received its final form in time to receive the slain of Otterburn. Chillingham church was enlarged and altered in the twelfth century. In the thirteenth the old churches of Bywell St Andrew, Corbridge and Ovingham were all greatly enlarged and there were substantial additions to the priory church at Hexham. The church of St Aidan at Bamburgh is also primarily of this period.

[45] *N.C.H.,* Vol. XIV, p. 226.

The landscape of regression, 1300–1600

"Northumberland has more castles, fortalices, peles, bastles and barmikins than any other county in the British Isles"[46] thanks to the centuries of war, raiding and brigandage which began in the reign of Edward I. By Tudor times, and in part because the new monarchy undermined the authority of the old nobility of the north, it was necessary to have at least one strong tower, and often more than one, in most of the villages and hamlets throughout the county. "There is more theft, more extortion by English thieves, than there is by all the Scots of Scotland," reported the bishop of Carlisle in 1522.[47] At the very end of the sixteenth century landowners were still building strongholds instead of country houses. The tower of Dues Hill Grange, above the Coquet near Hepple, was built in 1612. The tower of Coupland, in Glendale, was a little later in date and was probably the last private stronghold in England to be constructed in the old medieval manner.

The early Norman castles consisted of stockades on artificial mounds of earth. The most impressive of these castles is the motte at Elsdon, constructed by the Umfravilles in the heart of their lordship of Redesdale and strategically commanding one of the most important communications centres near the Border. The castle was strongly sited on a ridge above the burn in close touch with Dere Street and the tracks running east and west between Redesdale and Coquetdale. Elsdon, however, was too remote and presumably too liable to be cut off. It was abandoned in favour of Harbottle.

Stone castles did not appear till the reign of Henry II, whose stone keep at Newcastle replaced an earlier Norman work (Plate 10). Even in the thirteenth century there were

---

[46] B. Long, *Castles of Northumberland* (1967), p. 1.
[47] *Letters and Papers of Henry VIII*, Vol. III, Pt 2, p. 985.

only ten important castles in the county, of which Bamburgh, Norham and Wark on the Tweed, Harbottle in Coquetdale, and Newcastle, were in royal hands. A castle had also been constructed at Berwick but this was handed over with the town to the Scots by Richard I.

Baronial castles included Alnwick and Warkworth, commanding the crossings of the Aln and the Coquet and blocking the increasingly important coastal route between Newcastle and Berwick. Farther south the baronial castles of Morpeth and Mitford guarded the crossings of the Wansbeck and formed the outer defences of Newcastle twelve miles to the south. The keep of Newcastle, commanding the lowest crossing of the Tyne, was supported by the equally impregnable castle of the Umfravilles at Prudhoe.

In the thirteenth century the majority of the Northumbrian landowners lived in halls surrounded by wooden palisades, banks or hedges, and sometimes by a moat. A minor hall-house of this type was at Fawns, in the high fields above Kirkwhelpington. The best remaining example is Aydon Castle above its deep dene north of Corbridge. This remained basically the house of a country gentleman fortified in troubled times at the end of the thirteenth century.

The record of those times is written in stone on the face of Northumberland. Work on churches, which had been a marked activity of the eleventh and twelfth centuries, dwindled almost to nothing outside the walls of Newcastle and Alnwick. The Northumberland countryside enjoyed neither the wealth nor the security which made possible the fine village churches elsewhere in later medieval England. The churches seen today, as at Embleton, Whittingham and Stamfordham, are largely the result of sometimes over-enthusiastic nineteenth-century restoration, such as that which demolished much of the pre-Conquest work at Whittingham.

The beginning of the Scottish wars in 1297, and the anarchy which followed Bannockburn, was followed by a rush to transform the old manor houses into castles. The prior and convent of Tynemouth were authorised to fortify the priory before the outbreak of war, in 1296, and so began the evolution of the imposing fortress on the headland guarding the Tyne. The manor houses of Ford and Etal were fortified in support of the royal castles guarding the line of the Tweed. The manor house at Chillingham, captured and destroyed by the Scots in 1296, received a licence to crenallate in 1344. Famous castles, such as Blenkinsopp under the fells above the North Tyne, and Bothal on the Wansbeck, were constructed during this period. Langley Castle, the centre of a small barony and technically a tower-house rather than a castle, was built in the mid-fourteenth century. Langley was strategically placed to command the fords above the Tyne west of Hexham and the tracks leading south over the fells. The gate upon the bridge at Haydon was "kept constantly barred, chained and locked" by the barons of Langley.[48] Sensitively restored by the historian Cadwallader Bates, Langley retains much of the atmosphere of the time among its trees under the Stublick Moors.

The most impressive of all the Northumbrian castles, even in its ruined state, is Dunstanburgh, a gatehouse castle with the black cliffs of the Whin Sill and the sea at their feet incorporated into the defences (Plate 11). The massive curtain wall and the gatehouse keep emerge most dramatically in all their arrogant strength at the point where the path from Craster climbs out of the dip which was once a marshy valley. They should be seen on a day of storm when the sea-spray flies over the towers. Dunstanburgh does not really enter into the strategic scheme of Northumbrian castles. It was originally constructed for Thomas, earl of Lancaster, in the early years of the fourteenth century, probably more for his own purposes than as a defence against the Scots.

[48] J. Hodgson, *History of Northumberland,* Part II, Vol. III, p. 378.

The castles of Warkworth and Alnwick came into the hands of the Percies in the fourteenth century. Alnwick is imposing and famous, and today stands essentially as it was completed, though it was extensively restored in the eighteenth and nineteenth centuries. Despite its plundering as a source of building materials in the seventeenth century, Warkworth remains the finest achievement of medieval military architecture in Northumberland, built as much for the comfort of a rich and powerful owner as for defence.

A pele, or peel, originally meant a defensive enclosure with a ditch, palisade or mound. The term was applied to the enclosure, and not to the building within. But by the end of the sixteenth century almost any strong tower might be called a pele and it is in this sense that the term is used in Northumberland today. According to a list drawn up for Henry V, in 1415, Northumberland had at least seventy-eight such towers 100 years after Bannockburn. These included the famous vicars' peles, which can be seen today at Corbridge, Chatton, Elsdon, Embleton and Whitton. At Alnham a tower for the security of the vicar became necessary by 1541. It is now a Youth Hostel. At Corbridge, an open town and repeatedly burnt by the Scots, the vicar's pele is a strong and forbidding building close to the church (Plate 12). It was built in about the year 1300 with stones from the convenient quarry of Roman *Corstopitum*. The tower at the east end of Main Street dates from about 1600. Country vicars faced the risk of being carried off by the Scots and the vicar of Kirkwhelpington had to appear with horse and armour at the muster of 1538.[49] Stawood Pele, west of Hexham, is a genuine pele within an enclosure, standing high on the crest of a wooded spur between the West Allen and the Harsondale Burn.

The destructive raids with which Henry VIII pursued his Scottish policy were returned in kind. In Tudor North-

[49] J. Hodgson, *Muster of Northumberland for 1538*, f. iii, MS. copy in the Library of the Society of Antiquaries of Newcastle upon Tyne.

umberland some kind of stronghold became essential for any man of property. The wealthier farmers of the period built simple defensive structures consisting of a lower storey where stock, and especially the horses, might be taken for protection, and an upper storey reached by an outer stair-case, where the family at least might hold out till morning. Peles of this type abounded in the wilds of North Tynedale and Redesdale, along Tarset and Tarret Burn, as at Gate-house (Plate 13) and Black Middings. The pele at Hole Farm in lower Redesdale is a good example. At Ninebanks the tower incorporated in the farm by the roadside above the East Allen was originally a more ambitious building than the small peles which abounded in Redesdale and Tyne-dale, but it is a reminder that insecurity extended to the southern confines of the county in Tudor times.

Bastle houses were constructed for men of relative wealth and social standing. The word *bastle* comes from the French *bastille*. Doddington Bastle in the centre of the village was constructed as late as 1584 for a member of the great Border family of the Greys. It remained in good condition until the 1880s. It is a large, stone house three storeys high, with walls three feet thick, and was designed for a reason-able degree of comfort by the not very rigorous standards of late Tudor Northumberland. At Chillingham, close to the southern boundary wall of the Park, Hebburn Tower is a fine bastle which replaced a larger tower-house at some time in the sixteenth century. Standing among the great oaks and ash trees of the park, clasped by the strangling cables of ivy, Hebburn Tower is the classic 'ivy-mantled tower' of a Gothic landscape.[49a]

[49a] The publication of *Shielings and Bastles,* Royal Commission on Historical Monuments—England (1970), was too late to be of assistance in work on this chapter. Whether or not the term 'bastle' should properly be applied to all defensible farmhouses regarded as bastles by the authors, the book is indispensable for the study of buildings, unique in England, which evolved in Tudor Northumberland under the pressure of chronic inse-curity.

Peles and bastles were intended to do little more than resist a brief raid, or at least to preserve the life of the owner and his family, even though the stock might be driven off, until neighbours might be summoned to ride to the fray. At the hamlet of Downham, high above the Bowmont near Mindrum, a tower of the Ogles was completed in time to hold off a raiding party in 1596, though they "hewed at the gate of the barmikin with axes"[50] all through an October night. Incidents of this kind did not assist the economic development of the countryside of Tudor Northumberland, and by the end of the reign of Elizabeth I most of the county had reached its nadir. Leland reported that only "crooked old trees and shrubs" remained in the Cheviots.[51] The forests had long vanished along Tweedside and the inhabitants burned sea-coal. In Elsdon, in 1604, it was reported that there were no woods of any value except on the higher ground where it "hath been, and still is, wasted and decayed by the inhabitants of Scotland".[52]

The destruction of forests was an almost universal activity in England generally during the sixteenth century. In Northumberland the process had been intensified by shifting cultivation, large-scale grazing and war. By the second half of the century the inhabitants of townships in Bamburghshire were reduced to leasing areas of Chatton "to have sufficient heather and furse for their fuel".[53]

Sheep on the fells

For centuries before the Norman Conquest sheep had been the primary cause of the clearance of the Northumbrian hillsides. Their presence on the remote fells was in itself an indication that the primeval wilderness was in retreat. Flocks could not graze where wolves were numerous, and

[50] *N.C.H.*, Vol. XI, pp. 85–6.
[51] *Itinerary,* 1769 ed., Vol. VII, p. 67.
[52] *Survey of the Debateable and Border Lands,* p. 108.
[53] *N.C.H.*, Vol. XIV, p. 211.

the grants of grazing rights to the monks of Newminster during the thirteenth century suggest that even in the wilds of Upper Coquetdale the wolf had been brought close to extinction. Goats are even more destructive of vegetation than are sheep and were not always looked upon with favour. In 1297 the monks of Newminster were granted grazing rights in the neighbourhood of Ulgham *ad omnia animalia sua, exceptis capris.*[54] A few goats, the wild descendants of domesticated ancestors, still survive in Northumberland today in the more inaccessible areas, such as the heights of Cheviot itself. Large herds of cattle moved between the seasonal grazing grounds. In the thirteenth century Newcastle was a major port for the export of leather.[55] The chronicler of Edward III's expedition of 1327 found Northumberland "a wild country full of barren wastes and great hills, and extremely poor"; but he added, "save for livestock".[56]

Newminster, as befitted a daughter-foundation of Cistercian Fountains, was prominent in the production of wool; and from its charters it is possible to form a picture of the flocks grazing their way into the far hills. The bare fells and scree of Kidland, and all the hills between the Coquet and the Border, owe their present appearance, or at least as it was before recent forestry operations, primarily to Cistercian sheep. In 1181 the monks were granted grazing rights in the lordship of Kidland "between Alwin and Clennell and thence by the Kidland Burn to the south as far as the great road of Yarnspeth by the wood to Yarnspeth Burn".[57] The wood has long vanished, though it is now being replaced by conifers. Yarnspath Law, 'the hill of the eagle's path', is the broad-backed fell above the Usway from Usway Ford to Fairhaugh.

'The great road' was Clennell Street, now in many places an almost imperceptible depression in the bent, elsewhere

[54] 'Newminster Cartulary', *Surtees Society*, Vol. LXVI (1876), p. 284.
[55] C. M. Fraser, *The Northumberland Lay Subsidy Roll of 1296* (1968), p. 8.
[56] Quoted by R. Nicholson, *Edward III and the Scots* (1965), p. 25.
[57] N.C.H., Vol. XV, p. 429.

improved for the purposes of modern forestry, which climbs above Alwinton to the ridge above Kidland Dene and then slants down the side of Yarnspath Law to the ford across the Usway and the ascent to the Border ridge.

By the thirteenth century the sheep farms and shepherds' cottages of Kidland and Upper Coquetdale had their predecessors in the heart of the fells. At Barrow Burn the monks had their own fulling mill. In the deep valley of the Usway is the shepherd's cottage of Batailshiel Haugh at an altitude of some 900 feet (Plate 14). Its site was once a shieling belonging to one Henry Bataille, who lived in the latter half of the thirteenth century and gave to a certain Henry the Carpenter the site which is now the farm of Linshiels at the mouth of the Ridlees Burn.[58] At the neighbouring farm at Quickening Cote during this period there was a settlement where the valley of the Ridlees Burn broadens under the hills above the junction of the burn with the Coquet, between Linbriggs and Linshiels. Here, in 1317, Richard Horsley was empowered to dedicate in *mortmain* 100 acres of arable land and sixty acres of meadow to maintain a chaplain to serve his chapel in the manor of Aldenscheles. Aldenscheles was the original name of Quickening Cote higher up the Ridlees Burn. The site of the chapel and the small settlement has been identified between the round *stell* and the Ridlees Burn, east of Linshiels, where they are guarded by the red flags and minatory notices of military operations. They are now little more than foundations close to the remains of a large enclosure of earth and stone.

It has been suggested that this site above the Ridlees Burn was originally Celtic in origin, reoccupied in the Middle Ages and then abandoned during the Scottish wars.[59] The remains are not spectacular and they are

[58] *N.C.H.*, Vol. XV, p. 487.

[59] See *N.C.H.*, Vol. XV, p. 468 and footnote pp. 467–8 for a description of this site and its history. I am also much indebted to Mr Edward Miller for his guidance and comments.

Plate 11 Dunstanburgh Castle

Built for Thomas, Earl of Leicester, in 1313–16, and improved by John of Gaunt *c.* 1380. The castle was built on the Whin Sill headland where the cliffs were a sufficient defence on the seaward side. The work of the 'over-mighty subject' of the period, Dunstanburgh had little strategic importance. The photograph shows traces of extensive medieval ploughing.

Plate 12 The vicar's pele, Corbridge
Built of Roman stones in about 1300 at the beginning of 300 years of Border
warfare and very necessary for the protection of a relatively important man in
an unwalled town. There are vicars' peles at Alnham, Embleton, Elsdon,
Shilbottle and Ponteland.

Plate 13 Gatehouse pele, North Tynedale
A strong house designed for defence against raiders, and built in the latter half of the sixteenth century. Access to the family's living quarters was provided by the outside staircase. Stock were kept in the lower room. Windows were as few and as small as possible.

Plate 14 Batailshiel Haugh, Upper Coquetdale

The name of this remote shepherd's cottage on the Usway is derived from the Bataille family who owned land in the area during the twelfth and thirteenth centuries. *Shiel, shield* or *shielding* is a word of Norse origin. Originally meaning summer grazing, it was also applied to temporary buildings occupied by shepherds and others, such as the fishermen of North Shields.

difficult to interpret: but they convey a memory of human settlement and endeavour in the remote hills.

In the reign of Henry VIII it was reported that there were no longer any buildings in the lordship of Kidland. Upper Coquetdale is too well supplied with routes across the Border, as the drovers knew, and as the shepherd knows today. The deep secluded valleys, or hopes, under the round hills of Kidland were unsuitable for the organisation of mutual defence. As the Tudor commissioners explained in 1541:

> the said valleys or hopes of Kidland lieth so distant and divided by mountains one from another that such as inhabit . . . cannot hear the fray, outcry or exclamation of such as dwell in another hope or valley upon the other side of the said mountain nor come to assemble to their assistance in time of necessity.[60]

Even after the Union of the Crowns, in 1603, security on the Border deteriorated in the time of the Commonwealth. It was not till the late seventeenth century that much of Northumberland became safe for isolated ventures in farming. The fine Georgian farm at Shillmoor, in Upper Coquetdale, is a memorial to the final establishment of peaceful conditions.

Deserted villages

The high tide of settlement began to recede in the fourteenth century after the anarchy which followed Bannockburn and the devastation caused by the Black Death. It has been circulated that towards the end of the century the density of population averaged only 17 persons to the square mile, a marked increase since the average of 5·4 at the end of the eleventh century, but very small compared with the figures

---

[60] Ibid., p. 451, quoting report of 1542.

of 37 for Yorkshire or the 58 of Leicestershire.[61] Scots raids may have had little permanent effect, but they must have inhibited economic progress throughout all rural Northumberland. Records show that Tynemouth Priory was having increasing difficulty in finding tenants by the early sixteenth century. There was a marked decline in arable farming and much evidence of the destruction or dwindling of villages caused by economic change, a trend which continued until the nineteenth century. The long decline in arable farming was such that by 1933 only 33,000 acres of Northumberland were under corn.

Sites have been abandoned at all periods of Northumbrian history and are found at all levels, from the coastal plain to an altitude of some 700 feet. They range from Old Yeavering, royal manor of Anglian kings, to villages at Low Buston and Humshaugh, removed to improve the amenities of eighteenth- and nineteenth-century estates. Some give shadowy glimpses of the Dark Ages, as at Ollerchesters in Redesdale, or record the remote manor of a minor medieval landowner, as at Fawns near Kirkwhelpington. Many tell the story of the remote settlements and shielings in the remote hills, as at Memmerkirk, or the site of the chapel within the mounds of the Roman camp at Chew Green, where Dere Street crosses the Border. Memmerkirk was no more than a shieling, a medieval long house where excavation has revealed fourteenth-century pottery,[62] and now scarcely to be discerned amid the tussocks between the junction of the Yoke Burn and the Sting Burn under the ascent to Cushat Law. There are other signs of similar sites in Kidland; and probably a similar origin can be ascribed to the foundations among the bent under Cunyan Crags, north of the Breamish. There is a marked concentration of deserted villages on sites which must have been marginal

[61] J. C. Russell, *British Medieval Population,* p. 313.
[62] B. Harbottle and R. A. S. Cowper, 'An Excavation at Memmerkirk', *A.A.,* 4th series, Vol. XLI (1963).

for arable farming in the wide central uplands between Dere Street and the Great North Road (Fig. 11).

Some sites were abandoned for more favourable alternatives, as at Old Felton, now a single farm off the Great North Road, which was probably abandoned in favour of the crossing of the Coquet marked by the medieval bridge of Felton. Others represent failures in new ventures in urban settlement, as at Bamburgh and Warkworth new towns. Many are sites cleared by landlords in the eighteenth and nineteenth centuries to improve the landscaping of their estates, as at Kirkharle, Biddlestone and Haughton.

The great majority of deserted villages represent the dwindling of rural communities which began in the sixteenth century, when landlords no longer required armed retainers and turned to devote to the development of their estates new wealth and methods backed by much of the legal and social power of the older Border feudalism. A few villages disappeared completely. The majority were reduced to a single large farm. This process continued throughout the eighteenth century and into the nineteenth. Doddington in Glendale was assessed at the relatively high figure of £65 6s. 2½d. in 1296. It was still a prosperous village in the eighteenth century with handloom weavers and a weekly cattle market. Now consisting of two large farms and a handful of cottages, Doddington experienced a marked decline in population, from 339 in 1801 to 153 in 1901, and this decline seems to have been hastened by the enclosure of Doddington Moor by agreement in the eighteenth century.

Redesdale and North Tynedale were particularly heavily populated in Tudor times. The sites of peles which were once the homes of a substantial household are numerous. At Evistones, above the Sills Burn near High Rochester, there was a settlement large enough to support six or seven strong houses of the pele type.[63] In the 1630s there were

[63] J. Hodgson, *History of Northumberland,* Part II, Vol. I, p. 135, and p. 84 for following statement.

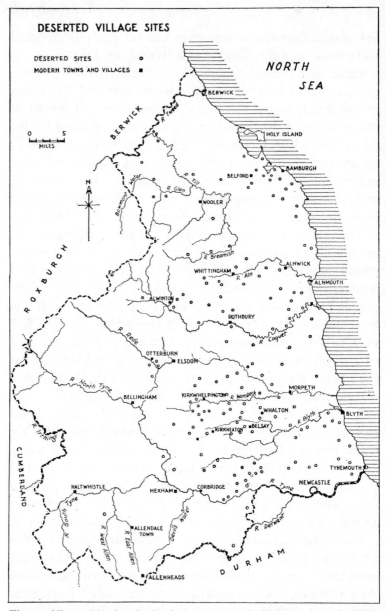

Fig. 11. All over Northumberland except among the high western moorlands are found the sites of deserted medieval villages and settlements. Most of these represent the peak of the colonisation of the waste in the thirteenth century. From these are derived the large areas of old ridge-and-furrow which can still be seen in many places today. There is a large concentration in the central highlands between the Tyne and the Wansbeck, now primarily a grazing country. This map is based on the Deserted Medieval Village Research Group's list of 1963, which shows a total of 165 sites.

still eleven corn mills below the moorlands of Elsdon and Corsenside, though they had been reduced to one, at Elsdon, by the 1820s.

Depopulation of parts of Northumberland was becoming marked by the reign of Henry VIII, though perhaps not as much as the muster rolls might suggest. Landlords were taking demesne lands into their own hands and were turning to pastoral farming. By 1537 most of the arable land of Tynemouth Priory had been converted into pasture, as at Backworth, where only 250 acres of arable land remained compared with 1000 acres of grazing. The process was hastened by the new entrepreneurs who acquired the former ecclesiastical estates. Robert Delaval bought up the whole of the former priory's Hartley estate, "purchased the freeholders lands, displaced the said tenants, and converted their tillage to pasture".[64] Today the curves of ridge-and-furrow east of the abandoned railway at New Hartley remain as vestiges of old arable farming (Plate 15).

Chirmundesden, once one of the 'ten towns of Coquet-dale', disappeared some time in the sixteenth century. A few tumbled stones and mounds amid rushes, gorse and tree stumps indicate the original site on a small plateau. It lies high above the Coquet within the great amphitheatre of hills from the Rimside Moors and Simonside to the Har-bottle Crags and the smooth slopes of Clennell. The site is close to a junction of pathways suggesting here, as else-where in Northumberland, the ghosts of ancient tracks now abandoned to the grazing cattle, the peewits and the curlews. At Wreighill, on the hills overlooking the junction of the Coquet and the Grasslees Burn, are traces of the foundations of a village which grew up around the grange and gardens of the monks of Newminster. The village disappeared without trace in the seventeenth century, possibly on account of plague. At Reaveley, now a single farm near Ingram, the foundations of a medieval settlement are

[64] *N.C.H.*, Vol. IX, p. 124.

visible under a small grove of oak and ash. This too faded quietly out of history in the sixteenth century.

Excavations at West Whelpington, on the edge of a crag above the Wansbeck at an altitude of 700 feet, have revealed a group village of stone houses, each with its croft, grouped around what was once a village green. Some of these houses were occupied in the twelfth and fourteenth centuries. One house was constructed in Tudor times.[65] Occupation of West Whelpington seems to have ended in the early eighteenth century when, according to an oral tradition, the whole of the village came into the hands of one man who then evicted fifteen farmers.[66] Today, large areas of ridge-and-furrow on the moorlands and rough pastures above the Wansbeck show the outlines of the village fields and indicate that there were centuries of arable farming on these uplands.

Fallowfield, where the hills below the Roman Wall slope south towards the Tyne, was the site of a village abandoned in 1595. Here the mounds of old foundations are close to the single farm which replaced the medieval village. Lead was worked on Fallowfield Fell in the seventeenth century and coal-mining followed until the nineteenth. Medieval ridge-and-furrow can still be seen among the gorse and rough pastures, and among the thickets of birch, alder and hazel, which also conceal the abandoned mine workings and heaps of spoil.

At Humbleton, in a fold of the Cheviots near Wooler, the medieval village, assessed at over £39 in 1296, was grouped round the small triangular green, which now lies within the framework of by-roads.

Most of the farms of Northumberland are the lineal descendants of medieval villages and have been formed by the concentration of the original holdings into the hands of

---

[65] H. G. Jarrett, 'The Deserted Village of West Whelpington', *A.A.,* 4th series, Vol. XL (1962).

[66] J. Hodgson, *History of Northumberland,* Part II, Vol. I, p. 198.

one individual. Despite the need for armed men this process was widespread in Tudor times. At Outchester, on the hill above the Waren Burn near Belford, excavation has revealed the existence of a village which consisted of two rows of houses in the fourteenth century.[67] By 1580 one Thomas Jackson of Berwick, who held a mortgage on the property, had expelled the tenants and put the land to pasture. At Hetton, in Glendale, Jackson also made use of a mortgage to convert the best lands to pasture.[68] Elsewhere the Muster Rolls show that the increased exactions of landlords at this time were often advanced as the reason for the lack of 'furnishing' of horse and armour, as at Beal and Haggerston.

Today the most obvious sign of these deserted villages is usually old ridge-and-furrow, such as the fine sweeping curves north-east of the farm of East Trewick, once the site of a village, at the point where the road from Walton to Belsay dips to the crossing of the Blyth. At Low Buston, near Warkworth, the mounds representing former houses and crofts are visible near the spring on the plateau above the Hounden Burn. Low Buston village was removed by an improving landlord about 1780, and here, too, ridge-and-furrow near the Warkworth road recall ancient arable farming.

The ebb and flow of settlement is a continuing process. Blawearie, abandoned in the nineteenth century, is a farm standing high on its windy ridge at the edge of the rocks and heather of the moorlands between Chillingham and Old Bewick, amid its sycamores, hawthorn and rhododendrons where the recesses of the great rocks still form a natural *stell*. At Reaveley Hill, near the site of a prehistoric settlement, a recently abandoned shepherd's cottage stands crumbling on the skyline, a gnarled willow and a hawthorn

[67] 'An Excavation at Outchester, Northumberland', *A.A.*, 4th series, Vol. XLIII (1965).

[68] *Calender of Border Papers,* Vol. I, 'Muster of the East Marches', pp. 16, 17; and p. 19 for Beal and Haggerston below.

appearing unexpected on the moorland mark the site of its abandoned croft, a modern version of the tumbled stones and rabbit-mined mounds of Celtic homesteads and medieval shielings on the hills of Northumberland.

Country houses and parks

After the Union of the Crowns in 1603 the Northumbrian landowners began to feel sufficiently secure to convert their strongholds into mansions designed for domestic comfort rather than for defence. There are a few Jacobean great houses replacing or adjacent to some older tower; but it was not till the eighteenth century that improved security and increased wealth influenced domestic architecture on any substantial scale. Aydon Castle, above Corbridge, is a medieval mansion, a fortified house rather than a castle. In design it "represents the amount of space and comfort which could be afforded in the Border country (and indeed anywhere in England) about 1300".[69] Here, above the deep dene of Aydon Burn, are the hall and solar of a medieval country gentleman, protected by the burn itself and with a defensive wall on the more accessible side. It is essentially a domestic group of buildings, belonging to the years before the Scots raided deep into Northumberland and little affected by later changes of architectural taste.

Aydon's neighbour, Halton (Plate 16), was also a small manor house in origin; its history suggests that it stands on the site of the wooden hall of an Anglian thegn. The tower was added in the fourteenth century. The house on its eastern side followed in the late seventeenth. This compact group of grey buildings, set off by their trim lawns and beech hedges, on the hills above the Tyne, provide a striking example of the continuity of rural history. They lie south of the Roman cavalry fort of *Hunnum*, which provided stones for their construction, and were the centre of

[69] N. Pevsner, *Northumberland*, p. 77.

a pre-Conquest estate which was held until the thirteenth century by the Saxon tenure of *thegnage*.[70] Below Halton the little burn forming the township boundary was once also the boundary of Halton South Field; it was very probably selected as a convenient line of demarcation when the first Anglian thegn received a grant of an estate within the royal manor of Corbridge.

The course of history expressed by the medieval stronghold followed by a Jacobean mansion, and then by the classical building required by later wealth and taste, appears in the sequence of buildings at Belsay, each a superb example of its period. Here the imposing tower-house, probably the finest in the north of England, is fourteenth century. Adjoining is the Jacobean mansion of 1614. Behind are the fine eighteenth-century stables. The latter was superseded in its turn by the cold perfection of the Doric house constructed by the young John Dobson from the designs of the owner made during a honeymoon in Greece. Belsay Hall was completed in 1817. To improve the lay-out of gardens and grounds the village was removed and rebuilt in an Italian style on its modern site. The deep quarries from which the stone was cut were converted into one of the finest 'Gothic' gardens in England, such as would have delighted the heart of Jane Austen's Catherine Morland, where the path winds under the rocks overhung by ferns and great trees.

Chipchase Castle (Plate 17) tells the same story of the transition from war to peace. It begins with the tower, probably constructed in the mid-fourteenth century, which replaced an unfortified manor house during the period of ruinous Scots raids and local brigandage after Bannock-burn. The big Jacobean mansion was added in the reign of James I, its wide expanse of windows, their shape subsequently altered in Georgian times, forming a significant contrast to the narrow slits in the tower at its western

[70] W. Percy Hedley, *Northumberland Families,* Vol. I, p. 258.

corner. Jacobean mansions, however, were rare in North-umberland, and pele towers were still being built at about the time the house at Chipchase was under construction. The true country house came late to Northumberland—100 years or more after those in the Midlands.

Deep in North Tynedale the tower of Hesleyside was for centuries the stronghold of the chiefs of the Charltons. To Hesleyside is attributed the custom of bringing a spur to the table as a sign that the larder should be replenished by a raid. The medieval tower was domesticated to some extent in the seventeenth century, but the greater part of the house is the work of the eighteenth. It is now a dignified classical mansion standing in grounds laid out by 'Capa-bility' Brown (Lancelot Brown 1715–1783). Here there is little but the setting of the hills to recall the old lawless society of medieval Tynedale.

The greatest country house in Northumberland, and the supreme example of the new wealth, security and prestige of the eighteenth-century aristocracy, is of course Alnwick Castle. The marriage of Sir Hugh Smithson to Lady Eliza-beth Percy, heiress to the last of the Percies of the old line, and Smithson's creation later as duke of Northumberland in 1766, brought to Alnwick one of the wealthiest land-owners in England and began an enduring tradition of enlightened landlordism. The castle was restored by the first duke and the grounds planned in accordance with eighteenth-century taste. This was not to the taste of the naturalist Pennant who commented that, "The apartments are large, and lately finished in the Gothic style with a most incompatible elegance. The gardens are equally inconsis-tent, trim in a highest degree, and more adapted to a villa near London than the ancient seat of a great baron."[71] The grounds were laid out by 'Capability' Brown, who also planned the sites of many of the small woods and copses visible today on the hilltops in the vicinity of Alnwick.

[71] T. Pennant, *A Tour in Scotland* (1776), Vol. I, p. 358.

The fourth duke (1847–1865) and his architect Salvin rebuilt the castle in its present form.

The rebuilding of Alnwick Castle in the first half of the nineteenth century was one of the finest achievements of Victorian Gothic. The new blends with the old, and the two elements combine to create one of the largest and finest country houses in England. A less happy work of the same period was Beaufront, near Hexham. Beaufront designed by John Dobson, and described as an "elegant building of the domestic castellated style",[72] is a tribute by the affluence of Northumberland to the Middle Ages seen through the eyes of Sir Walter Scott or Bulwer Lytton.

Most of the Northumbrian landlords avoided imitation Gothic. The ancient tower of the Fenwicks at Wallington was succeeded by the fine Italianate mansion of the Blacketts, which was completed about 1750 in the midst of an ordered countryside created from the waste during the same period. The tower of the Swinburnes at Capheaton was replaced by the baroque building which exists today. Netherwitton Hall is a dignified Queen Anne building on the site of a medieval tower, and forming with vicarage and church what is in Northumberland a rare picture of the traditional rural scene.

The new great houses required the setting of a park or extensive grounds. In the hands of a master like 'Capability' Brown, the whole of the surrounding countryside was treated as a complete scheme of landscaping. Villages were removed to conform with the grand idea, even for the relatively small-scale landscaping and rebuilding at Nether-witton and Shawdon; and at Biddlestone, the Osbaldistone Hall of *Rob Roy*.

Parks were originally created for hunting, and as the food reserves of feudal magnates with large domestic and military households. The oldest trace of a park boundary in Northumberland is the remains of the thirteenth-century

[72] W. W. Tomlinson, *Comprehensive Guide to Northumberland* (1968), p. 134.

park wall, which can still be seen in the bracken and heather close to the inscribed stones and the mounds of the ancient settlement of Lordenshaws. Chillingham was emparked at some date in the fourteenth century. Much of it still gives a good impression of a medieval hunting ground, particularly the area known as Robin Hood's Bog. Here the alder thickets and great trees under the moorland escarpment are the home of the famous wild cattle, descendants of the herds which roamed Northumberland in ancient times, contemporaries of the wolf, the beaver and the bear. Scotswood and the Scotswood Road on industrial Tyneside derive their name from one Richard Scott, who was licensed to empark the west wood of Benwell in 1367.[73]

A park has existed at Warkworth since the second half of the thirteenth century. It was enlarged by the fourth earl of Northumberland in about 1480. It was then called Sunderland Park, Sunderland meaning 'the south land' south of the river. By the end of the fifteenth century it was enclosed by a fence. Today Warkworth Park is a thin strip of fine trees on the steep slopes above the river. The original southern boundary can still be traced, since humans, like badgers and deer, tend to follow the same routes throughout generations, if allowed to do so. The modern footpath follows the line of the deer park fence from the gate under the south-western tower, the Carrickfergus Tower, of the castle to the boundary hedge at the back of the gardens along the Morwick Road. From this point the hedge follows the old line westwards. The boundary then becomes the north side of the Waterhaugh Road to the bottom of the hill above the Coquet, where it is continued as a hedge boundary crossing a field to the river.

The modern township of Acklington Park represents a deer park which was first mentioned in 1248, when it contained 140 deer. It was formed within a loop of the Coquet and so was easily enclosed by a fence on one side. The park

[73] *N.C.H.,* Vol. XIII, p. 217.

was well timbered with oak and ash at the end of the six-teenth century but all the deer had been destroyed by 1616. Here, too, the medieval boundaries have survived in the form of modern roads and footpaths. North of Acklington Park Farm the boundary fence followed the eastern side of the road which descends to the Coquet at Brainshaugh. South of the farm it is represented by the line of old oaks and tree stumps on the eastern side of the lane and is continued as a raised bank forming field boundaries near the ruins of Low Park Farm and Station Wood. Place-names such as the farms of High Park and Low Park, North Park Wood and South Park Wood, recall the original use of this area.[74]

In the Middle Ages deer were an economic crop. Accounts for Acklington deer park in 1471 include items for new palings, posts and rails, and the enclosure of a field as winter pasture for the deer. In the eighteenth century such parks were an indication of the wealth and status of their owners. Rothley deer park was the creation of Sir Walter Blackett, who constructed the big stone wall that exists today, as well as the sham ruins of Rothley Castle. Sir Walter was M.P. for Newcastle for forty years, and his deer are said to have been required to provide venison for the freemen of the city.

The finest park in Northumberland, and one of the largest in England, is the park at Alnwick, which was extended to take in the ruins and grounds of Hulne Priory and was not completed until the first half of the nineteenth century. The enclosure of the park involved the diversion of the old road to Eglingham, in about 1830, and the construction of the fine boundary wall which flanks the modern Eglingham road. Alnwick Park, together with the surrounding woods and copses, was the outcome of a prodigious programme of landscaping extending over some sixty years during which public footpaths were closed and roads diverted. The park

[74] *N.C.H.,* Vol. V, p. 378.

reached its zenith, about 5000 acres in area, in the days of the third duke (1817–1847) of whom it was said that "his style of living was stately and magnificent, but somewhat exclusive, having more of the courtly formality of a petty German prince than the social freedom of an Anglo-Norman nobleman".[75] The dukes of Northumberland resolutely refused to allow the new railways to interfere with their amenities, much to the advantage of posterity who can enjoy the beauties of the park, reduced in changed circumstances to about 3000 acres, while Alnwick station has been closed.

The last of the old-style parks of Northumberland is Billsmoor, which was enclosed in the early nineteenth century. Today it survives as an ambitious stone wall and gateway on the east of the road between Elsdon and Hepple.

Villages did not always harmonise with the carefully planned landscape of castle or mansion, gardens and park. Accordingly many were removed. Haughton village was destroyed when the park was made in about 1816. All that remains today is the scant ruins of the medieval chapel in the grounds of the tower-house above the North Tyne. Capheaton village was replaced, in the late eighteenth century, by the row of single-storey cottages at the roadside. At Biddlestone the old village had to make way for the new classical mansion and grounds of the Selby family under the hills. In recent years Biddlestone Hall has been demolished in its turn and today the most conspicuous feature of the neighbourhood is a large quarry.

Improving landlords

The monumental survey of landed estates made in 1873 revealed that a far greater proportion of the total area of Northumberland, excluding the wastes, was occupied by

[75] G. Tate, *History of the Borough, Castle and Barony of Alnwick* (1866), p. 364.

large estates than was that of any other county in England
except Rutland.[76] The proportion for Northumberland was
fifty per cent. It was fifty-three per cent in Rutland; but
Rutland, the smallest county in England, was dominated
disproportionately by the estates of the duke of Rutland
and the marquess of Exeter. The third county in terms of
area occupied by large estates was Nottingham with only
thirty-eight per cent.

All the Northumbrian landowners, great and small, were
active improvers of their estates in the eighteenth and nineteenth centuries, using their power derived from ownership
of villages and wide areas of land, backed by the influence
derived from the habits of an older feudal society, and by
the new wealth created by economic expansion, particularly
in the coal industry. These men formed the modern landscape out of a generally treeless and hedgeless countryside
of moorlands and unenclosed fields. They built the stone
and slate farms. They planted woodlands, shelter-belts and
fox-coverts.

Hedges were not unknown in medieval Northumberland;
in Tudor times they had been encouraged for military purposes. Whittonstall, near the Durham boundary, means
'the homestead with a quickset hedge'. A government order,
made in 1561 for 'fortifying' the Borders, provided for the
hedging of township crofts and for impeding access to them
by means of "narrow ways, hedges and ditches".[77] But in
the early eighteenth century most of the Northumbrian
landscape was one of unkempt villages, often "mere clusters
of turf-covered huts, surrounded by open fields . . . in a
wilderness of whin, broom and heather".[78] If variety of
botanical species in a hedge is an indication of age the

[76] F. M. L. Thompson, *English Landed Society in the Nineteenth Century* (1963),
p. 32, Table II.
[77] Quoted by J. Raine in *The History and Antiquities of North Durham* (1852),
p. 31. See also J. Hodgson, *History of Northumberland,* Part II, Vol. I, p. 359.
[78] R. C. Bosanquet, 'John Horsley and His Times', *A.A.,* 4th series,
Vol. X (1933), p. 149.

hedges of Northumberland should be relatively modern, as indeed they are. As late as the 1770s the naturalist Pennant, returning from Scotland, described the country south of Cornhill as "open, destitute of trees and almost of hedges".[79]

In the first half of the eighteenth century Sir William Loraine of Kirkharle, the birthplace of Capability Brown, is said to have planted 24,000 forest trees, 488,000 quicks and 580 fruit trees, besides building farms, draining and clearing,[80] in developing the encumbered estate inherited from his father and the lands bought up out of the forfeited estates of his Jacobite neighbours. The first Sir William Blackett, owner of the manor of Winlaton and its collieries, lessee of lead-mines on Alston Moor, and with shares in collieries at Newburn, Brunton, Fallowfield and Acomb, was the prototype of the new Northumbrian industrialist-landowner. His son, the second Sir William, bought the sequestrated estates of the Fenwicks and rebuilt Wallington. The present house was constructed by Sir Walter Calverly Blackett, who remodelled "many square miles of North-umberland by road-making, building and planting"[81] between 1730 and 1770. The fields, roads and woodlands of the Wallington countryside are primarily his creation, and the attractive bridge which carries the public road over the Wansbeck was designed to conform with his new landscape.

Ford and its neighbourhood, with its fields, woodlands and copses, are wholly a creation of the second half of the eighteenth century. At the time of the accession of George III, the 7000-acre estate was unenclosed and mostly moor-land. There was scarcely a tree, apart from a few near the castle. Lord Delaval constructed thirteen of the solid grey stone farms such as exist, with later improvements, today. He fenced and drained and made the large regular fields with their neat quickset hedges.

[79] T. Pennant, op. cit., Vol. II, p. 279.   [80] J. Hodgson, op. cit., p. 247.
[81] R. C. Bosanquet, op. cit., p. 63.

Plate 15 Ridge-and-furrow, Holywell Dene

This photograph gives a good impression of the extent of arable farming in Northumberland during the Middle Ages. It looks east towards St Mary's Island lighthouse and the houses of Hartley. Much of this area passed into the hands of the Delavals in the sixteenth century when tenants were evicted and their holdings converted from arable into pasture. It is Boulder Clay country, overlying the coal measures.

Plate 16 Halton Tower

Once the centre of a large estate which was still classified as held by *thegnage* tenure in 1166. The tower is mid-fourteenth century and like many buildings near the Wall is constructed of Roman stones. On the right of the tower appears the house built in the late seventeenth century.

Plate 17 Chipchase Castle

Chipchase Castle, on the North Tyne, is a good example of the transition from war to peace in Northumberland. The tower is fourteenth century. The Jacobean house was added in 1621 at a time when large windows were no longer a dangerous liability in the house of a Northumbrian landowner. Chipchase belonged to the Herons, a famous family in Border history.

Plate 18 Cushat Lane, near Hexham
Cushat Lane, near Lowgate, Hexham, is a disused enclosure road constructed when Hexham East Common was enclosed in 1753. It runs through a typical enclosure landscape.

Plate 19 Blanchland

A planned stone-roofed village built by the trustees of the estates of Lord Crewe, Bishop of Durham, after 1752 on the site of the Premonstratensian abbey. The gatehouse was built about 1500 and the building shown on the right of the photograph formed part of the abbey. The eighteenth-century village was constructed for lead-miners.

The moorlands and open fields around Swinburne Castle, and Dere Street on the hills above, were enclosed and planted with "multitudes of quick-fences and plantations"[82] by the Swinburnes, who also took the lead in developing North Tynedale. Among the hills west of the Great North Road, Charles Bigge of Longhorsley constructed "above eight miles of drains and eleven miles of hedges, planted considerably, fenced in the natural wood on the sides of the Linden Burn and Tod Burn, rebuilt and repaired all his farmhouses".[83] Here the hill pastures flanking the old coach road to Tod Burn and Rothbury still show traces of their moorland origins; ragged lines of gaunt hawthorns mark the original late eighteenth-century enclosures.

An improving landlord of a characteristically eighteenth-century cosmopolitan type was Horace Paul, who served in the Austrian army and became a count of the Holy Roman Empire as Count Horace St Paul. After four years in the British embassy in Paris he eventually returned to his Northumbrian estates, in 1787.[84] Count St Paul rebuilt the old house of Ewart, in Glendale, and created a model estate in what was then one of the most backward parts of the county. His work is a precise, man-made landscape. The lines of his fields, roads and woodlands recall something of the formality of eighteenth-century warfare in their precise, geometrical lines. Today part of the eighteenth-century design has been obliterated by the requirements of the airfield laid out during the war of 1939–45, but much remains as it was laid out by Count St Paul (Fig. 12).

Contemporaries of St Paul were the brothers George and Mathew Culley, originally from Denton, near Darlington. They learnt their craft from Robert Bakewell, of Leicestershire, and then settled in Glendale, first at Coupland and later at Fowberry Tower. The Culley brothers bred the

---

[82] Hodgson, op. cit., p. 71. [83] Hodgson, op. cit., Vol. II, p. 96.
[84] See *N.C.H.*, Vol. XIV, pp. 183–9 for the summary of an eventful career.

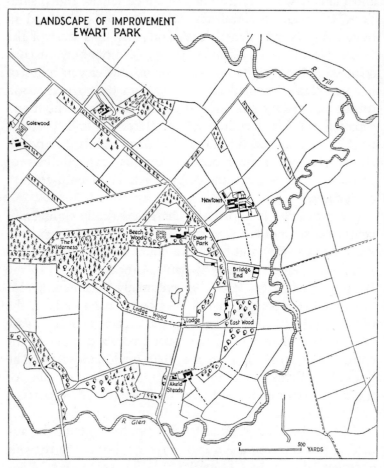

LANDSCAPE OF IMPROVEMENT
EWART PARK

Fig. 12. The gardens, woods and fields of the Ewart Park estate in Glendale are the creation of the improving landlord Horace St Paul, Count St Paul of the Holy Roman Empire. The precise geometrical patterns are the acme of eighteenth-century planning in an area which was mostly unimproved and unenclosed in the earlier half of the century. The features of the north-west corner of the estate have been obscured by the construction of an airfield during the last war but there has been no major change in the remainder.

Border Leicester sheep. They ditched, drained, hedged and embanked, coverting into arable fields and pastures the acres of broom which had once been the scene of a famous ambush in the year 1513. At near-by Chillingham the Yorkshireman John Bailey, engraver, artist, mathematician and surveyor, was steward to the Tankervilles, collaborated with George Culley in *A General View of the Agriculture of the County of Northumberland,* and created the wide fields east of Wooler along the Till.

Horace St Paul died in 1812, Mathew Culley in 1813, and John Bailey in 1819. They were the creators of the landscape in the heart of Glendale as it is seen today, transforming country of which a visitor wrote:

> The corn land, which is very little in quantity compared with meadows and grazing grounds, lays mingled with the other over the open faces of the vales, without any fences; to protect which many an indolent herdsman stands for hours wrapped up in his plaid.[85]

By virtue of their wealth, social position and example, the dukes of Northumberland stood at the head of the improving landlords of Northumberland in an era of agricultural advance and colonisation. It is recorded that the first duke planted some two million trees, including the afforestation with conifers of some one thousand acres of Corbridge Fell, the beginning of the great woodlands between Blanchland and Dilston visible today. The first duke undertook a programme for the rebuilding of farms which has in practice resulted in the rebuilding of almost every farm once every 100 years, and is one of the reasons why old farm buildings are rare in Northumberland. The Commissioners for Greenwich Hospital, who acquired the forfeited estates of the earl of Derwentwater after the rising of 1715, also planted trees on a great scale, remodelled farms and cottages, and

[85] W. Hutchinson, *A View of Northumberland* (1778), Vol. I, p. 258.

constructed churches for the new parishes of Simonburn, as at Thorneyburn and Greystead.

Arthur Young commented with approval on the work of Abraham Dixon, owner of Belford, in the second half of the eighteenth century, who planted plantations and hedges, and built farms. Dixon also "applied himself with great spirit to rendering the road to Belford, north and south, as good as possible; this he effected as far as his influence extended, and would not have left a mile of bad road in the country, had others been as solicitous as himself about so important a subject".[86]

Arthur Young also praised the high standards of farm management in Northumberland, though he found it "very melancholy to ride through such vastly extensive tracts of uncultivated good land, as are found in every part of this county".[87] Capital, labour and the great authority of Northumbrian landlordism were applied with increasing momentum to the transformation of a countryside ruined by centuries of war. The wilds of Kidland were repopulated and farms or shepherds' cottages rebuilt on their medieval sites, as at Shillmoor and Fairhaugh. Improvement brought good returns. Even allowing for changes in the value of money the rent received for the 17,000 acres of Kidland is a fair summary of agricultural or pastoral progress in the years of peace. In 1541 Kidland was leased for a nominal 20s., which does not appear to have been paid. In 1631 rents amounted to £5. They had risen to £400 by 1731 and to £3000 by 1800.[88] The returns from the Craster estates in Bamburghshire nearly doubled during the first half of the eighteenth century.

The improvements undertaken by Northumbrian landlords from the eighteenth century onwards formed a colonisation of the waste on a scale such as had not been

[86] Arthur Young, *A Six Months Tour through the North of England,* 2nd ed. (1771), Vol. III, p. 38.

[87] Ibid., p. 91.

[88] D. D. Dixon, *Upper Coquetdale* (1904), pp. 55–6.

seen since the thirteenth century. Their last achievement in the old grand manner was Cragside, famous for its woods and rhododendrons among the rocks above the Coquet at Rothbury. Cragside was the creation of the first Lord Armstrong, inventor, engineer and armaments manufacturer, who raised Newcastle to the peak of its industrial fame and, with less happy results, rebuilt Bamburgh Castle.

Later enclosure

The needs of defence had perpetuated an archaic military society in Northumberland, and throughout the Tudor period landlords were concerned to ensure the presence of their customary tenants, mounted and properly equipped, at the musters. In 1580 Lord Burghley was informed that "There is no lease in [Northumberland], but with provision to find horse and armour for each tenement, to be held by an able man".[89] The landlords of Tudor Northumberland were, however, as interested in obtaining maximum economic benefits from their land as were their colleagues elsewhere; economic grievances and the exactions of landlords were not the least of the causes of the northern rebellion known as the Pilgrimage of Grace. The old theoretical equality of holdings in the common fields had long since disappeared. Farms had become concentrated, usually in the strong hands of the nobility and great landlords; the needs of defence in the Tudor north did not prevent the eviction of farmers and the transformation of arable land into pastures.

After the Union of the Crowns, in 1603, landlords lost no opportunity of eradicating the old customary tenancies. The seventeenth century offered new economic opportunities. In 1619 the Delavals, bent on developing their coal, evicted the remaining smallholders of Cowpen.

[89] *Calendar of Border Papers*, Vol. I, p. 34.

It has been pointed out that when enclosures in Northumberland were effected by private Act of Parliament between 1729 and 1844, the frequency with which the area is described as within manor and barony suggests the pressure of feudal influence which must have often carried conclusive weight in securing agreement.[90] The weight of this influence would have been the easier to bring to bear because the number of individuals involved was so small, and often they were all members of the same landowning class united by a common interest in improved agriculture. When the common fields of Earsdon were divided, in 1649, there were only eight customary tenants to consider. At Beadnell, where the arable fields were divided by agreement in 1701, the whole township, except for two small holdings, was in the hands of five landowners. The enclosure of the common fields of Hedley, in 1767, required no more than an agreement between the duke and duchess of Northumberland and Ambrose Surtees.

In England as a whole there were over 2500 enclosure acts, affecting some two and a half million acres, between 1761 and 1844.[91] Only seven related to Northumberland, and even these were primarily concerned with commons, involving the transformation of rights of common into private holdings, often of great size, defined by the great stone walls on the fells today. Between 1729 and 1731 forty-five private Acts of Parliament were obtained for these purposes in Northumberland. Sixteen of these accounted for over 32,600 acres between 1801 and 1831. They included great tracts such as 5000 acres of Tosson, Hepple and Elsdon in 1805, 4200 acres in Corsenside east of the North Tyne in 1807, and 6000 acres of Rothbury Forest in 1831. In the nineteenth century enclosure was facilitated by the General Enclosure Act of 1845 and subsequent legislation. Twenty-

[90] W. E. Tate, 'A Handlist of English Enclosure Acts and Awards', Part 26: 'Northumberland', *Proceedings of Soc. of Antiquaries of Newcastle upon Tyne*, 4th series, Vol. X, No. 1 (1942).

[91] W. G. *Hoskins, The Making of the English Landscape* (1965), p. 143.

three orders of enclosure were made, in accordance with the new procedure, affecting close on 80,000 acres, mostly moorland, and including 7460 acres of the Hareshaw moors above Bellingham, 12,056 acres in Knarsdale west of the South Tyne, and 3130 acres of Plenmeller Common near Haltwhistle.

Enclosures of the commons on this scale supplemented the work of the Northumbrian landlords who, throughout the nineteenth century, were consolidating and rationalising the arable fields by means of large enclosures enclosed by hawthorn hedges, and by the construction and improvement of roads. The enclosure of Hexham and Allendale Commons, by private Act of Parliament in 1800, affected a vast area, estimated to comprise 42,000 acres, extending from the road between Hexham and Langley in the neighbourhood of Stublick Moor southwards across the moorlands and bogs to the Durham border; almost the whole of the country between the Devil's Water and the West Allen. It also involved the demarcation between Hexham parish and its former chapelry of Allendale by means of boundary stones across the moors. The East and West Commons of Hexham had been enclosed earlier, in 1753 (Plate 18). They comprised over 4000 acres between the West Dipton Burn and the South Tyne opposite Newbrough.

Enclosures on this scale involved the remodelling of the countryside below the fell tops and higher moorlands, which were left as stinted grazing, or as grouse moors. Over 650 allotments were made to about 280 individuals. Land was set aside for roads and quarries. Stints were carefully regulated. A two-year-old horned beast, five one-year-old sheep or eight lambs under one year formed one stint. A two-year-old mare or gelding formed two stints.

These enclosures, between 1753 and 1800, created the typical wide fields and the straight roads of Sunnyside and Yarridge, near Hexham Race Course and East Nubbock.[92]

[92] Northumberland County Record Office. Enclosure Maps ZGI xxxii/1 and xxxii/2.

The roads have wide verges. On either side of the road from Low Gate to Stublick enclosure fields form a regular rectangular pattern. Small copses of windblown firs were planted as coverts and shelter-belts. The long lines of boundary walls span the moorlands, and draw sharp lines along the slopes between the stinted pastures and grouse moors of the higher fells and the enclosures below.

The big moorland enclosures of this type are a feature of North Tynedale, especially on Hareshaw Common above Bellingham, and in the area of Sandysike and Blackburn Common further to the north. Here the long lines of the major boundary walls are ruled precisely across the landscape. Some of the finest examples are derived from the last of the great moorland enclosures of Northumberland, the enclosure of the 12,000 acres of Knarsdale Common in 1859. Here, between the South Tyne and the cold, wet heights of the Pennine ridge near Cross Fell, the stone walls climb from the Knarsdale Burn and its tributaries up to the cotton grass and bog, the country of curlew and golden plover. These walls form the last stage in the colonisation of an inhospitable waste which in Knarsdale, in Middle English 'the dale of the rugged rock', began at some date after the Norman Conquest.

Near Newcastle enclosure of the great Shire Moor began with the 1900 acres of Killingworth Moor, by private Act of Parliament, in 1790 and this laid down the road system which has lasted until today. By the award of 1790 a public highway, fifty feet in breadth, was to be constructed from the Salter's Bridge north-east over the common to the White House Bridge and was to be called the Salter's Bridge Road. This was the origin of the road now called Salter's Lane. Two other fifty-foot roads became the Great Line Road joining the Salter's Road to the modern Whitley Road and the Benton Road, now Benton Lane, thus providing a north-to-south connection between Killingworth and Long Benton.

Prestwick Carr was drained by an award of 1860 under the General Enclosure Act of 1845 and subsequent legislation. The last of the great areas of primeval marsh in the county, the carr consisted of about 1000 acres north-east of Ponteland. In summer it was an area of scattered pools amid furze and heather with wide stretches of good grass grazed by geese and cattle.[93] It is best studied from the ridge road to the north between New Horton Grange and Berwick Mill, above the quiet levels with the straight roads of enclosure between their wide verges and hedges, the drainage ditches full of meadowsweet and churring sedge warblers among the rushes. One of the original enclosure roads is now disused and has reverted to a grassy track. In winter the Black Pool holds sufficient water to recall something of the original appearance of the carr though cattle graze in the peaty fields among the feeding peewits. The hawthorns rise tall and ragged from the hedges forming the boundaries of the nineteenth-century fields.

Throughout all Northumberland the landlords were free, from the beginning of the eighteenth century, to mould the county into a pattern dictated by the requirements of improved agriculture. The process was facilitated by the prevalence of large estates and its success was demonstrated by the rise in rents. The rent of Spindlestone, in Bamburghshire, rose from £800 a year in 1735 to £3,250 a year by 1840.[94] When the topography allowed, as it usually did, roads were driven straight across country. On Tweedside, between Norham and Horncliffe, enclosed by agreement in the latter half of the eighteenth century, the fields today give the appearance of having been ruled by set-square in a draughtsman's office. The enclosure of Tarretburn Common and Smiddywell Rigg, in the heart of the pele country of North Tynedale, created, in 1809, the same regular field

[93] D. Maddison, *An Historical and Descriptive Account of Prestwick Carr and its Environs* (1830).

[94] J. Grey, 'View of the Past and Present State of Agriculture in Northumberland', *Trans. Royal Agric. Soc.* (1840), p. 160.

I

patterns, with stone walls instead of hedges. The pattern is reproduced on the fells of Hartleyburn, enclosed in 1864, and by the enclosures on Melkridge Common, near Halt-whistle, enclosed eighty years previously.

By the end of the eighteenth century the Board of Agri-culture was informed that the whole of the county capable of cultivation was, in general, enclosed by live hedges, except in parts of Glendale where enclosure was then in progress.[95] The practice was sufficiently new for it to be subject to comment by visitors, one of whom reported that:

> The fences most generally used for new enclosures are earth mounds, at the base of which, and on the edge of the ditch out of which they are raised, are planted the quicks, usually upon an upturned sod, six inches high. In some parts the injudicious mode of cutting the quicks every year prevails, this makes the fence look neat and snug, but it never grows so thick and impenetrable as when left to nature and cut at proper intervals.[96]

Today, most of the hedges are 'neat and snug'.

Landlords often insisted that their tenants should en-courage the growth of trees in the hedges. This is the origin of many trees in Northumberland, especially along the hedges of minor roads. When Warkworth Moor was enclosed in 1857 the whins were stubbed and cleared but meticulous instructions were issued on behalf of the duke of Northumberland for the planting of trees on the steeper banks, and for the planting of the quicks "upon a cast three feet high and four feet wide at the bottom, with a proper slope and backed with sods".[97] Some of the finest

[95] J. Bailey and G. Culley, *A General View of the Agriculture of Northumber-land* (1800 ed.), p. 64.

[96] E. Mackenzie, *An Historical, Topographical and Descriptive View of the County of Northumberland* (1811 ed.), Vol. I, p. 135.

[97] Northumberland County Record Office, Warkworth Parish, ZG1 xxxii/4.

hawthorn hedges in Northumberland today are in Whittingham Vale, where the fields were already "well fenced with
quicksets" in the 1770s.[98]

Peace and enclosure encouraged the construction of the
isolated farms amid the newly enclosed fields and the
reappearance of isolated shepherds' cottages and sheepfarms in the wilds of Kidland. At Matfen, the farm of
Thornham Hill was originally constructed after the enclosures of the seventeenth century in the middle of a newly
consolidated holding at some distance from the village.[99]
Farms, such as Heathery Edge, Shildon Hill and Well
House Farm, appeared after the enclosure of Shildon Common, and the draining of Shildon Lough in 1749. The fine
house and farm of Grindon Hill amid sheltering trees at the
edge of the Stanegate, on the uplands between Haydon
Bridge and the Wall, are a product of the era of peace and
enclosure. The two farms called Make me Rich, one near
Capheaton and the other near Bellasis Bridge, both appeared
in the latter half of the eighteenth century.

Planned villages

The Georgian landlords who removed villages to conform
with the aesthetics of the new country houses and parks
also applied their capital and the contemporary principles
of good estate management to the planning and construction
of new villages and the complete reconstruction of old ones.
Nathanial Crewe, Baron Crewe and Lord Bishop of
Durham, held the great see of Durham for forty-seven years
and died, aged ninety, in 1721. A man of great wealth, he
bought from the heavily indebted Forsters the properties
of Bamburgh and the Blanchland estate, which the Forsters
had acquired after the dissolution of the monasteries in
1539.

[98] W. Hutchinson, *A View of Northumberland* (1778), Vol. I, p. 230.
[99] W. Percy Hedley, 'The Manor and Township of East Matfen', *A.A.*,
4th series, Vol. XXII (1944), p. 113.

The trustees of the Crewe estates after the bishop's death rebuilt Blanchland in the middle of the eighteenth century, secured the recognition of Blanchland as a separate parish, and transformed the choir of the old abbey into the parish church. Blanchland has become one of the great tourist attractions of modern Northumberland, a cluster of homogeneous stone buildings constructed of the mellow brown sandstone of the Pennines, and roofed with the heavy stone slates which are the characteristic roofing material south of the Tyne.

Blanchland should be approached from the south by the road which descends from the high fells of Stanhope and crosses into Northumberland by the bridge across the Derwent. From the approach to the bridge the village is revealed, a brown cluster sheltered by the woodlands on the banks of the Derwent and the slopes which rise to the heather of Bolbec Common and Blanchland Moor. The village was rebuilt for the lead-miners, whose old shafts and workings abound along the Shildon Burn and who themselves, in the eighteenth century, continued a tradition of mining at Blanchland and Shildon which had begun in the Middle Ages. The whole of the space closed on the north by the fine late-fourteenth-century gatehouse once formed the great courtyard of the abbey bounded on the east by the abbot's lodging, now the Lord Crewe Arms Hotel (Plate 19).

The modern road from Blanchland to Hexham is the product of the early nineteenth century. The medieval road is represented by the track which emerges from the great plantations of conifers of Slaley Forest to cross Blanchland Moor and descends to the Shildon Burn below Pennypie House, once an inn for drovers.

A more sophisticated planned village, and still a fine example of eighteenth-century architectural taste, is Stamfordham. The village, 'the *ham* at the stony ford' appears late in history, and the church, substantially reconstructed in the nineteenth century, does not appear to be older than the thirteenth. The common lands of the township of Heugh, in which Stamfordham was included, were divided in 1735 at a time when Sir John Swinburne, of Capheaton, owned half the area, and Balliol College, Oxford, most of the remainder. The award of 1735 provided that the green of Stamfordham should be enjoyed by the small group of landowners together with "their tenants and farmers, and by the inhabitants of such houses as are or shall be built upon the said town green, with the consent and direction of Sir John Swinburne and Balliol College".

The result is still one of Northumberland's finest examples of harmonious architecture in brick and stone. This harmony has, unfortunately not been maintained by some later buildings, though it may be observed that the architect of the Presbyterian church, of 1860, experienced no difficulty in designing a modern building which yet conformed with the unity imposed by eighteenth-century planning. "The tranquil skyline formed by the roof ridges gradually builds up from each and towards a centre where the doctor's house, higher than its neighbours, gracefully and naturally assumes the role of focal point in the street."[100] The market cross, erected at the expense of Sir John Swinburne, the eighteenth-century pond and the fountain complete the period picture of the small centre of an agricultural district, designed at a time when so much of the Northumbrian countryside was being remodelled.

The Swinburnes were noteworthy for their share in this remodelling during the Georgian period and in the early years of the nineteenth century. In addition to the small new village of Capheaton and Stamfordham, they developed their coal interests in North Tynedale, constructing roads and bridges, and the little hamlet of Mounces situated at

[100] F. Austin Child, 'A Record of Stamfordham', *A.A.*, 4th series, Vol. XXIII (1945), a valuable study of the village from which the quotation from the award of 1735 is also taken.

the edge of the moors where Sir John Swinburne's road along the Akenshaw Burn into Liddesdale leaves the North Tyne.

Ford, in Glendale, is a nineteenth-century planned village; a sharp contrast to Stamfordham, it is a study in Victorian Gothic, a mannered suburb set down near the Border. This village was the pride of Victorian Northumberland as exemplified by Tomlinson, author of the well-known *Guide to Northumberland* first published in the 1880s: "the cosy-looking, homelike cottages, half hidden in foliage and trimmest of gardens . . . present a picture of rural peace and retirement".[101] Fittingly Ford was rebuilt under the inspiration of Louisa, countess of Waterford, and Queen of Beauty at the famous Eglinton Tournament of 1842.

Ford's near neighbour Etal is an altogether less ambitious planned village, laid out between the ruined castle above the Till and the manor house. Etal Manor was built in 1748 and took its final form some twenty years later. The white-washed cottages, some thatched and others roofed with slates, together with the Bull Inn, forms an unpretentious and pleasing group of eighteenth-century buildings under the tall trees. The church, designed by Butterfield and built in memory of one of the children of the duke of Clarence, later William IV, is less suitable in the Northumbrian context. Its historic importance lies in the authentic touch of mid-nineteenth-century property and propriety which it conveys.

Simonburn, a larger village, was rebuilt by the Allgoods in the eighteenth and nineteenth centuries. The core of the village is the green, planted with oak, lime and chestnut, surrounded by mainly eighteenth-century whitewashed houses and cottages, functional buildings in the good taste of their period. The church, though much restored by

[101] W. W. Tomlinson, *Comprehensive Guide to Northumberland* (1968 ed.), p. 521.

Salvin and others, yet remains an integral part of the village scene. In origin Simonburn church is one of the oldest in Northumberland and it contains a link with its little-known past in the fragments of an ancient Anglian cross. The existing village, shaped in 'the Age of Improvement', remains faithful to the spirit of the Northumbrian landscape.

Cambo and Wallington were both rebuilt by the Blacketts during the late eighteenth century and in the nineteenth: both are fine examples of the villages constructed by improving landlords to conform with the architectural scheme of a remodelled Border tower in its garden and park, and at the same time providing better standards of housing. Cambo is a small jewel with the ordered simplicity of stone and slate houses and a pleasing church constructed in 1842. The new village was originally laid out by Sir Walter Blackett in about 1740. The full range of its buildings, which extend into the twentieth century, form an object-lesson in the combination of improvement with architectural grace. The post office is in a building of 1818, which itself was a reconstruction of a small Border tower.

Rock, south-east of Embleton, is the latest, and perhaps the last, of the villages planned by landlords with wealth and architectural taste in the old tradition. The village is built on a limestone outcrop characteristic of this part of Northumberland between the A1 and the sea, and is the centre of a small estate which has formed a township within the same boundaries since the time of Henry I. Rock Hall, now a youth hostel, was originally a small tower of the usual Northumbrian type, to which a domestic mansion was added in the seventeenth century. This house was reconstructed in the early nineteenth century. The estate came into the hands of Charles Bosanquet, a wealthy West Indian merchant, who reconstructed the village and rebuilt the little twelfth-century church. The cottages aligned along the wide grass verges have been rebuilt since the original nineteenth-century reconstruction; some, such as the post office, are modern. All have maintained the harmony of the old and the new in a single concept of hall, church and village, with the large farm and estate offices on the outskirts grouped round the mill-pond shaded by its trees, the whole comprising a range of building from the twelfth to the twentieth century.

The creation of the planned villages of Northumberland is a continuing process and has many forms. All over the county villages were rebuilt during the Victorian period, as at Chatton. The majority of the farm hamlets, such as the massive groups of buildings at New Bewick and Fenton Town, are nineteenth-century. The colliery villages of the late eighteenth century and later were themselves planned villages of a utilitarian type, such as Percy Main. Nineteenth-century industrialism even influenced the design of farms, as at Chollerton. In the twentieth century the Forestry Commission has continued the story, in a modern idiom, with the new villages of Byrness and Kielder amid the forests of North Tyne and Redesdale.

Rural building

A visitor travelling from Wooler to the Border in 1776 noted that "the cottages of the lower class of people are deplorable, composed of upright timbers fixed in the ground, the interstices wattled and plastered with mud, some thatched and others covered with turf . . . a hearth stone on the ground for the peat and turf fire".[102] Dwellings such as these were little different from the huts in which the peasants of Northumberland had lived in the Middle Ages, frequently burnt in Border warfare and easily rebuilt. In the eighteenth century they were being rapidly replaced by improving landlords. By the second half of the nineteenth century stone and slate were being used throughout the

[102] W. Hutchinson, op. cit., p. 258.

county for the reconstructed farms and the cottages of shepherds and farm-labourers.

Stone had also been used as a building material since ancient times, as for the walls of the Celtic huts and homesteads during the Roman occupation. Lord Dacre reported regretfully of the Scottish side of the Border in 1524, that there was "little left upon the frontiers except old houses, whereof the thatch and the coverings taken away, so that they cannot be burnt".[103] The Scots were engaged in similar activities south of the Border. Accordingly Beal, on the flat coast facing Holy Island, contained in 1560 "certain little houses of stone and lime that some of the tenants have built for their own safeguard against the thieves of the borders".[104]

Many of the peles of Northumberland were in fact fortified farmhouses. The peles at Gatehouse and Black Middings were buildings of this type. A very old form of rural building in Northumberland was the long house, a rectangular building housing occupiers and stock under one roof. This architectural style appears to have been introduced from Scandinavia and remains have been excavated on the site of the medieval settlement on Ingram Hill. These closely resemble ancient houses, dating from the sixth to the eighth centuries, near Stavanger in Norway.[105] There was a long house at Memmerkirk, in the angle between the Yoke Burn and the Sting Burn. Long houses were still being constructed in the early nineteenth century and the foundations of one are visible beside the pele of Black Middings, above the Black Burn in North Tynedale.

In the late eighteenth century, and even in the early nineteenth, other buildings of a primitive type still survived. At Holburn in the 1770s many of the old cottages "were built chiefly with oak trees which in many cases

[103] J. Raine, *The History and Antiquities of North Durham* (1852), p. 16.
[104] Raine, op. cit., p. 303.
[105] A. H. A. Hogg, 'Further Excavations at Ingram Hill', *A.A.*, 4th series, Vol. XXXIV (1956), pp. 158–9.

rested upon the ground and were joined at the tops, so as to form a kind of sloping roof".[106] At Alwinton there were 'buildings with roughly hewn oak beams and couples, the ends of which were sunk in the ground'.[107] Dwellings such as these would have been an archaic survival even in the Middle Ages. Excavations on the site of the abandoned village of West Whelpington have revealed relatively substantial stone-built medieval cottages.

Thatch, usually heather thatch, was the normal roofing material. At Rothbury in 1760 the houses were roofed with sods and thatch. During the nineteenth century thatch was nearly everywhere replaced by slate; the thatched cottages which give to Etal a touch of southern England are now exceptional.

The vigorous programme of rural development undertaken by landlords in the eighteenth and nineteenth centuries involved the reconstruction of the older farms and cottages throughout the county and the construction of new buildings in utilitarian stone and slate. The relative scarcity of villages necessitated a permanent labour force. The Northumbrian hinds, or agricultural labourers, were usually married men living in rent-free cottages around the farm. They received free carriage of coal, at pit-head price, pasturage for a cow, grain or wool at harvest and shearing. The hind undertook to provide a woman worker, or a boy, to work in the fields at a fixed wage; these were bound by their agreements to work for a year and were known as bondagers.

The large Northumbrian farms, particularly in Bamburghshire and Glendale, are therefore self-contained hamlets, a massive group of buildings with associated labourers' cottages. They are the descendants of the ancient manors and smaller estates where the landed gentry lived

---

[106] E. Mackenzie, *An Historical, Topographical and Descriptive View of the County of Northumberland* (1825 ed.), p. 382.
[107] D. D. Dixon, *Upper Coquetdale*, p. 217.

surrounded by their dependents. Willimontswick in the South Tyne valley, is a fine example of this type of farm, adapted in the seventeenth and eighteenth centuries from an older stronghold. The entrance to the inner courtyard, which in the rebuilt nineteenth-century farms is often through an arch in service buildings, at Willimontswick is through a medieval gatehouse; and the farmhouse itself incorporates a medieval tower.

Rudchester, near Heddon on the Wall, is an impressive farm of the same pattern with the massive stone buildings grouped round an inner court. The site itself is ancient, the name is derived from the Old Norse, 'Rudda's *ceaster*'; but the buildings seen today are of eighteenth-century construction, using stones from the Roman Wall and incorporating a medieval building.

A smaller, more utilitarian but equally impressive, farm of this type is Buteland, high above the North Tyne, a strong and uncompromising group of stone and slate buildings round an inner court continuing in nineteenth-century idiom the defensive traditions of an isolated farm settlement in the remote hills.

The great farms of Elford, near Bamburgh, and Stamford, north of Long Houghton, are examples of the big isolated farms which impressed early nineteenth-century visitors to Bamburghshire. At Chollerton the farm, laid out in the same period, is an agricultural version of the contemporary colliery villages which were being constructed in the coastal plain. In the foothills of the Cheviots near Wooler, the village of Ilderton is virtually one farm, its buildings constructed in the usual massive tradition. Ilderton is perhaps the best survival in Northumberland of a self-contained medieval farm settlement rebuilt in the eighteenth and nineteenth centuries.

Farms of a different type are linear in design instead of being built round a courtyard. The design is ancient, a descendant of the medieval longhouse. Whiteley Shield

Farm, situated at an altitude of over 1200 feet above the West Allen, is an impressive example of this type of farm and appears to be basically seventeenth-century in date. A thick-walled building with a heavy stone roof to shelter both inmates and stock, sheltered by the great sycamores of the dales, Whiteley Shields sits close to the hillside, gripping the rock to withstand the gales of the high fells.

Whiteley Shields was the home of a small farmer. In Northumberland generally until the eighteenth century there was a wide gulf between the fortified settlements of the landed gentry and the dwellings of most of their tenants, many of whom lived in the primitive structures described at Horton and Alwinton. More substantial farmers usually lived in peles, such as those at Gatehouse in Tarsetdale and Hole Farm in lower Redesdale. In the early nineteenth century Rothbury Forest was scattered with dwellings of this type, all of which have disappeared. In the eighteenth century it became possible to build farms for tenant farmers and shepherds' cottages without thought for defence. Most of these smaller buildings have been rebuilt since the eighteenth century, especially on the wide Percy estates, but Longlee Farm, near Denwick, remains a good example of a farm of this period.

James Caird, though reporting with approval on the standards of Northumbrian agriculture in 1850, criticised severely the state of labourers' housing which, he said, was sometimes worse than "in some of the most wretched villages in Ireland".[108] Caird wrote at a time when a vigorous rebuilding programme was in progress. The Commissioners of Greenwich Hospital were constructing free-stone cottages with walls two feet thick, roofed with Welsh slate, their ground floors paved with Aberdeen flags. The characteristic rows of labourers' cottages, which are still common today, were built at this time. It was generally accepted that "in the case of large farms or collieries, where

---

[108] J. Caird, *English Agriculture in 1850–51,* 2nd ed. (1852), p. 390.

a great number of cottages are required, the expense of building them singly or in pairs . . . is sufficient to condemn the plan, unless founded on proved or absolute necessity".[109]

The attractive cottages constructed on this plan at Capheaton were designed in conformity with the architecture adopted on the estate; and there is a pleasing row at Brandon White House just north of the Breamish. Later and more dour examples are to be found at Grindon, on the uplands south of Norham, and at Old Mousen near Belford.

Red pantiles were used for roofing, particularly north of the Aln. The unfortunate George Collingwood of Esslington, who lost his estate for his share in the rising of 1715, used pantiles for his rebuilding programme at that time. They form the roof of the small Georgian Ridge Farm at Bedlington. But by 1840 slates were replacing both thatch and pantiles. It was noted that "Blue slate from Wales or Westmorland forms the universal covering of all buildings of recent date, and the homely thatch and unseemly red tiles are now the exception, though within the last sixty years little else was to be seen."[110] Whether red tiles are 'unseemly' is a matter of opinion. They are used to good effect at Berwick and Warkworth, and appear on individual houses and cottages throughout the county in the coastal areas from the Tyne to the Tees. The great majority of the buildings of Northumberland are however austerely constructed of stone and slate (Plate 20). The materials are left to speak for themselves, and usually do so with a dignity which is not impaired by adventitious trimmings. These traditional materials and styles create buildings which are often difficult to date. In Warkworth and Corbridge stone buildings of the early eighteenth century and the late nineteenth are in harmony. Glanton, which in its present form is

[109] J. Grey, 'Cottages for Farm Labourers in Northumberland in 1845', *Journal of the Royal Agricultural Society* (1845), p. 243.

[110] J. Grey, 'View of the past and present state of Agriculture in Northumberland', *Trans. Royal Agric. Soc.* (1840), p. 190.

primarily the creation of the early nineteenth century, is a particularly good example of the unadorned simplicity of natural materials.

South of the Tyne the traditional roofing material, apart from the now vanished heather thatch, is the heavy stone slates cut from the various forms of the Pennine sandstones which lend themselves most readily to splitting. These stone slates are rare north of the Tyne valley. Blanchland is a well-known example of a stone-roofed village. Roofs of this type are numerous in Allendale Town, at Allenheads, particularly the Allenheads Hotel, and in the former mining village of Catton; and stone is still used to roof farms in this area.

The use of dry-stone walling in Northumberland goes back to the Celtic settlements of Roman times. Stone boundary walls were constructed in the Middle Ages, as for the deer park wall at Lordenshaws near Rothbury, and for the boundary walls of the thirteenth-century monks of Newminster on Barrow Law. None of the great stone walls visible on the Northumbrian moorlands today appear to be older than the eighteenth century. They are part of the landscape of enclosure. Dry-stone sheepfolds and *stells,* abound in the Cheviots (Plate 2). There is a good example, one among many, at the junction of the Housedon Burn and the Usway near Fairhaugh. The same technique was applied in the construction of the illicit whisky-still, known as Rory's Still, above Davison's Linn.

To watch the construction and repair of dry-stone walls today is to see one of the oldest traditional skills in the north, though in modern conditions stone walls are expensive and wire fencing is spreading rapidly across the moors. The same skill in the handling of stone which built the peles was used in the construction of lime kilns in the eighteenth and early nineteenth centuries, as in the almost megalithic structure of the kiln by the former drove road on Sandysike Rigg above the Tarret Burn.

SELECT BIBLIOGRAPHY

Allsop, B. and Clark, U. *Historic Architecture of Northumberland* (1969).

Beresford, M. *The Lost Villages of England* (1966).

Beresford, M. *New Towns of the Middle Ages* (1967).

Hunter Blair, P. *The Origins of Northumbria* (1948).

Hunter Blair, P. *An Introduction to Anglo-Saxon England* (1966).

Butlin, R. A. 'Northumberland Field Systems', *Agricultural Review*, Vol. xii, Part II, (1964).

Cameron, K. *English Place Names* (1961).

Collingwood, R. G. *Roman Britain* (1966).

Divine, D. *The North-West Frontier of Rome* (1969).

Ekwall, E. *The Concise Oxford Dictionary of English Place-Names* (1960).

Gray, H. L. *English Field Systems* (1959).

Hodgson, J. *History of Northumberland in Three Parts*, 7 volumes (1820–58).

Hutchinson, W. *A View of Northumberland,* 2 volumes (1778).

Long, B. *Castles of Northumberland* (1967).

Mackenzie, E. *A Historical, topographical and descriptive view of the County of Northumberland,* 2 volumes (1825).

Mawer, A. *The Place Names of Northumberland and Durham* (1920).

Northumberland County History Committee. *A History of Northumberland* (N.C.H.), 15 volumes (1893–1940).

Pevsner, N. *The Buildings of England: Northumberland* (1957).

Proceedings of the Society of Antiquaries of Newcastle upon Tyne (P.S.A.) 5th series, 32 volumes (1855–1956).

Raine, J. *The History and Antiquities of North Durham* (1852).

Richmond, I. A. *Roman and Native in North Britain* (1958).

Rivet, A. L. F. *The Iron Age in Northern Britain* (1966).

Royal Commission on Ancient Monuments (England), *Shielings and Bastles* (1970).

Society of Antiquaries of Newcastle upon Tyne. *Archaeologia Aeliana* (A.A.), 1st to 3rd series, 50 volumes (1822–1924); 4th series from 1925 to date.

Tate, W. E. 'A Handlist of English Enclosure Acts and Awards', Part 26: 'Northumberland'; *Proceedings of the Society of Antiquaries of Newcastle upon Tyne*, 4th series, Vol. x, No. 1 (1942).

Tomlinson, W. W. *Comprehensive Guide to Northumberland*, reprint of 11th ed. (1968).

Young, A. *A Six Months Tour through the North of England*, 2nd ed. (1771).

3. The urban landscape

The golden age of the boroughs

AT THE TIME of the Norman Conquest no town in North-umberland approached even the very modest scale of urban development reached by contemporary Winchester, Coventry or Exeter. City life fostered by the Roman occupation of Britain had found an uncongenial soil in the environment of the northern frontier. Carlisle and *Corstopitum* had been the only urban centres of any significance along the whole length of the Wall, or indeed anywhere north of York. *Corstopitum* was rebuilt for the last time in A.D. 369; when the Wall itself was abandoned shortly afterwards as a factor in frontier policy the town could not survive the loss of the stimulus once provided by imperial troops. Some urban life may have lingered on for a time, but only in "an ill-built town of hucksters and mechanics whose mean shops intruded on the noble ruins of the Antonine age, a town of vanishing wealth on the edges of a sinking empire".[1]

At the important bridge-head of *Pons Aelius* no evidence has yet been adduced to prove the existence of even a rudimentary settlement between the evacuation of the Roman fort and the construction of the Norman castle in the eleventh century. When, in the early fifth century, the Romans handed over responsibility for the peace of the North to local chieftains, the ordinary tribesman reverted to his traditional way of life, in which even rudimentary towns played no part.

After the Anglian settlement Bamburgh, Warkworth, Corbridge, Rothbury and Newburn-on-Tyne became the administrative centres of great royal estates. They amounted to no more than small villages, by modern standards, defended by a wooden palisade, hedge or mound, and con-

[1] *N.C.H.,* Vol. X, p. 11.

taining the wooden hall of the king and, in due course, a church.

Bamburgh, named after Bebba, the wife of Aethelfrith, was the leading royal 'city' according to Bede; and according to a twelfth-century tradition was "most strongly fortified . . . not very large, being of the size of two or three fields."[2] Its strength lay in its site and in the inadequacy of contemporary siege warfare; before the Conquest there was nothing comparable to Henry II's keep. Scott's description of "King Ida's castle huge and square", in *Marmion,* is a much-quoted anachronism.

Newburn, generally said to mean 'the new burgh', was new in relation to an older settlement on the Roman Wall called by Bede *Ad Murum,* which was probably the modern Walbottle. Its site is the usual one favoured by the Anglians below the higher crests of the hills and above the river haughs. Its importance lay in its control of the fords across the Tyne, where the Scots crossed the river in 1644.

Anglian Corbridge, situated less than a mile from the convenient quarry provided by *Corstopitum,* retained its strategic importance, which the Romans had so unerringly recognised, until the Norman development of the coastal route between Newcastle and Berwick.

After the consolidation of Norman rule north of the Tyne the growth of urban life was encouraged by a period of relative peace and by the policy of the magnates. Small towns evolved under the protection of royal and baronial strongholds, as at Newcastle and Alnwick, or were deliberately founded, as at Warkworth and Alnmouth. At Hexham a small medieval town developed under the stimulus of the medieval abbey; but with an absentee overlord, the archbishop of York, Hexham lacked the encouragement given to, say, Bury St Edmunds by its abbots, and it suffered severely from repeated Scots raids.

[2] Simeon of Durham quoted by C. J. Bates, 'The Border Holds of Northumberland', *A.A.,* 3rd series, Vol. XIV (1891), p. 227.

In Northumberland, as elsewhere in England, the thirteenth century was the great age of the development of towns, markets, and fairs. But the county remained overwhelmingly rural, even by medieval standards. In the sixteenth century Northumberland contained only eight market-towns—Alnwick, Bellingham, Berwick, Haltwhistle, Hexham, Morpeth, Newcastle and Wooler.[3] There were sixteen in Cumberland and forty-five in the larger county of Devon.

Berwick did not finally become English till 1482, after changing hands thirteen times in three centuries. By that time the frontier town, described in the thirteenth century as "a second Alexandria, whose riches are the sea and the water its walls",[4] had been ruined. The walls constructed by Edward I significantly enclosed a much greater area than did the later Elizabethan fortifications. The northern line of the Edwardian walls ran from the river below the station, the site of the medieval castle, to the Bell Tower on the edge of the Magdalen Fields, and thus included the whole of the area along the line of the Castlegate between the Scotsgate and the station (Fig. 13, Plate 21).

After the Norman Conquest the main strategic route between Tyne and Tweed was shifted eastwards from Dere Street to the line of the present A1. Castles were built to guard the river crossings and towns developed under their protection. Morpeth, fourteen miles from Newcastle, one of the earliest of these post-Conquest boroughs, was in existence by 1138. The borough was granted a market in 1199. The ford over the Wansbeck was commanded by the castle on the steep ridge to the south of the river and was supplemented in the thirteenth century by one of the earliest medieval bridges in the county. The medieval borough developed along the axis of the wide Bridge

---

[3] *The Agrarian History of England and Wales*, Vol. IV, p. 468. Corbridge was in fact a market town through its association with the great fair of Stagshaw Bank.

[4] J. Scott, *Berwick on Tweed* (1888), p. 13.

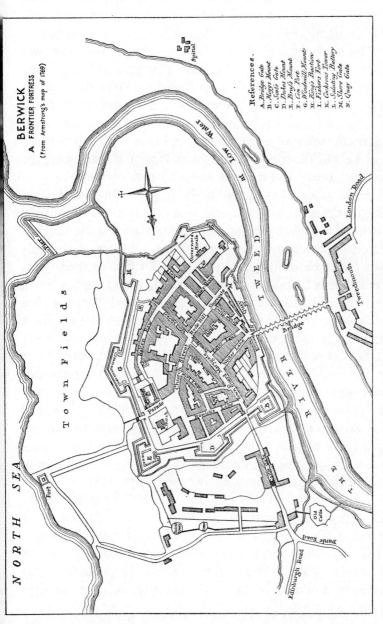

Fig. 13. Berwick is one of the finest examples of a fortified town to be found in Europe. Its medieval walls enclosed a larger area than do the still-existing Elizabethan walls constructed between 1558 and 1590. The former took in the area north of the Edinburgh road, the modern A1. The bridge, completed in 1624, is now known as the Old Bridge. The Town Fields, also called Magdalen Fields, still show good examples of ridge-and-furrow.

Street, on the north bank of the Wansbeck, between the Oldgate on the west and the thirteenth-century church of All Saints, near the Bridge Charity Museum, on the east.

The construction of the bridge enabled Morpeth to outgrow its rival Mitford, where the Bertrams had built their castle to guard the higher crossing of the river. Mitford lay apart from the direct route between Newcastle and the north, and the castle itself was eventually abandoned. Morpeth managed to prosper, even in the sixteenth century, and Leland described the town as long and well-built, the streets paved, "a far fairer town than Alnwick".[5]

At Alnwick, as at Morpeth, the river was used as the first line of defence for the castle against an invader from the north. An ancient centre of communications, the original Anglian settlement, 'the *wic* on the Aln', was probably based on the triangular space now formed by Bondgate, Fenkle Street, and the Rothbury road, where the town hall and the Northumberland Hall are situated. Here, it has been suggested, "there was once a green-village with a fairly large triangular green".[6] A simple motte and bailey castle was built on the hill above the river by the early years of the twelfth century. This was replaced soon afterwards by a stone structure. The construction of a baronial stronghold near the junction of ancient tracks above the river, and the existence of a great feudal establishment encouraged trade. The origins of the borough of Alnwick are uncertain but a charter had been granted to the burgesses by one of the Vesci lords of Alnwick between 1157–1185.

The modern traveller entering Alnwick from the south, through the fine fourteenth-century gateway known as the Hotspur Tower, enters what is still essentially in plan a medieval town centred on the broad Bondgate and the triangular space by the market. The buildings are primarily eighteenth and early nineteenth-century, built in the days

[5] *Itinerary,* (1769 ed.), Vol. VII, p. 62.
[6] M. R. G. Conzen, *Alnwick, Northumberland* (1960), p. 18.

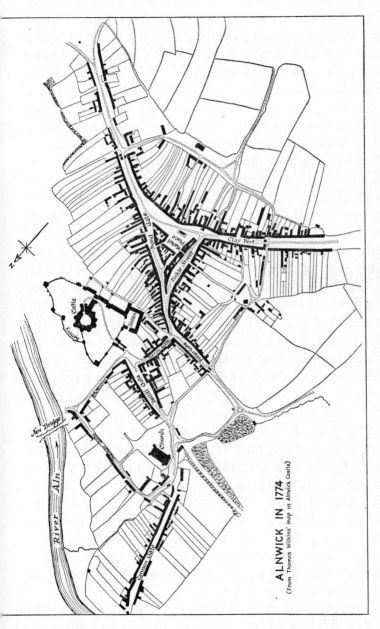

ALNWICK IN 1774
(From Thomas Wilkins' map in Alnwick Castle)

Fig. 14. Alnwick developed from a nucleus around the triangular green, itself an ancient track-junction, of the Anglian settlement called the *wick*, or 'farm', on the Aln. The medieval town grew up under the protection of a major baronial fortress, built shortly after the Norman Conquest, and received borough status in the second half of the twelfth century. The original burghal plots were well marked in 1774, but many can still be traced today.

when Alnwick flourished as a local capital and a ducal residence, a market town and social centre for a wide rural area. The medieval burgage-plots lined the sides of the triangular medieval street system, Bondgate, Fenkle Street and Clayport Street, as their successor houses do today, with their fronts on the broad space where the business of the borough was conducted (Fig. 14). Behind them their crofts radiated outwards towards the walls, forming long and narrow strips, some of which still exist as property boundaries today.[7]

To the north of the town the present line of the A1 emerges from the narrow streets into the broad space of the Bailiffgate, opposite the entrance to the castle, before turning down the Peth to cross the river at the Lion Bridge, the later eighteenth-century successor to the medieval bridge which was originally situated downstream in a position more directly dominated by the castle. The wide space of the Bailiffgate and the absence of the narrow plots of typical medieval tenements, such as those in the neighbourhood of the Bondgate, suggest a history that was distinct from that of the medieval borough. The area of the Bailiffgate was probably "largely, if not wholly, occupied by militia or by people assembled for administrative purposes", a suburb of the castle whose inhabitants paid rent to the castle reeve and not to the town reeve.[8]

The medieval town of Alnwick developed gradually around an existing road system to which its inhabitants had to conform. In contrast, Warkworth is still a textbook example of a planned medieval borough (Fig. 15, Plate 22). Warkworth makes a shadowy appearance in the eighth century, when it was a residence of the Northumbrian king Ceolwulf, to whom Bede dedicated his *Ecclesiastical History*. Little is known of the history of the manor until the twelfth century when it was granted by Henry II to one of the

---

[7] Conzen, op. cit., has made a detailed study of medieval Alnwick to which the author is indebted.

[8] Conzen, op. cit., p. 21.

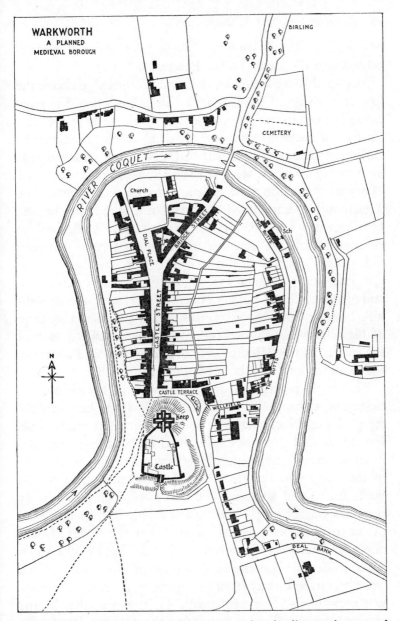

Fig. 15. Warkworth was originally the centre of an Anglian royal estate and is situated on a ridge within a loop of the Coquet. A castle was built after the Norman Conquest. The borough was founded *c.* 1200 and was planned along the axis of a single street between the castle and the church. Its plan is identical with that of the less successful borough of Norham, which was also laid out in the late twelfth century between the castle and the older church. In both cases the church had pre-Conquest origins and must have influenced medieval planning. Modern Warkworth retains its original burghal plots on either side of Castle Street, especially on the east.

de Vesci lords of Alnwick. In the fourteenth century it passed into the hands of the Percies.

Medieval Warkworth was laid out on the ridge above the lowest crossing of the Coquet at the point where the river emerges from its gorge into the tidal creeks of its estuary. At the foot of the ridge, opposite the dene which gave access to Birling and the north, the fortified bridge, still standing, was built in 1379. This crossing of the river was a link in the series of tracks connecting the Anglian coastal settlements from Tynemouth to Bamburgh. Widdrington, on the plain behind Druridge Bay, belonged to the royal estate of Warkworth in Anglian times; and the line of the ancient route between Warkworth and Widdrington is suggested by the series of footpaths and green lanes which, though in part overgrown, still provide a direct ridge-walk from Warkworth to Broom-hill. The northern end of this route, now the lane to the farm of New Barns, is aligned directly on the southern gate of the castle. In the Middle Ages this lane provided access to the demesne lands of the lords of Warkworth.

The castle is situated on the summit of the peninsular ridge and occupies virtually the whole space between the steep slopes which descend to the Coquet on either side. On the north, below the castle, the ridge broadens. Here the medieval town was founded between the castle at the top of the ridge and the church of St Lawrence close to the waterside at the bottom. The castle itself unquestionably occupies the strongest position available within the bend of the river. It is perhaps curious that the bailey should not have been placed on the north side, leaving the town space to develop on the level ground to the south, which was also farthest away from the direction from which attack was most likely. It is very probable, however, that by the eleventh century there was already a substantial village at the north side.[9] The church of St Lawrence, described as being

[9] W. Douglas Simpson, 'Warkworth; a castle of Livery and Maintenance', *A.A.,* 4th series, Vol. XV (1938), p. 120.

Plate 20 Great Whittington
A typical Northumbrian village constructed of stone and slate. One hundred years after the Norman Conquest it was still held by the Saxon tenure of *thegnage*.

Plate 21 Berwick

A frontier city. The photograph shows the Old Bridge, nearest the river mouth, constructed 1611–24; the Royal Tweed Bridge, completed in 1928, in the centre; and the Royal Border Bridge, built by Robert Stephenson in 1847–50. The castle of Edward I was situated above the point where the Royal Border Bridge reaches the north bank of the Tweed. The photograph shows clearly the line of the Elizabethan walls which make Berwick one of the finest fortified towns in Europe.

Plate 22 Warkworth

A planned medieval borough within a loop of the Coquet and set out along the axis of a single street between the castle and the church, as in the abortive borough of Norham. The gardens to the right show clearly the original burghal plots. The small village of Birling is shown beyond the river at the top of the photograph; to its right is the site of one of its common fields where Warkworth Newtown was founded in the thirteenth century. The line of the medieval deer park fence is represented by the modern footpath running diagonally to the left across the ridge-and-furrow from the tower at the bottom left-hand corner of the castle.

Plate 23 Bamburgh

The site of the first Anglian settlement in 547, this stronghold on the Whin Sill outcrop became the capital of Northumbria and later an important royal castle. The keep was built by Henry II. The castle was extensively restored for Lord Armstrong in 1894–1905. The photograph shows part of the triangular village green.

unique in Northumberland in being a large, fairly complete Norman church,[10] was completed in substantially its present form in the early twelfth century. It is likely that the Norman church was on the site of the church founded by Ceolwulf in the early eighth century; if so, there would have been a settlement in the neighbourhood before the construction of the castle.

The medieval borough had emerged in the twelfth century in the reign of Henry II. Seventy-seven houses and plots were planned. The lay-out, unlike Alnwick, was a formal composition in medieval town-planning. The burghal houses were placed on either side of the broad street descending the hill from the castle to the church and the bridge. Behind the house-fronts on the east many of the long narrow gardens sloping down towards the river still retain the boundaries and dimensions of the original plots. Their eastern boundary is the narrow footpath which slants up the hill between garden hedges and stone walls. This path is marked in the map drawn for the manorial lord, the earl of Northumberland, in the early seventeenth century. Beyond the footpath, and above the modern road to Amble, is the area known as the Butts, a word with several related meanings; in this context it meant the place where the burgage tenements abut upon the boundary.

The Percies transformed the castle into a fortified palace; their work of the fourteenth and fifteenth centuries is commemorated by the Percy Lion on the tower forming the entrance to the great hall. The borough itself grew slowly. In 1296 Warkworth was smaller than Corbridge, and smaller even than Bamburgh. Today it is primarily an eighteenth-century town within the confines of the original medieval boundaries. Bridge End House, close to the southern end of the medieval bridge, is a fine example of an early eighteenth-century house built in the days when peace had come to Northumberland and country gentlemen gathered

[10] N. Pevsner, *Northumberland,* p. 311.

for business and social occasions in their local centres. Even the buildings of the later nineteenth century, such as the house dated 1887 on the north of the square near the church, have in the main continued the traditional treatment of Northumbrian stone. The eccentricities of suburban villadom have been confined to the areas along the Waterhaugh road to the south of the town, on what was once the demesne land of the medieval lords of the manor.

North of Warkworth, at the mouth of the Aln, the little seaside town of Alnmouth repeats the regularity of a medieval planned borough. The site is similar to that at Warkworth (Fig. 15), a narrow ridge between the river and the sea which was once part of the common belonging to the village of Lesbury. Little is known of the early history of Alnmouth. There was certainly an Anglian settlement here before the Conquest. Among the sandhills south of the town beyond the river mouth are the remains of a pre-Conquest church which, under Norman influence, was named St Waleric, after St Valéry near the mouth of the Seine. This site was cut off from Alnmouth when the river changed course after floods in 1806.

Alnmouth, once also called Newbiggin, was founded in the second half of the twelfth century by the Vesci lord of Alnwick. It was mentioned as a borough in a charter of 1147 and so was one of the earliest of the new boroughs founded after the stabilisation of Norman rule in Northumberland. In 1207 King John authorised Eustace de Vesci of Alnwick to make a port and to hold a market. For a time the new borough prospered. Alnmouth was assessed at £55 8s. 9d. in 1296, more than the assessment of Morpeth.[11] In the fourteenth century the borough dwindled and by 1567 it contained only sixty inhabitants, including twenty fishermen. In the early eighteenth century the town was still derelict, but it later revived as a port, particularly

---

[11] C. M. Fraser, *The Northumberland Lay Subsidy of 1296*, p. 96.

for the corn trade, and became the coastal terminus of the so-called Corn Road.

Alnmouth is an example of the foundation of a new medieval settlement on the boundary of a parish (Fig. 16). Seen today from the west, or south across the saltings and mudflats, it retains the appearance of a close-packed medieval town between the river and the sea. The burgage plots were laid out symmetrically on either side of the road on the line of the medieval track from Lesbury, which curves round on the higher ground to the east of the Aln. Until the construction of the Duchess's Bridge, in 1864, the road formed Alnmouth's only direct channel of communication with Lesbury and Alnwick.

The northern boundary of the medieval town began at the modern roundabout, where the road from Alnmouth station joins the approach road from the north from Foxton Hall. On the east of the main street the burghal plots behind the houses are still in part visible on the ground, in the form of the narrow properties sloping steeply to the modern road on the edge of the links below. Access to the links on this side was maintained by the lanes shown on the plan of 1614. These still exist as Crow's Nest Lane and Pease Lane. On the west of the main street the modern gardens have modified the original medieval lay-out, though the general appearance remains unaltered in the form of the gardens which descend to the edge of the saltings by the river. A lane entering Argyle Street above the Aln Boat Yard appears to have been on the line of the western boundary of the town in medieval times.

Alnmouth today is largely the creation of the nineteenth century, when the construction of the railway opened up its links and sands to the middle-class of Newcastle. Argyle Street with its red roofs and gables, and Osborn House, dated 1900, are characteristic of this period.

Warkworth and Alnmouth have both retained their original medieval town-plans. Bamburgh, as an Anglian

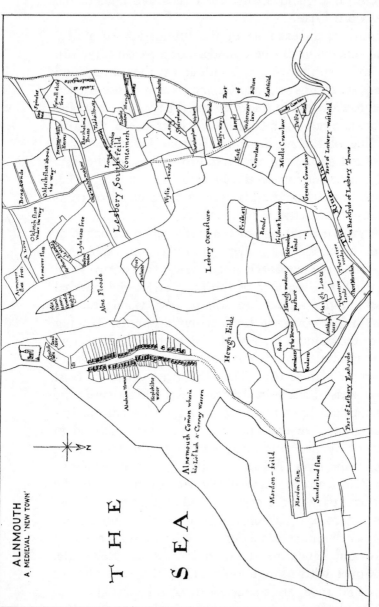

Fig. 16. Alnmouth was one of the earliest of the medieval new towns of Northumberland. It was founded in the twelfth century on the southern edge of Lesbury parish. The town was laid out along the axis of a single street, as at Warkworth and Norham. This map shows Alnmouth in 1624 and was drawn with the south at the top. The medieval church at that time was still joined to the town by a line of sandhills, before the river changed course in 1806. Lesbury South Field in 1624 was mostly divided into pastures and the approach to Alnmouth was by means of a track along the

stronghold older than either, is largely a planned early nineteenth-century village. The original Anglian settlement was on the Whin Sill outcrop above the sea, but this village is unlikely to have survived the construction of the keep by Henry II. After the Norman Conquest Bamburgh became a major royal castle and inherited the religious traditions derived from association with St Aidan and St Cuthbert. Monastic buildings were built close to the present church of St Aidan; and in 1265 the Dominicans founded the establishment now represented by the farm of Bamburgh Friars, which contains medieval stonework.

In the hopeful atmosphere of the thirteenth century the new village which had grown up below the castle developed sufficiently for Henry III to grant it exemption from the jurisdiction of the royal sheriff and of the constable of the castle. In 1295 the small borough, like Corbridge, sent two representatives to the Model Parliament; but by the end of the thirteenth century the Scottish wars had begun. The burghers were soon under the necessity of removing to the castle not only their food stocks, goods and chattels but also the timber frames of their houses.[12] Any prospect of a revival of urban development vanished in the great siege of 1464 during the Wars of the Roses.

Bamburgh today is the creation of the trustees of the Crewe Estate, a typical green-village grouped round a triangular green, where the market was held in the Middle Ages, and with a good row of cottages built by the trustees in 1802 (Plate 23). The *Northumberland County History*, however, suggests tentatively that the main street of the medieval borough may have been the Spittle Gate, the road named from the thirteenth-century leper hospital, which in fact lay outside the borough since its property owners in 1296 did not pay the borough rate.[13] It is possible that this road is represented today by the path which runs at the back of the houses and gardens in an easterly direction from

[12] *N.C.H.*, Vol. I, p. 124.   [13] Ibid., p. 113.

the Ingram road and which passes close to the fifteenth-century dovecote behind the Lord Crewe Arms Hotel. There are indications that the road may have been continued by the line of gates which give access to the Seahouses road opposite the ascent to the gateway of the castle.

Corbridge, though lacking the glamour of Bamburgh's history and situation, is considerably more interesting as a study in urban settlement. If any shadow of the urban life of Roman times survived into Anglian times—and there is no overt evidence of survival—it would have been at Corbridge. As an Anglian royal manor it appeared for the first time in historical records in 786, when a bishop of Mayo was consecrated in the church. The manor remained royal property until the reign of King John. It then passed into the possession of the Fitz Roger lords of Alnwick, who later adopted the surname of Clavering. Corbridge itself is the only place in Northumberland to incorporate in its name at least part of the name of its Roman predecessor, the great fort and supply base of *Corstopitum* from the stones of which so much of Corbridge has been built. Despite its strategic importance on the crossroads of Roman Northumberland, Corbridge was always an undefended town. No castle was erected at the important medieval bridgehead. The town grew as an important commercial centre and suffered badly from Scots raids.

Seen from Dilston haughs south of the river, Corbridge appears as a compact huddle of stone houses and slate roofs on the steep bank above the Tyne. The original Anglian core is the area about the church, the vicar's pele and the market, some fifty to sixty feet above the Tyne on dry and well-drained glacial drift, and only some half mile from the Roman ruins which supplied ready-shaped building stone. Approached from the west, along the riverside lane which once formed part of the Carelgate, the Saxon church tower stands high on the skyline on the far side of a declivity, the

Foul Syke of medieval times, which would have been deeper before it became filled with the detritus of succeeding centuries.

The modern street known as Watling Street bears no relation to any Roman road system though it provides a congested access for holiday traffic to Dere Street and the North. The name Watling Street did not appear at Corbridge till the sixteenth century. But the short descent now known as Well Lane, to the west of the market place, is the ghost of one of the oldest roads in the county. Now a pleasant walk where blackcaps sing in summer and the sandpipers bob by the waterside, the rough stones underfoot are the remnants of a route which was still in use as a main road in the eighteenth century. This is the Anglian Carelgate (Plate 24), the Carlisle road, which crossed the burn near the mill and climbed Sherdon Brae to join Agricola's military road which the Anglians called the Stanegate.[14]

The Roman bridge across the Tyne above Corbridge disappeared during the Dark Ages and the main ford across the Tyne was south of the existing bridge. The ancient approach to the ford, used by the cattle which thronged Corbridge in droving days, is the short length of stone-walled lane leading off the Newcastle road at the eastern end of Main Street and descending to the meadow by the river.[15] In 1235 Simon, lord of Dilston, the small barony cut out of the Corbridge waste south of the river after the Conquest, gave permission for the construction of the southern end of a bridge upon his land. This was the predecessor of the fine bridge which stands today. The citizens of Corbridge were given permission to build a road from the southern bridge-head to join the Holepath— 'the hollow way'. This thirteenth-century road became in due course the modern Station Road.[16] The burghers were

[14] R. P. Wright, 'The Stanegate at Corbridge', *A.A.*, 4th series, Vol. XIX (1941), p. 194.
[15] R. Forster, *History of Corbridge and its Antiquities* (1891), p. 99.
[16] *N.C.H.*, Vol. X, p. 64.

also confirmed in their rights to a footpath downstream 'to the wood', still a pleasant walk on the south bank of the river from the bridge to Farnley Scar.[17]

By the eve of the Scottish wars, in 1296, Corbridge had become the second town in Northumberland, though with an estimated population of a mere 1500 persons. Its trade was mostly in leather, hides and shoes, and in iron. Its streets were designed for a busy trading town, for pack-horses, sheep and cattle. Hill Street, a remarkably wide street by medieval standards, was in existence by the four-teenth century, and was known variously as the Fish Market, Horsemarket and Hidemarket. The fine Main Street, known as the Smithy Gate in the Middle Ages, was well-fitted for the flocks and herds of pastoral North-umberland travelling south from beyond the Wall by the line of Dere Street, and for traffic across the Tyne by the moorland tracks to the mines of the Alston Moors and the Allendales.

Medieval Corbridge lived as much by agriculture as by trade; the framework of the town fields and pastures as they existed in the Middle Ages is still visible. South of the Tyne lay the extensive grazing grounds and waste finally en-closed in the eighteenth century. The arable fields were situated north of the river. Cow Lane, from its junction with the Stagshaw road, and Milkwell Lane, from the Aydon road near the modern police station, pass through what was once the North Field of Corbridge and com-bine to cross the ford of the Cor Burn before the ascent to the Leazes, the ancient pastures in the neighbourhood of Leazes Cottage and Leazes Lane. The East Field filled the space between the Aydon road and the Tyne. After the enclosures of 1779 the consolidation of holdings led to the appearance of narrow rectangular fields in this area. A few of these still remain, and the name of Eastfield House recalls the medieval field in which the house was built

[17] *N.C.H.*, Vol. X, p. 64.

after the division and enclosure of the field. The West Field was situated west of the modern A68 and extended across the Cor Burn to the present boundary between Corbridge and Sandhoe.

Until recent years Corbridge has been largely confined within its medieval boundaries. The northern limit of the medieval town was what is now called St Helen's Road. Beyond the road was the site of St Helen's chapel, and the manor house of the Clavering lords of the manor built in the thirteenth century south of the ditch which marked the northern boundary of the original borough. This area until recently consisted largely of gardens and allotments. The eastern limit of the medieval town was Prince Street, in the Middle Ages Prendestretland, which gave access from the bridge to the Aydon road. West of Corbridge, near the junction of the Cor Burn with the Tyne, the mill has an ancient history. It is the successor to the mill where Ralph the Miller was assessed at the substantial sum of fifteen shillings in 1296.[18]

On the hills to the north, below the point at which Dere Street passes through the Wall at the Portgate, the moorland pastures of Corbridge became the site of the most famous fair of Northumberland, the Stagshaw Bank Fair, which was in existence at the beginning of the thirteenth century, at a time when the king's agent purchased supplies of horseshoes and nails for the army advancing into Scotland. In the early nineteenth century Stagshaw Bank Fair was still renowned for the sheep and cattle brought south by the Scots drovers to the stances south of the Portgate. Much of the site today is still open common of gorse and heather among the stone-walled pastures of eighteenth-century enclosure.

Hexham grew out of a community offered a livelihood by employment and trade at the gates of St Wilfred's famous

---

[18] *N.C.H.,* Vol. X, gives an interesting account of medieval Corbridge with a map of the fourteenth-century town at p. 113.

seventh-century church. The town became the administrative centre and market for a wide area, which in fact was both unadministered and notoriously lawless by the time it was brought under direct control of the Crown in 1572. Hexham today is still a harmonious concept of urban architecture constructed, for the most part, in the mellow local stone. It stands high above the haughs of the Tyne within a setting of wooded hills, its centre still the space under the abbey walls approached by narrow streets climbing from the lower levels.

St Wilfred's church was constructed on a commanding site on the spur between the Cockshaw Burn, which flows north in its wooded dene towards the Carlisle Road, and the smaller burn which descends from the vicinity of High Shields. The seventh-century grant to St Wilfred included the originally wide area of Hexhamshire,[19] which also formed the parish of the church of St Andrew. In the Middle Ages Hexhamshire became a regality, a semi-independent territory which passed into the hands of the archbishops of York after the Norman Conquest and was administered by the archbishop's bailiffs. Their monuments are the strong and impressive fourteenth-century prison and the fifteenth-century Moot Hall which, with the abbey, dominate the medieval town and together tell the story of its origins and history.

Hexham became noted as a centre for grain and livestock. The term 'Hexhamshire measure' denoted a full measure.[20] The lead mines in the fells were worked in the thirteenth century, subject to payment to the archbishop of York. The town stood apart from the main medieval roads but was in close proximity to the Stanegate, and to the moor-

[19] In the nineteenth century the area comprised only the parishes of Hexham and Whitley. In the Middle Ages Hexhamshire included the townships of Rowley, Bingfield, Ettington, Keepwick, Fallowfield, Bewclay, Sandhoe, Anick, Wall, Acomb, Ninebanks, Catton and Allendale as well as Hexham. *N.C.H.,* Vol. III, Part 1, p. 1.

[20] A. B. Wright, *An Essay towards a History of Hexham* (1823) p. 31.

land tracks into the wilds of Allendale and Alston, over Bolbec Common to Blanchland and so to Stanhope and Weardale.

Hexham (Plate 25) in origin is an unplanned town. Though an ancient borough by repute there is no trace of burghal plots, nor of the orderly lay-out of medieval Warkworth and Alnmouth. It developed as a settlement at the gates of St Wilfred's church and its successors on the small area of level ground approached from the Tyne by Market Street, once the main street of the town, and by the steeper ascent of Hallstile Bank. Hallstile Bank leads into the mid-eighteenth-century Alemouth (Alnmouth) Road. The market place itself was at one time much larger than it is now, before the erection of the buildings forming an island on its northern side. "Hexham's approaches from east and west", commented a local historian, "have all the inconvenience and contempt of order which distinguishes the buildings of our ancestors".[21] Those words were written in an age which tended to regard history as the record of progress, but they are just as regards lack of formal planning.

Comparison between Hexham and an Italian medieval city is inevitable. At the top of the ascent of Market Street, with the twelfth-century priory gate in Gilesgate, the seventeenth-century houses and the Regency building occupied by the post office, the market is still an enclosed and secret place between the abbey and the stark medieval strongholds. St Mary's Chare, containing some fine bow-fronted Georgian shop windows, provided the main access to Battle Hill, and to the wide streets of Hencotes and Priestpopple, the sites of fairs until the eighteenth century.

Newcastle upon Tyne was the first, and overwhelmingly the most successful, of the medieval new towns of Northumberland. No trace of an Anglian predecessor has yet been discovered. By the time of the Norman Conquest the

[21] Wright, op. cit., p. 20.

Roman bridge was in ruins, though its piers remained and were used by the new rulers of the north. In 1080 Robert Curthose selected the plateau above the Roman bridge-head as the site of his new castle and by so doing exercised a decisive influence on the future development of Northumberland. A civilian settlement rapidly came into being under the shelter of the castle. By the end of the thirteenth century Newcastle had an estimated population of 3970.[22] This was far smaller than contemporary York, which had a population of over 10,000, but it was already twice that of Corbridge, then the second town in Northumberland.

The natural strength of the site has been partially obscured by Victorian urban growth, and still more by twentieth-century development, though the city still rises from the bank of the Tyne in an imposing series of levels. For some 300 years the citizens of Newcastle have been seeking to overcome the difficulties in communication caused by its rugged topography, especially by the burns in their denes flowing towards the river from the high ground to the north. Many of the steep slopes and declivities have in fact been smoothed away, but the natural conditions which influenced the siting of the Roman bridge-head and the Norman castle can still be seen and studied, especially by the pedestrian climbing from the Close towards Hanover Street up Tuthill Stairs, or from the Sandhill to the castle area by way of Dog Leap Stairs.

The city developed from an area around the north end of the first medieval bridge, itself on the line of the Roman Bridge and now represented by the Swing Bridge, and from the area immediately north of the Norman military and religious precinct south of Collingwood Street and Mosley Street (Fig. 17).

The Lort Burn rose in the Leazes and, following the line of St Thomas's Street and Prudhoe Place, turned south down the deep ravine of Dean Street to reach the river

[22] D. L. W. Tough, *Last Years of a Frontier* (1928), p. 62.

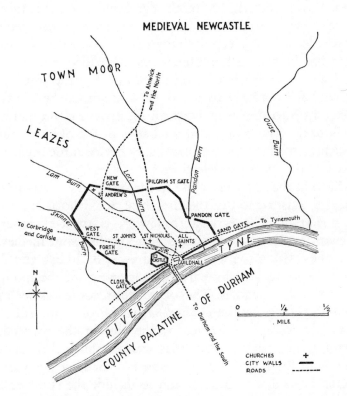

Fig. 17. The Normans used the piers of the Roman bridge to carry their wooden structure across the Tyne. It was guarded on the north bank by the new castle on the high ground between the Side and the Tyne. At the edge of the river, south-east of the fortified area, was the level area known as the Sandhill, where the commercial life of the city developed. The map shows the concentration of medieval routes in this area. This was continued by the nineteenth-century bridges. The two routes to the north followed the line of the Bigg Market–Newgate Street, and Pilgrim Street. They joined at the future Barras Bridge. Dean Street was the dene of the lower reaches of the Lort Burn, crossed by the High Bridge and the Low Bridge.

under what is now the Tyne Bridge. Its lower reaches were tidal. It was joined by the Lam Burn which entered the Lort Burn from the west near the junction of Grey Street and Market Street. Of more significance for the future development of the city was an unnamed burn, which descended by the steep declivity of the Side to the bottom of what is now Dean Street, and provided the natural defence of the castle area on the north. On the south the ground fell abruptly to the river. Westwards there was a steep drop to the levels between the river and the railway station, the low ground on the banks of the Skinner Burn which formed the western boundary between the medieval city and the manor of Elswick.

Beyond the Side, but close to the castle, there was room for the construction of the church of St Nicholas. Its date is uncertain. The earliest stonework is twelfth century. Newcastle was originally one parish, but had four medieval churches within the walls. St Andrew's, St John's and All Saints were technically parochial chapelries of the mother church of St Nicholas. They were still recorded as such in Ecton's *Thesaurum Rerum Ecclesiasticarum* of 1754. All the churches were in existence by the end of the thirteenth century. The parish boundaries were established by about 1220 and the highly irregular shape of St Nicholas parish seems to be due to the decision to include the commercial and administrative centre of the city.[23] There was a long projecting salient bounded on the east by the Lort Burn and taking in the area between the modern Mosley Street and High Bridge Street. On the west the boundary followed the line of the Bigg Market to the junction of St Nicholas Street and the Side. None of the other boundaries displayed the same eccentricities. All Saints covered the area between the Pandon Burn and the Lort Burn. St Andrew's comprised the northern part of the city north of the line of the Lam Burn. St John's took in the remaining south-west

[23] F. W. Dendry, *Three Lectures on Old Newcastle* (1921), pp. 7, 8.

corner to the western boundary of the city, the Skinner Burn.

Newcastle rapidly became the only city of any significance between York and Berwick. By the early years of the thirteenth century, little more than 100 years after the construction of the Norman castle, the city had a mayor.

A major factor in the development and prosperity of Newcastle was the completion, in 1306, of the walls which Leland, in the sixteenth century, described enthusiastically as "surpassing all the walls of any city in the realm and most of the cities of Europe".[24] Henceforward Newcastle remained impregnable until captured by a Scots army, with the support of the Parliamentary leaders in London, in 1644. The gates and most of the walls have long been demolished; but a good impression of their original appearance is still given by the length still standing between Stowell Street and the Westgate Road where the Morden, Heber and Durham towers are situated. To the east of the city the tower on the Wall Knoll, above the City Road, gives the best view of the rugged topography in the neighbourhood of the Pandon Burn.

This topography caused, and still causes, difficult problems in communications, particularly lateral communications. The Yorkshire squire Sir William Brereton, who visited the city in 1635, commented that, "This towne (a great part of itt) placed upon the highest and steepest hills that I have found in any great towne: these so steepe as horses cannot stand uppon the pavements."[25]

Below the castle communications with Durham and York were maintained by the bridge on its Roman foundations on the line of the existing Swing Bridge. Communications with the north lay along the ridges leading up from the river, along the line of Newgate Street and Pilgrim Street. The route to Carlisle and Hexham was the Westgate

[24] Leland's *Itinerary* (1769 ed.), Vol. V, p. 60.
[25] *Surtees Society*, Vol. XXIV (1915), p. 16.

with access by easy gradients to the castle area. Between Pilgrim Street and the west was the deep dene of the Lort Burn and its tributary down the Side. In consequence Newcastle developed from two centres, the quays east of the bridge, which blocked access for shipping to the higher reaches of the river, and the small area of level ground at the mouth of the Lort Burn; and the higher, but relatively level, ground north of the castle and St Nicholas.

The dene of the Lort Burn was bridged in the Middle Ages by the Higher and Nether Bridges, situated where High Bridge Street and Lower Bridge Street respectively join Dean Street from the west. The contours have long since been smoothed away in the northern section but there is still an almost imperceptible descent from Upper Bridge Street. Lower Dean Street is one of the most dramatic streets in any town in England, a deep canyon under the tall nineteenth-century buildings and the great railway viaduct. It was probably in this area that the first warship known to have been constructed on the Tyne was built, the galleon completed for Edward I in 1292. Small boats were moored, until the Lort Burn was paved over in 1696, at the bottom of Painter's Heugh, at the time of writing a narrow and dirty cul-de-sac on the east of Dean Street. It is improbable, however, that the name has any connection with a boat's mooring.[26]

Above the viaduct the steep and narrow ascent of the Side curves up the slope between Milburn House and the castle to reach the level ground near the Black Gate. For centuries the Side provided the shortest means of access between the two important commercial areas of the city (Fig. 17). Paved at the end of the seventeenth century, it was crammed with shops through which the coaches and waggons forced their way; it was still regarded as one of the principal streets of the city in the eighteenth century.

[26] J. Brand, *The History and Antiquity of Newcastle upon Tyne* (1789), Vol I, p. 338.

Plate 24 The Carelgate, Corbridge

Now a footpath by the Tyne, the Carelgate, or Carlisle road, called the Stanegate, from the Middle Ages till the mid-eighteenth century. The photograph is taken looking east towards Corbridge. Roman *Corstopitum* was on high ground behind the hedge on the left.

Plate 25 Hexham

An unplanned town which developed around the open space, now the market, at the east end of the church originally built by St Wilfred *c.* 675–80. On the far side of the market, opposite the east end of the abbey buildings, is the tower-house built for the Archbishop of York, lord of the manor, in the late fourteenth century.

Plate 26 A flue chimney, Stublick Moor

These tall chimneys are a characteristic feature of the Pennine moorlands of
Northumberland, monuments to an industry which prospered in the eighteenth
and early nineteenth centuries. Lead-mining in the Allendales ceased in 1899.
The chimneys were intended to disperse noxious fumes.

Plate 27 Dukesfield smelt-mill
The ruins by the Devil's Water of the largest of the smelt-mills owned by Sir
William Blackett in the eighteenth century. The lead ore was carried to Dukes-
field by Galloway ponies from the mines in the Allendales.

From the height of the Tyne Bridge the medieval city can be evoked out of the medley of roof tops and chimneys between the river and the steep slopes up to the Moot Hall, All Saints Church and Manor Chare. Most of the Sandhill remained an open space until the end of the eighteenth century, though it was fringed with merchants' houses. Magnificent examples of sixteenth and seventeenth century architecture exist here today. In this area the Guildhall was built in the fifteenth century, to be replaced by Robert Trollope's building in 1655–8. Behind the quayside to the north were the narrow and close-packed lanes, called Chares, for the most part destroyed by the great fire of 1854. There is now little left to recall them but a handful of names.

The Chares ran in parallel lines from north to south between the Sandhill and the original line of the city wall along Cowgate Street and the Broad Chare. When, in 1299, Newcastle annexed the prosperous village of Pandon above Pandon Dene it was necessary to extend the wall eastwards to include the village forming a salient under the heights above the City Road. Pandon Street curves in marked contrast to the straight lines of the Chares. The Broad Chare was broad because it could occupy the space once filled by the original line of the wall.

North of what are now Collingwood Street and Mosley Street, Newgate Street, the direct route from the castle to the north, ended as a wide wedge-shaped area with its base under St Nicholas. This level space, close to the military headquarters and communicating with the port area by the Side, grew at an early date into the higher of the two principal commercial areas of the city. It has been much modified by eighteenth- and nineteenth-century planning, but its lay-out is still essentially medieval. It is still a market centre; its street names, the Bigg (Barley) Market, the Cloth Market and the Groat Market, the narrow length of Pudding Chare, recall its early medieval origins. To stand in the Groat Market today when the stalls of the street traders are thronged, and to look down the curve of the street to the cathedral and the castle, gives some impression of the origins of this part of Newcastle in the days when peasants and traders from the open country beyond the walls first congregated beneath the twin monuments of Norman rule.

Until the mid-eighteenth century the commercial development of Newcastle was confined to the area south of High Bridge Street and Pudding Chare, forming an arc between Pilgrim Street and Westgate Street. The Edwardian walls to the north of the city were situated along the southern side of the Gallowgate and Blackett Street from St Andrew's Church, immediately within the wall, to the junction of Croft Street and New Bridge Street. The main north-to-south thoroughfares of the city emerged at the New Gate and the Pilgrim Street Gate, the former immediately to the east of St Andrew's, and the latter at the point where Pilgrim Street meets the junction of Blackett Street, Northumberland Street and New Bridge Street. The greater part of this area was occupied by the buildings and extensive grounds of the religious institutions, such as the thirteenth-century hospital and nunnery of St Bartholomew, which occupied most of the space between Newgate Street and Pilgrim Street north of High Bridge Street. The approximate position of the Priory is the short length of Nun Street. The Franciscans established themselves in the angle between Pilgrim Street and High Friars Street. After the Dissolution of the Monasteries these estates fell into private hands and the great gardens which succeeded them eventually provided the land for Newcastle's major achievement of town planning in the early nineteenth century.

North of Newcastle, between Barras Bridge and Jesmond, the extensive Town Moor, covering some 900 acres, remains as a unique inheritance from Newcastle's medieval past. It was acquired by charter from King John, at the beginning of the great period of Northumberland's medieval history. The fee-farm accepted by King John in 1213 was £100 a year; this was paid until 1885, when it was finally commuted for a capital sum. Edward III confirmed that the burgesses and their heirs should hold the land "as appurtenant to the town with all the profits thereof . . . with power to dig and have mines of coal thereon, and make their profit thereof in aid of the farm [revenue] of the town without impediment."[27]

Today the cattle on the Town Moor are a reminder of the pastoral pursuits of a medieval city, and of the times when the town neatherd blew horns in the city to give warning that the cattle were to be driven to the grazing grounds by the prescribed routes. South of the modern Ponteland road the name of the Nuns' Moor recalls the area where the nuns of the convent of St Bartholomew had rights of pasturage. The word *leazes*, of Anglo-Saxon origin meaning 'common pastures', survives, as a memory of ancient rights and practices, in the Castle Leazes and Leazes Park of today.

In 1400 Newcastle was recognised as a county with its own sheriff, though the castle itself remained a royal fortress. The city's prosperity behind its walls in the fifteenth century contributed to the completion of St Nicholas, the only ecclesiastical building in Northumberland to stand comparison with contemporary buildings in the more prosperous south. After the initial institution of the Norman garrison Newcastle had prospered as a wool staple with a "monopoly of the export of wool, hides and wool-fells for the four northern counties and Richmondshire".[28] Towards the end of the fourteenth century the citizens were already claiming that coal was "the mainstay of their trade".[29] The merchants living in the close-packed

[27] Quoted by E. M. Halcrow in 'The Town Moor of Newcastle upon Tyne', *A.A.*, 4th series, Vol. XXXI (1953), p. 150. This paper is an interesting summary of the history of the often menaced Town Moor.

[28] C. M. Fraser, 'North-East Trade 1265–1350', *Northern History*, Vol. IV, (1969), p. 55.

[29] Ibid., p. 65.

houses of the Sandhill and the Side were already laying the foundations of Newcastle's future as a major industrial city and port.

The industrial areas

The mining of coal and lead has an ancient history in North-umberland. At *Corstopitum* melted lead and fragments of ore were probably derived from the mines of Alston,[30] which was in Northumberland until the reign of Henry I. Lead and silver were worked on the Alston moors in the twelfth century and there were complaints that woodland in the lordship of Hexham was being destroyed by the miners. The lead-mining area of the northern Pennines comprised the high moorlands which lie across the modern boundaries of Cumberland, Durham and Northumberland from Allendale Town to Alston. Above the Nent in Cumberland, a mile from Alston, the name of Corby Gates farm is attributed to the medieval Corbriggate,[31] 'the Cor-bridge Road', where pack-horses from the Alston mines climbed the fells on their rough journey to Corbridge and the Tyne. From the Durham and Cumberland border to the Derwent and the Tyne the moorlands are scattered with the debris of a vanished industry; pits and mounds, fined down by wind and weather, half-hidden by heather and cotton grass; the shafts and flues; tall chimneys on the moorlands of Allendale, or standing sentinel among the grouse butts above Stublick Syke on the Langley Road (Plate 26); the great Blackett Level, four and a half miles in length and uncompleted, reaching the East Allen at Bridge End under Allendale Town.

The intensive exploitation of the Pennine lead mines began at the end of the seventeenth century with the

[30] A. Raistrick and B. Jennings, *A History of Lead Mining in the Pennines* (1965), p. 10.
[31] *N.C.H.*, Vol. X, p. 45.

assistance of Derbyshire miners. The Greenwich Hospital Commissioners, who had bought the sequestrated estates of the earl of Derwentwater after the failure of 'The Fifteen', built their smelt-mill near Langley castle in 1767. In 1729 Sir William Blackett began the exploitation of the Allenheads mine, which produced some 260,000 tons of lead concentrates between that year and the collapse of the industry in 1896.[32] Allenheads, at an altitude of 1400 feet, is the creation of the abandoned workings in and above the wood to the west of the church. Eastwards, across the wet moorlands of Byerhope Moss, runs the old pack-horse track, the Broad Way, by which the ore was once carried to the eighteenth-century smelt-mill at Dukesfield, now a grey ruin under the trees by the Devil's Water (Plate 27).

Shildon, near Blanchland, a stone-built, stone-roofed Pennine hamlet, is the descendant of the mining village which originated at some date in the Middle Ages. A nineteenth-century flue chimney still stands near the village above the burn and the woodlands below are pitted with old workings. On the road from Hexham to Penrith, Cupola Bridge, at the point where East and West Allen flow together to the Tyne, recalls the eighteenth-century furnace called a cupola.[33] The cupola itself is now no more than a few stones under the trees by the East Allen.

Allendale Town itself was the capital of the Northumbrian lead-mining (Plate 28). Pleasantly early nineteenth-century in appearance, with a fine square, its population halved between 1861 and 1901 with the decline of the industry. Across the river some two miles of old flues descend to the river below Thornley Gate. To the south on the high moors, where the road from Allenheads climbs to over 1800 feet near the county boundary, Coalcleugh preserves a memory of mining days: a small hamlet of

[32] Raistrick and Jennings, op. cit., p. 150.
[33] A low arched reverbatory furnace introduced from Wales about 1747; see Raistrick and Jennings, p. 124.

massive stone cottages and ruins under the sycamores, where the redshanks sound their alarm notes from fence and wall and the air in spring rings with curlews' calls.

Coal from outcrops on or near the surface has been consistently worked in Northumberland since at least the early thirteenth century and was much used for the manufacture of salt in the pans along the coast. Until the nineteenth century pits were mostly small and made little mark on the wide landscape. Even in the early nineteenth century the small pit at Widdrington employed only three to four men. Celia Fiennes, standing on a high hill two miles from Newcastle in the late seventeenth century "could see all about the country which was full of coale pitts".[34] This was an area where the High Main seam lay close to the surface and where there was a concentration of small pits before the centre of the industry shifted eastwards of Newcastle.

Today the small privately-owned colliery at Elsdon under the moorland ridges still gives some impression of the original scale and appearance of coal-mining, and its relation to the landscape, throughout most of its long history, just as Ashington and Lynemouth illustrate the modern development of the industry.

Throughout much of Northumberland are found the hummocks and depressions of small-scale mining, such as those favoured by modern picknickers above the Grasslees Burn between Elsdon and Hepple. Plashetts in North Tynedale was developed by the Swinburnes as a mining village about 1800. The road which exists today as a track up the Akenshaw Burn to Bloodybush and the Larriston Fells was constructed in part for the transport of Plashetts' coal. The colliery village of Scremerston, south of Berwick, is still, though the pit is now closed, typical of the larger Northumbrian pit-village of the nineteenth century in size and appearance.

Small pits were worked high up on the moorlands above

[34] *Diary of Celia Fiennes* (1888 ed.), p. 175.

Bellingham, below Hareshaw Head, where the old lines of the waggonways are still visible, crossing the Hareshaw Burn and descending the hills west of the burn, above the deep cleft of Hareshaw Linn, to Bellingham. For a time the adventurous enterprise of the nineteenth century appeared to be on the point of creating a new industrial centre in the heart of North Tynedale. The local ironstone was worked on a commercial scale, and the High Level Bridge at Newcastle contains twenty per cent of Redesdale iron.[35] But iron production, carried out in conjunction with the Bellingham coal pits, was abandoned by the middle of the century. The works were closed in the 1850s, leaving the moors to the curlews and the sheep.

In the early nineteenth century steam engines and coal pits were remarked upon by the rare visitor to the South Tyne valley. The collieries of Midgeholme and Hartleyburn employed 400 men. Mining debris is visible today at Lambley close to the Pennine Way under Hartleyburn Common and the heights of Cold Fell. The little village of Coanwood was a mining settlement in the remote hills; above the village, near Lane End, the rough pastures are pock-marked by old workings.

On the coast the ancient chapelries of Horton and Earsdon, south of the Blyth, lay at the heart of the great Northumbrian coalfield and have maintained a tradition of mining since the Middle Ages. "Its monotonous level stretches are for the most part varied by pit heaps and wagonways, and by colliery villages of one prevailing type."[36] Yet it is an area which enjoys to the full the spaciousness of the Northumbrian landscape. The primarily brick-built mining villages of the nineteenth century, Dudley, East Cramlington, Seghill and Shankhouse among them, lack aesthetic appeal; but they were compact, essentially

[35] T. M. Hoskison, 'Northumberland Blast Furnace Plants in the Nineteenth Century', p. 75. (Paper read to the Institute of Journalists, London, 13.3.1946.)
[36] *N.C.H.*, Vol. IX, p. 1.

villages with a life of their own, in a rural setting of wide fields where the pitmen could exercise their whippets.

Coal was worked at Cowpen in the fourteenth century and was used for the salt pans on the coast. The pits at Plessey, south of Stannington Vale, were one of the earliest fruits of the capital and energy devoted to coal by the business alliance of landed magnates and businessmen in the sixteenth century. The Plessey pit area has been greatly modified by open-cast mining, but the blackened cottage at Plessey Checks, the crossroad on the Bedlington road, marks the place where coal was checked on the waggonway, constructed about 1700, which carried the pits' output to Blyth. Coal on the coast at Hartley was vigorously exploited by the Delavals during this period and helped to finance the construction of Seaton Delaval Hall. To the west, New Hartley pit was one of the new deep pits opened in the early nineteenth century, as techniques improved and Northumbrian coal production began to rise to its climax. The memorial of that era lies among the cottage gardens: the old shaft, capped by masonry and hidden among the dahlias, which was closed after the great disaster of 1862, when over 200 men were killed. Now the railway is closed which once penetrated the heart of the coalfield, and willowherb encroaches on the track.

All over the coal measures nineteenth-century coal owners constructed new villages such as Percy Main above the Tyne, described in 1887 as "a village of modern growth containing several good streets of artisans' dwellings"[37] but now overtaken by the blight which follows the shift of industry, with a shattered chapel, opened for worship in 1902, as a symbol of growth and decay.

Ashington is the best example of a model pit village of the late nineteenth century which has survived, considerably improved, into modern times. In the 1850s

[37] T. F. Bulmer, *History, Topography and Directory of Northumberland* (1887), p. 343.

Ashington comprised one farm. Today its great slag heaps stand high on the uplands between the Wansbeck and the sea. Ashington was constructed as a model pit village in the 1880s. By 1887 there were 665 cottages arranged in eleven rows, with a tramway between each row to supply domestic coal and for the removal of ashpits. Ashington, scrupulously practical, made no attempt to soften the acerbities of the industrial planning of its day. Its early streets were numbers. By 1887 addresses in Ashington ranged from First Row to Ninth Row. These rows remain as the heart of a colliery town of 20,000 people, which now includes spacious examples of twentieth-century urban planning with wide and airy streets and new industries.

Pegswood, with its long rows of brick streets and the great slag heap close to the wooded dene of the Wansbeck, is also one of the later developments of mining urbanisation which has run its course; a dour mining town, it characterises the landscape of the Northumbrian coalfield, as its neighbour, Bothal, characterises the medieval past.

There are still many today who appear to imagine Northumberland as a congested area of smoking chimneys, slag heaps and industrial slums. This impression is based on the view of Tyneside from Gateshead, probably on a wet day. It is true, however, that the industrial and maritime activity of Northumberland, and the great proportion of its population, is concentrated close to the Tyne. Even in the early nineteenth century, Cobbett, pointing out that Northumberland had nearly one third less than the population of Suffolk though it was larger in area, added that "one half of its population have got together on the banks of the Tyne".[38]

The industrial belt created by coal and water transport begins at Lemmington, below Newburn, where glass manufacture had been carried on in the eighteenth century and a remnant of an eighteenth-century glass factory still exists.

---

[38] W. Cobbett, *Rural Rides* (1908 ed.), Vol. II, p. 387.

By the early nineteenth century a visitor was describing Lemmington as a "Sheffield in miniature", in a place which had consisted of no more than a handful of houses and some coal staithes until the Northumberland Glass Company was founded in 1787.[39]

Towards the end of the eighteenth century the exhaustion of the more accessible coal around Newcastle itself, and the great improvement in mining techniques, led to the development of the deeper High Main coal between Newcastle and the coast, the great source of London house coal. New collieries were opened, as at Flatworth, Billy Mill and Percy Main, with their waggonways and railways to the staithes on the Tyne, particularly in the neighbourhood of Whitehill Point. It was not, however, till the second half of the nineteenth century that industrialism began to absorb and annihilate the little villages along the Tyne. The Tyne Commissioners were constituted in 1850. Their first major work was the construction of the Northumberland Dock in 1857. This was followed by the construction of the Albert Edward Dock in 1884.

Works such as these altered the shore-line and obliterated the little villages of Howdon Pans and Coble Dene, once the centres of a salt industry. Miles of railway lines now spread out across the area between the Howdon Road and the river; together with oil installations and industrial debris they overlie the lines of the waggonways and colliery railways which came down to the staithes between Willington and Howdon. Coble Dene is little more than a name on the map east of the occupation road to the Albert Edward Dock. The last of the coal staithes remains at Whitehill Point. But the Northumberland Dock, which began the revolutionary change of topography and ancient settlement alike, has now been filled in, a site where linnets feed among the willowherb and thistles.

[39] E. Mackenzie, *An Historical Topographical and Descriptive View of the County of Northumberland* (1825 ed.), Vol. II, p. 485.

Walker, detached from Longbenton as a separate parish in 1846, was already a smoke-ridden industrial area by 1850. By then Low Walker, some thirty years before regarded as one of the most pleasant villages on Tyneside, had already disappeared under industrialism. Some signs of village origins still exist among the acres of urban streets. Lowfield Terrace, in the angle of Scrogg Road and the Walker Road, derives its name from the Low Field shown on an estate map of 1745. The long Scrogg Road commemorates another field of the same period, and the fields of the eighteenth-century Scrogg House Farm survive, though transformed, in the open spaces of Walker Park.[40]

Wallsend, the Roman *Segedunum,* has preserved its identity more successfully, as seen, for instance, from the ruins of the church of the Holy Cross within its iron railings above the dene. The site of the original village was the usual one popular with the Anglian settlers on the Boulder Clay. It lies on a hill within the bend of the Wallsend Burn. Described as "a very delightful village"[41] in 1770, its centre was the village green by the hall, now part of the Hunter Memorial Hospital. Half its original size, the green was preserved for posterity only by the vigorous efforts of the local population. With its trees and grass and the sedate surrounding buildings, with which the 1940 Health Centre conforms, the heart of Wallsend is still an early nineteenth-century village. Below Wallsend Station, in the neighbourhood of Buddle Street, are the packed brick streets of nineteenth-century industrialism and the modern shipyards of Swan Hunter, where the *Esso Northumbria,* of 253,000 tons, launched in 1969, continued the great tradition of Tyneside.

[40] F. W. Dendry, *Three Lectures on Old Newcastle* (1921), p. 38 and plate 10.
[41] W. H. Knowles, 'The Church of the Holy Cross, Wallsend', *A.A.* 3rd series, Vol. VI (1910), p. 192.

Ports and coastal towns

Apart from the Tyne and the Tweed there are no good natural harbours along the whole of the Northumbrian coast. The Northumbrian fishing boat, the coble, was designed for pulling up on a beach. Alnmouth was developed as a port for Alnwick in the early thirteenth century and reached its greatest prosperity in the eighteenth. In the eighteenth century, too, the activities of landowners included the development of the small havens along the coast where shelter had hitherto been provided by the outlying rocks. At Seahouses, south of Bamburgh, a small harbour was constructed at the end of the eighteenth century and was greatly enlarged by the Crewe Trustees in the mid-nineteenth. With room for 300 fishing vessels, Seahouses harbour was crowded in the heyday of the herring fisheries and yachtsmen were warned of difficulties in finding a berth when the fishing fleet was in.

Beadnell, further down the coast, had provided anchorage for small boats for centuries between the Snook, where the Anglian chapel of St Ebba was situated, and the links to the south. The little harbour was developed for the transport of lime, and the fine eighteenth-century lime kilns are still prominent above the harbour constructed by John Wood Craster towards the end of the century in about 1794. At Craster a haven was formed by the rocks known as the Muckle Car and the Little Car. The small harbour was constructed for the herring fishery in the nineteenth century.

In the eighteenth century the great expansion of the coal trade made it imperative to construct adequate ports. The Delavals, typical of the new class which had risen to wealth in Tudor England, were the first in the field with the construction of a harbour intended primarily as an outlet for their pits on the coastal plain. The harbour at Seaton Sluice was constructed at the end of the seventeenth century in brave defiance of the natural conditions on an exposed and rocky coast. Sluice gates were necessary at the head of the channel, and in the 1760s the harbour was further improved by the great cut through the rock, a work of almost megalithic grandeur befitting the family which had built Seaton Delaval. Seaton Sluice began to rival the developing port of Blyth and one of the Delavals wrote hopefully that "we should soon see a large town start up".[42] But the industrial activities of the Delavals at Seaton Sluice dwindled; the difficulties of creating a port there for expanding coal exports were insuperable. Seaton Sluice remains an impressive failure, a tourist attraction and a haven for small boats.

Blyth (Plate 29) went ahead to become one of the great coal ports of England, an uninspired red-brick and slate town not normally regarded as a tourist attraction but as significant a landmark in Northumbrian history as Holy Island and Bamburgh. It was famous for its steam-coal in the Age of Steam. Originally Blyth Snook and then South Blyth, the name is transferred from the river. The town began in the Middle Ages as a small settlement of fishermen and salt workers on the snook, between the narrow tongue of links above the river and a wide area of marshy land where the tidal Blyth Gut penetrated close to the modern Plessey Road in the vicinity of Croft Park.

Development as a port began in the early eighteenth century with the opening of the pits at Plessey and the construction of the Plessey waggonway which reached Blyth along the line of the Plessey Road and descended to the staithes below Ridley Street. The site of the waggonway is well marked as a sunken track[43] beneath the hawthorns climbing the slope to the east of Horton bridge and continued across the road as a footpath over the fields to New Delaval. Towards the end of the eighteenth century the

[42] *N.C.H.*, Vol. IX, p. 136.
[43] Recently mostly obliterated by road construction.

Plessey pits declined and were replaced by the pit at Cowpen. Much of the earlier development of Blyth was in Cowpen township west of Blyth Gut. Miners' cottages were first constructed in the Waterloo Road area, in Cowpen, in the 1820s. Connection with the port of Blyth was maintained by a bridge across the gut. In the second half of the nineteenth century the gut and its marshes were filled in. The name of Bridge Street alone recalls the tidal gut which separated Blyth and Cowpen in the vicinity of the modern market place.

Blyth was connected with the Percy Main colliery above the Tyne in 1847, and the construction of the modern harbour began in the 1850s. It was not, however, till the 1880s that the work was completed by the construction of the long piers and breakwaters which exist today. Coal exports leaped significantly, from 338,000 tons per annum in 1871 to four million tons by the beginning of the twentieth century. Shipbuilding flourished.

It was in this period, in the last quarter of the nineteenth century, that Blyth rose to its peak as a coal port and the bleak rows of brick streets were completed, such as Gladstone Street, Disraeli Street and Salisbury Street, near the now abandoned and dilapidated station; Croft Road, Coomassie Street and Wolsley Street near the Plessey Road. An unadorned and masculine town, its seamen known across the oceans of the world, a harbour where yachtsmen were warned against coal dust, Blyth is the creation of the Northumbrian coal industry at its height. Today the last of the coal staithes, the great staithe built by the N.E.R. on the Cambois shore, remains in proximity to the towering chimneys of the power station. Around the Seven Stars, the last relic of North Blyth, the machines prepare for the export of aluminium. Around the brick streets of late Victorian Blyth lie the modern housing estates and the bright gardens of Ridley Park.

Amble, at the mouth of the Coquet, was also constructed

in the nineteenth century, as a port for the pits opened at Radcliffe and Broomhill. The town contains an instructive range of some of the less attractive forms of urban architecture over a period of 100 years. At the end of the eighteenth century no more than a small village in the township of Hauxley, Amble grew rapidly after the completion of the harbour in the 1870s. Soon some 800 steamships and sailing vessels were transporting about 300,000 tons annually from the neighbouring collieries.

The port was completed in time for the high noon of Northumbrian coal. Its closure to coal shipments in 1969 marks the end of the era when coal was king.

North Shields first appeared in the thirteenth century as a small hamlet of fishermen's huts, or shields, on demesne land belonging to Tynemouth Priory. Its site was the mouth of the Spital Burn, which emerged from the dene in Northumberland Park and flowed under Tanner's Bank to reach the sea near the lifeboat station. The mouth of the burn is covered over by the North Groyne. Here a settlement was founded by the priory, for whom the inhabitants were to provide fish. Ships began to call for wool and hides; the settlement's rapid prosperity evoked the strong reaction of Newcastle in the form of an armed raid. For another 300 years Newcastle remained hostile to competition at the mouth of the Tyne. It was not till 1848 that the quarrel was finally resolved by the constitution of North Shields as a port.

Modern North Shields began with development by the owners of the former South Field of Tynemouth, divided in 1649, in the second half of the eighteenth century. The lead was given by Dr Thomas Dockwray, vicar of Stamfordham, who constructed Toll Square and Dockwray Square on the gorse-covered slopes above the modern Fish Quay. North Shields still bears the marks of town-planning of this period, for the development of the long rectangular areas which are so often the characteristic

shapes of the consolidated plots in the old common fields
produced the straight streets between the Tynemouth Road
and the steep bluffs above the river.

Dockwray Square and Toll Square have both been transformed by modern municipal housing. There is now no
trace of the "beautiful but angular buildings . . . mostly
inhabited by opulent shipowners"[44] described in 1825. The
square remains, but no longer "embellished with a border
of odiferous shrubs", and the modern flats, though convenient, are not beautiful. The "new, stately and elegant
lighthouse" constructed in 1808, the new High Lights,
remains on the open southern side of the square with a
magnificent view of the mouth of the Tyne.

The port area was developed along the narrow strip of
level ground along the line of Union Road and Union
Quay reached by a series of steep and often insalubrious
flights of steps, Stewart's Bank, Ropery Stairs, Linskill
Banks and Greive's Stairs, which lead to the Fish Quay and
the stone buildings constructed during the early period of
North Shield's modern development, such as the fine ashlar
faced buildings built for the duke of Northumberland in
1816 on New Quay. At the eastern end of the Fish Quay the
Low Lights was built in the early nineteenth century to
replace a seventeenth-century light at the mouth of the
Pow Burn.

North Shields still contains good examples of the civilised
architecture and planning which distinguished its early
growth during the Regency. Howard Street and Northumberland Square formed part of the fifty acres of the
South Field allotted to Lord Howard and sold to John
Wright of North Shields in 1796. Northumberland Square
has a dignity and spaciousness which contrasts sharply with
the neighbourhood of, for instance, Sibthorpe Street, and
the building now occupied by the town clerk is a nice
example of urban architecture at the time of Trafalgar.

[44] E. Mackenzie, op. cit., Vol. II, p. 445.

Plate 28 Allendale Town

Once the capital of the lead-mining industry of the Allendales, stonebuilt, and still to a great extent stone-roofed. Situated at a height of 1400 feet, it is now a popular resort for tourists.

Plate 29   Blyth

A nineteenth-century coal port developed from a small hamlet where salt was made in pans on the coast. North of the river is the power station of Cambois, a Celtic word pronounced as *kamus*, like the Irish *camus* meaning 'a bay'. In the creek to the right of the power station is one of the few remaining coal-staithes. Blyth no longer exports coal.

Plate 30 Whitley Bay
The development of Whitley Bay as a popular seaside resort followed the construction of the nineteenth-century railways, and especially the electrification of the coastal branch-lines in 1903.

Plate 31   Newcastle from the Tyne
The photograph shows the series of buildings which epitomise the history of the city. The old commercial centre of the Sandhill is dominated by the castle and the tower of St Nicholas. The viaduct introduces the Railway Age.

Plate 32   Grey Street, Newcastle upon Tyne
One of the finest city streets in England, Grey Street derives from the inspired planning of Richard Grainger and John Dobson in the 1830s.

Howard Street, though it has seen better days, contains some good early-nineteenth-century houses proportioned to the width of the street. Its Doric-style Scotch church of 1811 was built for the polite society of the day.

North Shields and Blyth grew as towns and became busy ports in the same period, but North Shields in the area above the quays was constructed in general for a wealthier class, as a stroll in Howard Street or Clive Street still reveals. Shipping was the main source of livelihood and wealth. Shipowners and master mariners were two major categories of employment in the early nineteenth-century directories. Substantial men, such as shipowners, surgeons and physicians, lived in Dockwray Square and Northumberland Square in the 1850s. Linskill Street, Howard Street, Percy Street and Norfolk Street were popular with master mariners. All are within an easy stroll of vantage points above the Tyne, the south side of Dockwray Square, or the top of Library Stairs, providing an opportunity to watch the busy quays and the river below, and the traffic at the mouth of the Tyne.

Modern North Shields is largely the creation of the latter half of the nineteenth century. It belongs to the heyday of the coal trade when colliers thronged the Tyne. A thriving fishing industry was encouraged by the construction of the Fish Quay in 1850 and its extension in 1887. The brick streets between the west end of Clive Street and the railway in particular date from the last quarter of the century. Today the town has more than its fair share of problems caused by economic change.

Towards the end of the eighteenth century improved roads, and new habits of leisure, led to the development of the coastal resorts within convenient reach of Newcastle, the area that was once part of the great ecclesiastical estate of Tynemouth Priory, comprising the townships of Tynemouth, Cullercoats and Whitley Bay. "Tinmouth and Cullercoats are now much in fashion; not a room empty. My

Lady Ravensworth and my Lady Clavering were a month at Cullercoats bathing" wrote a member of the Delaval family at this time. [45]

Tynemouth had begun as an Anglian abbey, a link in the long chain of religious foundations which fringed the coast of Northumbria from Whitby to Coldingham north of the Tweed. It was constructed on a strong and dramatic site on a peninsula thrust out into the North Sea, guarded on three sides by the waves and the cliffs, similar in situation to Dunstanburgh and Tantallon. After the Conquest the ruined Anglian foundation was given to St Albans, which constructed the priory church at the end of the eleventh century. At the end of the thirteenth century the monks obtained a licence to crenellate in time to offer a successful resistance to a Scots raid. The work was completed by the construction of the gate house across the narrow neck of the peninsula. Until the twentieth century the fortress was part of the defences of the Tyne.

Tynemouth was not regarded as a health resort in the Middle Ages. The church was of "wondrous beauty" but, wrote a monk, "thick sea-fret rolls in wrapping everything in gloom. Dim eyes, hoarse voices, sore throats are the consequence . . . the wind tosses the salt sea foam in masses over our buildings." [46] It is a picture with some relevance on a day when a north-east storm drives the surf over the great breakwaters, and castle and priory loom dark against the sea.

The fortress of Tynemouth implied a garrison, and garrisons during the Napoleonic Wars attracted polite society. This period, towards the end of the eighteenth century, led to the development of Front Street, still 'the village' of contemporary local usage, an eighteenth-century and Regency street, wide and well-proportioned, preserving an

[45] W. W. Thompson, *Historical Notes on Cullercoats, Whitley and Monkseaton,* p. 17.
[46] *N.C.H.,* Vol. VIII, p. 72.

individuality of its own though embedded in the huge suburban townscape which now stretches uninterruptedly from
the Tyne to the Brier Dene north of Whitley Bay. Front
Street leads straight to the gatehouse-keep of the castle and
the priory, beyond the row of neat eighteenth-century
houses on the south side of the street.

The railway reached North Shields in 1847 and Tynemouth was gaily decorated for the occasion. But even in the
1850s Tynemouth still consisted of no more than Front
Street with the addition of Bath Terrace and Allendale
Place, constructed during the early years of the nineteenth
century. They contain tall and dignified houses with iron
balconies and rooms with high ceilings providing ample
space for the well-to-do families visiting the sea. By this
time the fifty-three boarding-house and lodging-house
keepers of Tynemouth presaged the future of seaside resorts.
The life of Tynemouth was still concentrated in Front Street
with its five inns and hotels, two booksellers, a chemist and
a hairdresser.

In 1867 the Blyth and Tyne Railway Company extended
its line to a point close to the existing station of the North
Eastern. The new line was popular and Tynemouth began a
more vigorous period of expansion. In the 1870s there
began development of the area between Front Street and the
Long Sands, from Lovaine Terrace to Warkworth Street,
between Sea Banks, above King Edward's Bay, to Percy
Park Road. The Aquarium, Winter Gardens and skating
rink were constructed by 1878, a vast construction of
Victorian baroque at the edge of the cliffs designed to
attract visitors to the 'Brighton of the North' and now the
Plaza Ballroom. Inland from King Edward's Bay the great
crescent of Percy Gardens is formed of overbearing and
often over-decorated houses. In conception this development was imposing, but the late nineteenth century could
not reproduce the elegance of Bath or the strength of classical Newcastle.

North of the Long Sands the insignificant village of Cullercoats developed as a small port, at the end of the seventeenth century, for the export of salt from the local salt pans and of coal from collieries in Whitley and Cullercoats. The first pier was constructed in 1677, though it was subsequently heavily damaged by storms. In the early eighteenth century the salt trade dwindled and the collieries were closed. Cullercoats became a fishing village with a fleet of cobles based on the small harbour below the cliffs; but small-scale fishing dwindled in the second half of the nineteenth century with the rise of steam trawling based on North Shields.

With the construction of the Blyth and Tyne Railway in 1864 Cullercoats, like Tynemouth, began to grow as a seaside resort. As at Tynemouth, the vigorous period of development began in the 1870s. Only a shadow of the old village remains in the cluster of houses on Brown's Point above the little harbour. Houses spread south to form Beverley Terrace, and inland to the station. Huddleston Street, John Street and Eleanor Street formed the new Cullercoats and were in existence by the 1880s. The growth of Cullercoats was given further impetus by the new branch of the North Eastern Railway between Tynemouth and Monkseaton, completed in 1882. The existence of the prosperous new seaside resort was confirmed in the nineteenth-century manner by the construction of the vast church of St George, one of many churches built by the dukes of Northumberland, which was consecrated in 1883. A vast building in the style of thirteenth-century Gothic, St George's and the Plaza Ballroom are two great landmarks of urban growth in nineteenth-century Northumberland.

If any Northumbrian seaside resort can claim to be the Brighton of the North it is Whitley Bay. As late as 1851 Whitley township had a population of only 431. The development of the seaside resort began in the late 1860s after the construction of the Blyth–Tyne railway. By the 1880s the whole of the nucleus of modern Whitley Bay had been constructed, a long rectangle between the Whitley Road and the links bounded by the Esplanade on the north and the Grafton Road on the south. In 1864 the consecration of the attractive little church of St Paul's, at the junction of the Marden Road and Whitley Road, signified the new status and future prospects of the rapidly developing village. Nothing remains in Whitley of its earlier origins. The links have been tidied and tamed. It is essentially a new town of the nineteenth century born of the new facilities for cheap travel provided by the railways and transformed by the developments of the twentieth century (Plate 30).

North of the Blyth the development of seaside Northumberland is, as at Whitley Bay, primarily a feature of the modern landscape associated with the motor car and the caravan park. The magnificent sands and links of Bamburgh and Seahouses were attracting middle-class holidaymakers and historically-minded tourists well before the end of the nineteenth century; but they remained small and unsophisticated villages, offering little more than golf courses and a handful of bathing huts to their undemanding visitors, in addition to their coastal scenery and their positions as centres for the exploration of historic Northumberland. Alnmouth alone rose to the status of a small seaside-town which, however, scarcely outgrew the boundaries of its medieval origins on its ridge between the river and the sea.

Newcastle from the seventeenth to the nineteenth century

By the end of the sixteenth century Newcastle was firmly set on the course which was to take the city to the peak of its nineteenth-century reputation and prosperity. Coal shipments rose from 32,951 tons at the beginning of Elizabeth's reign to 162,552 tons at the end. By 1684–5 shipments increased to over 616,000 tons.[47] For the pitman, mining was becoming a full-time occupation. The great mine-owners and

[47] J. U. Nef, *The Rise of the British Coal Industry* (1932), Vol. I, p. 21.

coal merchants incorporated as the Company of Hostmen in 1600, the 'lords of coal', secured control over the city by the charter of the same year. In 1606 their empire was extended and the corporation of Newcastle was granted full admiralty jurisdiction over the river.

Since the Union of the Crowns in 1603 the city had begun to expand beyond the city walls. There was ribbon development outside the West Gate, and also outside the New Gate, along the line of what was called Percy Street by polite society in the mid-eighteenth century, but which ordinary people called the Sid Gate, the road to the Side.[48] Other suburbs had grown up north of the Pilgrim Street Gate. All these suburbs beyond the wall suffered severe damage when Newcastle was besieged and taken by the Scots in 1644.

Within the walls there were still large areas of open space, the orchards and gardens which had originally belonged to religious institutions (Fig. 18). Much of the space west of Pilgrim Street and north of High Bridge Street, the former property of the Grey Friars, had been acquired by Robert Anderson in 1580 and contained the great New House with its gardens, orchards and avenues. As Anderson Place it was purchased by the Blacketts, who converted it into a palatial property. Later acquired by a master builder, also named Anderson, it became a crucial area in Newcastle's early nineteenth-century town planning.

The economic and social life of the city was still confined to the narrow area between the river and the slopes above. On the Sandhill within a short stroll of the quays below the bridge, there still exists a group of houses built in Tudor and Jacobean times, in the age when the Hostmen were winning control of the coal trade, the city and the Tyne. The finest of the group, and the best known, is Bessie Surtees' House, the seventeenth-century city mansion from which Bessie Surtees eloped with John Scott, the future Lord Eldon, in 1793.

[48] J. Brand, *The History and Antiquities of Newcastle upon Tyne,* Vol. I, p. 423.

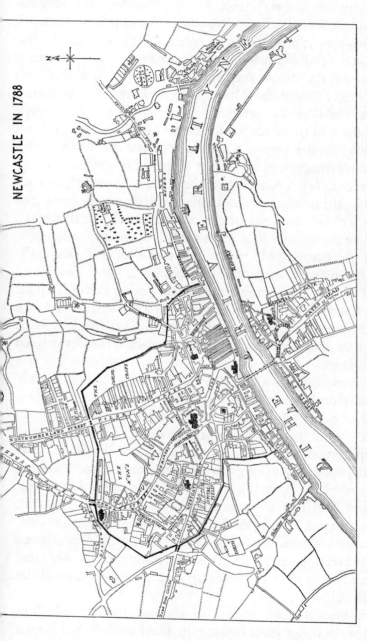

NEWCASTLE IN 1788

Fig. 18. (From J. Brand, *The History and Antiquities of Newcastle upon Tyne*, 1789.) The map shows the large areas of orchards and gardens used by Grainger and Dobson in the early nineteenth century to create a planned city. The future line of Grey Street is apparent north of the junction of Dean Street and Mosley Street. Pandon retains its distinctive street pattern within the south-eastern salient of the walls, which were extended eastwards after the absorption of the village by Newcastle in 1299. The Chares, congested lanes destroyed by the fire of 1854, are shown downstream of the bridge to the east of the Guildhall.

These buildings recreate in part the world of the business-men who were leading Newcastle in the van of the economic development of eighteenth-century Northumberland. Also on the Sandhill, belonging to the same era, and equally close to the quays and the shipping, the Guildhall was originally the medieval headquarters of the Gild Merchants. The building was extensively reconstructed by Robert Trollope in the seventeenth century. Downstream in Broad Chare, Trinity House, mostly of the first half of the eighteenth century, contains a fine chapel of the 1630s. Despite current development to meet the needs of twentieth-century traffic, the outlines of Newcastle of the Hostmen about 1700 can still be discerned in the modern landscape (Plate 31). Below the Tyne Bridge lies a medley of rooftops and chimneys, blackened walls, tall warehouses and small shops; the Guildhall with its prominent colonnaded east end added by Dobson, and behind it the ancient houses in the Sandhill; the Quayside and Broad Chare with Trinity House; in the background, the steep slopes rising to the heights above Pandon, and the Norman keep from which the city derived its origin.

Above the City Road, near Manor Chare, the brick Holy Jesus Hospital, constructed and endowed by the corporation of Newcastle in the 1680s, stands close to one of the main roads through the city. Renaissance in style, it is more in keeping with south-country gardens than with urban Newcastle, though it belongs to an age when the neighbouring Pandon Dene was still a famed beauty spot. Eastwards, below Wall Knoll Tower, stands the Keelmen's Hospital, built in 1701. It was paid for by the keelmen themselves, the men who worked the keels, or lighters, of the Tyne, shared in unequal partnership with the Hostmen in the great expansion of the city's trade and, when roused, sacked the Guildhall.

In 1745 the suppression of the last Jacobite rebellion ended the threat from beyond the Border which had been a background to the life of Northumberland for over 700 years. The walls of Newcastle were manned for the last time during the Napoleonic Wars, but their removal had begun in 1763 when the riverside wall was demolished. Within the walls the modification of the topographical landscape and the improvement of communications across the city had begun with the paving-over of part of the Lort Burn at the end of the seventeenth century. Finally Major George Anderson filled up the Nun's Dene which connected with the Lort Burn across his new property north of High Bridge Street. The first major improvement undertaken by the Corporation, and the precursor of the great works of the early nineteenth century, was the construction of Mosley Street, completed by 1750. In 1787 the lower reaches of the Lort Burn were finally buried under Lower Dean Street, and the narrow declivity of the Side lost its ancient importance as the direct route from the bridgehead to the market area north of St Nicholas. Henceforward traffic seeking the centre of Newcastle, or the Westgate and the new military road to Carlisle, could take the lower and wider part of the Side up the new Lower Dean Street into Mosley Street.

The West End of Newcastle at this period was the Close, the spur of high ground above the river to the east of Orchard Street. This area, "once the residence of the nobility and gentry of the town and district",[49] like most of Newcastle should be explored on foot, from the point where the Forth Banks road descends to the pavée of the Skinner Burn road to end at a public lavatory and the oily debris of an industrial river. It was an area of gardens and orchards until the end of the eighteenth century, as the name of Orchard Street implies. The Close is now an industrial road beside the river flanked by warehouses which reflect impressively, in a business idiom, the strength of Northumberland's traditional architecture under the steep climb

[49] R. J. Charlton, *A History of Newcastle on Tyne*, p. 266.

to Hanover Square. In Hanover Square, Clavering House survives from the eighteenth century in conjunction with the great railway viaduct of a later era.

Near the junction of the Westgate Road with Fenkle Street the Assembly Rooms, completed in 1776, were built, according to an inscription placed under the foundation stone

> In an age
> when the polite arts
> by general encouragement and emulation
> Have advanced to a
> state of perfection
> unknown in any former period.[50]

Charlotte Square, at the junction of Fenkle Street and Cross Street, still retains something of the atmosphere of this period.

Newcastle in the reign of George III was entering upon its great age.[51] In the early years of the nineteenth century the city launched out into one of the most sweeping and successful ventures of large-scale planning ever undertaken by any nineteenth-century town. It was the achievement of a classical culture working in conjunction with industrial and commercial enterprise.

The alliance of John Dobson the architect (1787–1865), Richard Grainger the builder (1797–1861) and John Clayton, solicitor and town clerk (1792–1890) proved a remarkable combination of practical men who grasped the possibilities of planning on a hitherto unparalleled scale and within a unified architectural frame. Grainger, educated at one of the charity schools endowed by Sir William Blackett, had all the energy and willingness to take risks characteristic of the men who were creating the England of the Industrial Revolution.

50 J. Brand, op. cit., Vol. I, p. 121.
51 See L. Wilkes and G. Dodd, *Tyneside Classical* (1964), for an informative study of Newcastle during this period.

Dobson, who had begun in his teens as an apprentice to a damask weaver, became a pupil of the architect David Stephenson, studied painting in London, and returned to Newcastle as the only professional architect between York and Edinburgh. John Clayton was a product of the wealthy and educated middle class of nineteenth-century England. As town clerk of Newcastle from 1822 to 1867, in succession to his father, he steered the city through the years of reform and urban renewal. A gifted amateur archaeologist, his memorial is not only his share in the construction of the modern city but the excavation and preservation of the Roman fort and bridge of *Cilurnum,* the modern Chesters, in the grounds of his house on the North Tyne.

The main problem to be faced by early nineteenth-century Newcastle was the improvement of communications within and through the city. Access between the riverside and the higher areas of the city was still difficult. By the end of the eighteenth century Newcastle's growing predominance as the industrial and commercial centre of the North, and the increase in wheeled traffic, had accentuated the pressures on the network of communications concentrated on the crossing of the Tyne. Within the walls the large areas of gardens and open spaces inherited from the medieval ecclesiastical estates provided a magnificent opportunity for the early nineteenth-century planners.

The population had increased from about 18,000 at the beginning of the eighteenth century to over 28,000 in 1801. Pleasant residential suburbs were growing up in the open country to the north of the walls. Eldon Place off Barras Bridge was a fine example of this period, "the last complete street of Georgian architecture in Newcastle",[52] until it was pulled down in the 1960s to make room for university buildings. One house only, where George and Robert Stephenson lived for a short time, remains in its new setting. Eldon Square, completed in 1826 and "designed

[52] Wilkes and Dodd, op. cit., p. 147.

clearly under the influence of Nash's spectacular work for the Regent",[53] presaged the self-confidence and imaginative sweep that were to transform the city. It was the first achievement of the new alliance between Grainger and Dobson. Now doomed to give place to the requirements of modern planning it is Regency in a northern idiom, strong in design and conception. Shortly afterwards Grainger completed the fine line of the Leazes Terrace designed by Thomas Oliver.

The major development of the Newcastle street system in the nineteenth century began with the construction of Blackett Street, which in 1812 was driven across the gardens and orchards of the Nuns from the site of the recently demolished New Gate to the head of Pilgrim Street near the junction of New Bridge Street. In 1834 Grainger acquired the key area of Anderson Place and made public his plans for future development, the first plans for the construction of a planned city centre ever put forward in Britain. By 1840 the grand design was completed substantially as planned. It involved the construction in five years of "nine new streets . . . the new market, the new theatre, the new dispensary, music room, lecture room, two chapels, the incorporated companies hall, two auction marts, ten inns, forty private houses and three hundred and twenty-five houses with shops".[54] Its supreme achievement was the magnificent curve of Grey Street from the focal point of the monument to Earl Grey, erected in 1838. Grey Street is one of the finest streets in any English city, a triumph of "architectural harmony and proportion"[55] (Plate 32). From the monument Grainger Street was driven in a south-westerly direction to meet the Westgate Road. Clayton Street, the last of the three main streets which were the base of the whole plan, was taken through the Nuns and the grounds of Anderson

[53] N. Pevsner, *Northumberland*, p. 222.
[54] Quoted in Wilkes and Dodd, op. cit., p. 73.
[55] Ibid., p. 91.

Place to Newgate Street, and thence to the Westgate Road, to provide a new means of communication between the growing residential areas of northern Newcastle and the rapidly developing industrial areas along the Tyne.

North of the cathedral, in the area between St Nicholas Square and Grainger Street, the old site of the medieval markets of the upper city was left virtually untouched, though it was modified in detail. The Bigg Market, Cloth Market and the Groat Market have retained a lay-out that forms a sharp contrast with the streets constructed by the early nineteenth-century developers; it is still basically medieval.

In the meantime, Northumbrian colliery owners had been experimenting with steam traction. In 1829 George Stephenson and his son Robert demonstrated the technical efficiency of the Rocket. Newcastle's position as a key centre of communications was confirmed by the completion of the railway to Carlisle in 1838, and by Robert Stephenson's High Level Bridge of 1849. For the North-Eastern Railway, Dobson designed the Central Station. The original design was modified, it was originally intended to include the headquarters of the company, but it is still one of the most striking achievements of the Railway Age and, like the new streets, expresses the self-confidence of Newcastle's great era. The construction of the station and the railway lines involved the destruction of many of the castle buildings and much of the remaining city walls; but the castle, the station and the High Level Bridge together form a picture of the city's history worthy of Turner.

The expansion of the city followed swiftly from the neighbourhood of the station westwards along the hills above the river. The area between the Elswick Road and the Westmorland Road is today one of the derelict areas of Newcastle, a place of closed and dilapidated houses, of smoke-blackened and neglected churches. In the 1850s the long lines of streets, Elswick East Terrace, Rye Hill, East and West Parade, were completed on a fine site above the river. They were constructed for the lower levels of the middle classes, potential Forsytes setting out on the road to fortune which would take some in due course to Gosforth and Jesmond. They included small manufacturers and brewers, agents and brokers, chemists and provision dealers, a civil engineer; and half a dozen solicitors, representatives of a professional class whose more prosperous members tended to be concentrated in Dean Street, Grey Street and Pilgrim Street.[56] The Rye Hill area is not an adornment to the modern city, but it marks a significant stage in Newcastle's nineteenth-century development in the age of Palmerston.

Westwards again was the manor of Elswick centred on a small village on the site of Elswick Park. The estate was bought by Grainger for over £100,000 with the intention of creating a planned industrial and residential area. Grainger, however, was experiencing financial difficulties and the estate was sold off piecemeal for development. Elswick Haughs had already become an industrial area, as the still standing eighteenth-century shot tower recalls. The spectacular development into a world-famous industria area began with William Armstrong's purchase of a couple of fields in 1847. The population of the township increased from 3500 in 1851 to 52,000 by the end of the century.

The construction of the great Elswick Works and the shipyards higher up the river below the Scotswood Bridge necessitated the construction of the miles of new streets of Benwell and Elswick, mostly in the last quarter of the nineteenth century. They formed a spectacular development of industrial Newcastle and concentrated in that area three quarters of the population of the city. The period of most rapid growth followed another of Lord Armstrong's achievements, the construction of the Swing Bridge in 1876,

[56] William Whelan & Co., *History, Topography and Directory of Northumberland* (1855).

significantly opened for the first time to enable an Italian ship to take delivery of a 100-ton gun at Elswick. Assured of access to the sea, the great industrial complex along the Tyne reached its peak. The regular lines of streets, extending down the slopes from Elswick Road to the river, remain as a memorial of that period of industrial growth, as significant in the development of Tyneside as Grey Street and Grainger Street.

North of Newcastle the open space of the Town Moor, vigorously defended against encroachment, prevented the otherwise inevitable expansion of the city to absorb Gosforth. South Gosforth remained a small village throughout the first half of the nineteenth century, with a colliery opened on the bank of the Ouseburn in 1829, an event which was celebrated by a famous ball given 1000 feet underground. In the High Street a terrace of houses dates from this period. South Gosforth developed as a well-to-do residential area towards the end of the nineteenth century, along the line of High Street, when streets such as Woodbine Road, Hawthorn Road and Ivy Road came into existence. Near the station a small group of streets such as Percy Terrace and Bowsden Terrace were built for artisans during the same period. South Gosforth was still a distinct village in 1914 and retains that characteristic today along the length of High Street north of the Grove.

West of the Town Moor Jesmond was developed as a middleclass residential area mostly between 1880 and 1914. In the 1880s the little village of Jesmond could still be described as "a quiet little place, shut in by sloping grassy banks and hanging woods", where haymakers could be watched at work in the fields in summer and the sandmartins nested in the banks above the Ouseburn.[57] Its peace, and its fame as a beauty spot, were protected by the big houses and gardens which monopolised the area, notably the house and gardens of Lord Armstrong. Towards

[57] R. J. Charlton, op. cit., p. 385.

the end of the 1880s the construction began of the last of the great middle-class residential areas of pre-1914 Newcastle, particularly in the neighbourhood of West Jesmond Station; long rows of solid houses, Fern Avenue, Lily Crescent, Holly Avenue, Larkspur Terrace and Mistletoe Road; Jesmond Road and Clayton Road. Rising wealth, and the emphasis on attendance at church or chapel, ensured the construction of, usually, massive churches to keep pace with the growing population: Dobson's Jesmond Parish Church completed in 1861; St George's, in the Osborne Road, completed in 1888, and the Gothic Holy Trinity of 1905 above the descent to the Ouseburn at the top of Benton Bank.

The streets and terraces along the line of Osborne Road and Jesmond Road arose during the climax of Newcastle's industrial development and, fittingly, were completed at about the time when the *Mauretania* first sailed down the Tyne. They belong to the era of the golden sovereign and domestic service, the electric tram (introduced into Newcastle in 1901), the straw boater and the demonstrations of naval strength at Spithead.

Churches and chapels

In Northumberland, as elsewhere, the nineteenth century was a great age of church building comparable in some respects with the twelfth and thirteenth centuries. In both periods there was an assumption that society in all its aspects was Christian; and so part of the vastly increasing wealth of the county was devoted to the restoration of old churches, not always with happy results, and the construction of new ones. There was much to be done. Rural churches in particular had been neglected since the seventeenth century. As late as 1862 the visitor to St Michael's at Alnham was greeted by "a green flash from mildewed walls, and by streaks of sky seen through the slates".[58] Window sashes

[58] *N.C.H.,* Vol. XIV, p. 563.

were rotten, admitting wind and rain. Fungi abounded within the building. Dissent had stepped into the gap left by the Church of England. The "rude and unguided Borderers", in Defoe's words, had become "most flourishing Congregations of serious Christians".[59]

One of the earliest buildings of the religious revival was Sir William Blackett's chapel built for his lead miners at Allenheads in 1703. This was replaced in 1825 by the existing building of St Peter's, a simple structure suited to the Pennine landscape, withdrawn on the hillside under pines and beeches and facing the debris of the lead industry across the valley. St Mary's, at Wooler, was rebuilt in 1763, replacing the older thatched church which had been in a dilapidated state since the early sixteenth century, a circumstance to which the spread of Dissent in the town was attributed. After a fire in 1863 it was again rebuilt, at a time when Wooler was receiving its modern form. Ilderton church is a complete rebuilding of the same period which involved the transformation of the medieval church into a plain structure that is yet impressive by reason of its size and simplicity.

More pretentious, and out of place in the Northumbrian landscape, were the new nineteenth-century churches built by wealthy landlords. Their medieval predecessors had also built churches; but now greater wealth and technical resources enabled Gothic churches to be erected in a few years instead of the more evolutionary construction of the past carried out by local craftsmen following long-descended skills and slowly adapting new styles to the local idiom. The church of Holy Trinity, in Whitfield, placed in an incomparable setting in the wooded dale of the West Allen, has a tall spire which provides an incongruous touch of the landscape of southern England in a parish of scattered farms.

At Matfen the church of Holy Trinity was completed in 1854 at the expense of Sir Edward Blackett, who also built

[59] *Memoirs of the Church of Scotland* (1717), p. 167.

Matfen Hall and reconstructed the village. Thus Matfen became a traditional village of the midlands and the south with the church and big house in close association; it has been suggested that "the church spire would look in place somewhere in the Nene valley".[60] It provides a sharp contrast with Whitley Chapel, constructed in 1858 in the wooded hills near Hexham: a plain grey building, with the Lord's Prayer, the Ten Commandments and the Apostle's Creed on its white-washed interior walls, by the road which climbs the hill from the Devil's Water. No monument of ecclesiastical architecture, it is yet a moving building, retaining the atmosphere and spirit of the ancient churches of rural Northumberland.

In church-building, as in much else, the dukes of Northumberland were prominent. The sixth duke built the towering church of St George's of Cullercoats, an experiment of the 1880s in thirteenth-century Gothic, built at a time when the new houses of Tynemouth was spreading northwards. The present church of St Hilda's, at Lucker, was constructed in the 1870s when the duke was also rebuilding the village; and it was he who was largely responsible for the dark and massive church of St John at Alnmouth, completed in 1876.

St George's of Cullercoats is a faithful reflection of its period, as are the grand nineteenth-century churches of Newcastle, such as Dobson's church of St Thomas at Barras Bridge. Jesmond Parish church, one of the last of Dobson's works (it was completed in 1861) is a solid expression of the Forsytism of mid-Victorian England, which was then colonising Jesmond. The tall campanile of St George's, Osborne Road, was built in 1888 at the expense of the gifted C. W. Mitchell, Lord Armstrong's partner. The church is a fitting monument to the Newcastle of the age of the Golden Jubilee. It is the creation of industrial power and wealth, as of the still-strong habit of religious observance.

[60] N. Pevsner, op. cit., p. 210.

Necessarily less ambitious churches were built in the rapidly expanding coal towns. The church of St Alban's at Earsdon, its tower a landmark of the coastal plain, was completed in 1837. Blyth was constituted a parish in 1883, and its parish church of St Cuthbert was completed in 1885, bringing to new docks and utilitarian brick streets the requisite flavour of ecclesiastical Gothic.

The Anglican revival was preceded by the growth of Dissent. The Covenanter William Veitch (1640–1722) had preached and wandered among the hills of North Tynedale and Redesdale during his years of outlawry. Much of the atmosphere of those times survives in the Presbyterian church of Falstone, which replaced a building of 1709. Here, as so often in the North, the shepherds were attended by their collies in church. In the same tradition is the Kielder Presbyterian church, of 1874, which looks south to the new village of Kielder above the stream where the flags flower by the old reivers' route to the Deadwater and the wind carries the scent of hay and pine.

Architecturally the churches of Falstone and Kielder are undistinguished; but both belong in spirit to the era when "Burns and the Bible . . . superseded the Ballads", the time of the Scottish occupation of the English Cheviots when "vulgarity had not yet invaded from the cities".[61]

Sharing the same simplicity of the older Nonconformity are the unadorned churches and chapels of the larger villages and the towns. The Presbyterian church in the village square of Embleton, built in 1833; the smaller Wesleyan chapel, of 1844, at Newbiggin, hidden behind the sea-front in Vernon Place. At Great Whittington, a substantial stone-built upland village, there is no Anglican church; its place is taken by the plain Wesleyan chapel of 1835. The tradition of these older buildings of Nonconformity is well maintained, in a modern style, by the Cullercoats Methodist church at the junction of the Farringdon and Marden roads.

[61] G. M. Trevelyan, *Clio, A Muse* (1930), p. 37.

In the towns and new residential areas towards the end of the nineteenth century Nonconformist churches began to vie with the Anglican buildings as evidence of wealth and respectability. The big Gothic Congregational church of 1874, with its tall spire, stands high above Front Street, Tynemouth. The massive Baptist church, of 1889, in Osborne Road, Jesmond, like its Anglican contemporary neighbour St George's, reflects the conditions of its time.

South of the Tyne the little Nonconformist chapels have been bequeathed by mining in the high fells. At Limestone Brae, by the roadside above the West Allen, the Methodist church faces west across the dale. It is a short distance from the Primitive Methodist chapel of 1857. Depressing and desolate when the rain sweeps down from the fells is the derelict Primitive Methodist Chapel, with cracked and damp-stained walls, built in 1863 at Lane End for the mining community of Coanwood above the South Tyne.

Roman Catholicism was kept alive in Northumberland by a handful of ancient families, such as the Charltons of Hesleyside, whose tower-house provided concealment for a priest. In a more tolerant age the Catholic church of St Oswald was built outside Bellingham. At Callally Castle, under the wooded crags near Whittingham, the Claverings maintained a chapel till the 1870s and then financed the construction of the existing church of St Mary by the roadside between Glanton and Whittingham. Similarly the Ogles and Delavals had maintained the faith at Newsham near Blyth, and the big church of St Wilfred, consecrated in 1862, continued the tradition in the dreary Waterloo Road of Blyth.

The Catholic church of St Mary, in Clayton Street, Newcastle, was designed by Pugin, whose vision sought the soaring aspirations of medieval Gothic in the industrial landscape of nineteenth-century England. The spire was added later and the great church, smoke-blackened like so many of the buildings of Tyneside, forms a conspicuous and impressive landmark near the Central Station. Its setting is industrial Tyneside; the acres of railway lines, the cattle market, the steep streets of Gateshead across the river. Church and station, different in architectural style as in purpose, yet stand in conjunction, creations of the two strands of the human spirit which created the Victorian North.

Public buildings

The small towns of Northumberland in their present form are largely the creations of the late eighteenth and early nineteenth centuries. Their public buildings continue the restraint and dignity of the traditional Northumbrian architecture in stone. They were built in an age when the landed gentry and wealthy businessmen accepted as a matter of course in architecture the classic rule of proportion. There is a noticeable lack of the sometimes overpowering and expensive town halls with which the rising cities of Lancashire and the West Riding expressed wealth and civic pride in the course of the Victorian age. Berwick is an eighteenth-century city within walls which represent the latest developments of military architecture in the sixteenth century (Plate 33). From the south, it is dominated by the classical town hall standing high above the river, with its tall bell tower which at first sight might be taken as the tower of a church. The town hall was completed in 1761 and contained the only peal of bells in the town. A thoroughly civilian building for a town learning to turn its back on a turbulent past, the town hall was also something of an architectural adventure for a place where the 'higher class' lived in a 'very retired manner' and exchanged 'the pleasing civilities of social life' only at the assemblies celebrating royal birthdays, and the Lamberton races.[62]

At Alnwick the town hall in the market place was completed in 1771. Alnwick Castle is an ancient stronghold as it should have been in the eyes of those who had read *Marmion*

[62] E. Mackenzie, op. cit., p. 302.

or *The Lay of the Last Minstrel*, but the town hall continued the transformation of the medieval town into the social, as well as the business, capital of a wide agricultural area at a time when the market was also a social occasion and horse traffic reached its final development. The tradition was maintained by the Northumberland Hall, also in the market place, constructed at the expense of the third duke in the 1820s. The great column surmounted by the Percy Lion at the southern edge of the town was erected in 1816 by a grateful tenantry to the second duke, who had reduced rents during a difficult period. Few landowners have enjoyed greater wealth and prestige than the dukes of Northumberland in the nineteenth century, and few have been more conscientious landlords. It is fitting that one of the most conspicuous landmarks in Alnwick should be this monument to the landed interest in its heyday which was renewing Alnwick, rebuilding villages and remodelling much of the modern Northumbrian landscape. The fourteenth-century gateway across the Bond Gate gives access to a town which in character belongs to the first half of the nineteenth century, where cobbles and lime trees, the hotels and inns, such as the White Swan and the Turk's Head, recall the white beaver hats of the age of Palmerston.

Morpeth Town Hall was designed by Vanbrugh and erected in 1718 at the expense of the earl of Carlisle; although heavily damaged by fire and substantially rebuilt in the nineteenth century it can still be fittingly described, in the language of early Victorian England once applied to the building, as "an elegant stone structure".[63]

Morpeth had quietly avoided the more turbulent aspects of Northumbrian history, though it had made a spectacular and uncharacteristic appearance in 1644, when it had enjoyed the distinction of being captured by Montrose. From the early eighteenth century Morpeth entered on a period of quiet prosperity which was increasingly based on

63 W. Whelan & Co., op. cit., p. 750.

its position, before the railway era, as the terminal market in Northumberland for the great droves of cattle from further north. By the nineteenth century the town was noted as a place of cheap and comfortable retirement for officers of the services. To this later period belongs the battlemented gateway of what was originally the County Gaol, designed by Dobson in 1822, by the main road south of the Wansbeck. This is an adaptation of Gothic which is particularly unsuitable for Morpeth. More in keeping with the town's history as a market, and an important posting stage on the Great North Road, is the fine Regency bow-fronted Black Bull facing the broad Bridge Street.

In general the public buildings of nineteenth-century Northumberland were utilitarian and undistinguished. Wealth was lavished on churches, bridges and private houses. In North Shields the smoke-blackened town hall and police station in Saville Street, a somewhat surprising Gothic building in the environment of North Shields, built "in the Elizabethan style" for the Improvement Commissioners, is one of the many buildings designed by John Dobson. It is a monument of the virtuosity of the architect and of the experimentation in design which, in the nineteenth century, led to the construction of so many buildings with incongruous touches of a pre-industrial age.

In Newcastle the ancient Moot Hall in the castle bailey was pulled down and replaced by the existing building constructed for the county of Northumberland in 1812. On a commanding site high above the river, with its great Doric columns and pediment, classic in inspiration and strong in execution, the building continues the story of Newcastle's development from the city's older and less uncompromising Guildhall in the Sandhill below. The new Moot Hall ushered in the great age of Newcastle's classical architecture and forms as significant a landmark in the city's development as the High Level Bridge, spanning the river below.

The classical tradition and culture which, hand in hand

with coal and engineering, created the modern Newcastle is repeated in the fine library of the Literary and Philosophical Society in the Westgate Road, near the Central Station. The name recalls the scholarly clergymen, surgeons and attornies of a more leisurely age. But the 'Lit. & Phil.' was a focal point for the academic, county and business society which combined to create modern Northumberland. Robert Stephenson was a member and left the society an important legacy. William Armstrong lectured there on electricity, in 1844, and later, as Lord Armstrong, donated the lecture hall. In the 'Lit. & Phil.' Collingwood Bruce gave the lectures which initiated the great age of research on the Roman Wall. The building stands for the many-sided achievement of nineteenth-century Newcastle.

From the Literary and Philosophical Society, too, came much of the inspiration which led to the construction of the Hancock Museum completed in the 1870s, the last important building in the tradition of Newcastle's classical period and, like so much in Newcastle, owing much to the munificence of Lord Armstrong. It was followed with a change in architectural style, by the original nucleus of the present university of Newcastle, in Queen Victoria Street near Barras Bridge. By the time the building was completed, in the early twentieth century, the classic tradition of Newcastle had been superseded. The style is Gothic. The front, completed in 1909, is described by Pevsner as 'Tudor-cum-Baroque'. Begun as a centre for education in physical science, Armstrong College was completed at a time when Newcastle had risen to the height of its world fame in shipbuilding and engineering. The Moot Hall of 1812 and Armstrong College of 1904 stand at either end of the period of Newcastle's most vigorous growth and achievement. They reflect the influence, direct and indirect, of the country gentleman, classical in inspiration as in architectural expression, and the more baroque tastes of the newer world of the great industrial magnates.

Surprisingly enough the corporation of Newcastle itself, which had the inspiration to back the grand design of Grainger and Dobson, built for itself no fitting memorial of the period. The Old Town Hall retains the classical tradition but is an uninspired building on a cramped site. It was built after the rejection of Grainger's own plans.

It was perhaps to be expected that wealth and economic achievement, combined with technical virtuosity and the exploration of new architectural styles, should contribute to a marked exuberance both in public and private buildings. The great private houses of the late Victorian industrialists were Gothic, like Jesmond Towers (now a school), or Tudor like Jesmond Dene House. A baroque wealth of ornament became fashionable. In Westgate Road the ornate Union Club contrasts with the classical style of the Central Station and the Literary and Philosophical Society building. In New Bridge Street the Laing Art Gallery, completed in 1904, is a fine essay in baroque with something of the strength characteristic of Vanbrugh's great house of Seaton Delaval itself. At the bottom of Dean Street the tall buildings constructed at the turn of the century have a wealth of ornament. It is a style which is carried to its limit in the ornately decorated roof of Emerson Chambers[64] in Blackett Street, a building which perhaps more than any other bears witness to the spirit of Newcastle in the days when Tyneside had become one of the great workshops of the world.

In the small colliery towns and villages, where brick was the usual, though not universal, material for construction, funds were not usually available for architectural virtuosity. At a time when Newcastle was leaving the classical tradition, Blyth was constructing brick buildings such as the Primitive Methodist Sunday School, of 1898, and the Blyth and District Social Club, of 1902, in Keelman's Terrace; a tradition followed, though less over-poweringly,

[64] B. Allsop, *Historic Architecture of Newcastle upon Tyne* (1967), p. 92.

o

by the Blyth Public Library with its bright brick and blue slates in a setting of geraniums and lobelias. As typical of the period is the Mechanics' Institute at the corner of Bridge Street and Front Street in Newbiggin. It is the usual red brick and blue slate building, relieved by stone facings and adorned with a turret, in sharp contrast with the simplicity of the older Railway Inn nearby.

The countryside outside the coastal coal area remained faithful to stone throughout the nineteenth century. In Wooler the Registry Office of 1839, the County Library of 1854 and the Mechanics' Institute of 1889 summarise much of the social history of England throughout the Victorian period. All three are stone buildings, architecturally conservative and unadorned, yet harmonising with the older cottages of Wooler, such as those in the neighbourhood of the Peth and Cheviot Street, as much a part of rural Northumberland as the pele tower post office of Cambo and the unspoilt simplicity of the inns and houses of early nineteenth-century Glanton.

SELECT BIBLIOGRAPHY

Allsopp, B. *Historic Architecture of Newcastle upon Tyne* (1967).
Beresford, M. *New Towns of the Middle Ages* (1967).
Brand, J. *The History and Antiquities of Newcastle upon Tyne*, 2 volumes (1789).
Charlton, R. J. *A History of Newcastle on Tyne*.
Conzen, M. R. G. 'Alnwick, Northumberland', *Institute of British Geographers, Publication No. 7* (1961).
Dendy, F. W. "Newcastle upon Tyne", *Lit. and Phil. Lectures* (1921).
Forster, R. *History of Corbridge and its Antiquities* (1881).
Hodgson, J. *History of Northumberland in Three Parts*, 7 volumes (1820–58).
Middlebrook, S. *Newcastle upon Tyne* (1950).
Nef, J. U. *The Rise of the British Coal Industry*, 2 volumes (1932).
Northumberland County History Committee, *A History of Northumberland* (N.C.H.), 15 volumes (1893–1940).

Pevsner, N. *The Buildings of England: Northumberland* (1957).
Raistrick, A. and Jennings, B. *A History of Lead Mining in the Pennines* (1965).
Richardson, W. *History of the Parish of Wallsend* (1923).
Scott, J. *Berwick upon Tweed* (1888).
Tate, G. *History of Alnwick,* 2 volumes (1866).
Wallace, J. *History of Blyth* (1869).
Wilkes, L. and Dodds, G. *Tyneside Classical* (1964).

4. Roads, bridges and railways

Except in the urban areas, where they have been overlaid by later developments, and among the wet mosses of the moorlands, an intricate pattern of trackways, drove roads, green lanes and bridle paths knits together the Northumbrian landscape, a pattern which has evolved since men first journeyed between hill fort and settlement and the cattle of the pastoral Celts trod out their paths to the grazing grounds. The term 'trackless moorland' is indeed misleading, except in a few areas such as the upper reaches of the Irthing, still a wild, wet country of sikes, flows and mosses.[1]

Some of these tracks have evolved over more than 3000 years, since the days when prehistoric man erected the barrows, such as Auchope Cairn, on the crest of the Border ridge. They exist in a great variety of forms and few can be dated with any certainty. Some are easy enough to recognise: the drift roads for cattle between walls of turf and stone descending the moorlands to Elsdon; or the walled lanes down the steep slopes of Knarsdale Forest constructed after the enclosure of 1864. Some are deep hollow ways in the heather, trodden down over the centuries and scoured by rain, where the nature of the ground enforced concentration of traffic, as at Lordenshaws and Witchy Neuk on Simonside, at Phillip's Cross on Catcleugh Hill; and Outer Cock Law, just north of the Border line, where Clennell Street and the Salter's Road together descend to the Bowmont.

Some tracks are shadows in the grass left since the years before Rome, like Clennell Street below the hill fort above Alwinton; some are now forestry roads, like the drove road through Slaley Forest; or appear as ruts in the heather on the Blanchland moors; or a Roman road tarred in recent years,

---

[1] As the *Border Guide* (1962), p. 76, points out: "trackless and marshy, with distance too great to be traversed with safety".

like Dere Street south of Chew Green. Some are associated with great rocks as landmarks, like the Kielder Stone on the Border line under Peel Fell, and the Pedlar's Stone on Black Law above the Holystone Burn; and with the remnants of medieval crosses: Steng Cross south of Elsdon; Comyn's Cross where the Pennine Way enters the forestry plantations from Haughton Common.

The Royal Commission on the Ancient Monuments of Scotland remarks of these trackways in the Border area that "in their choice of routes they affect high-lying ground, avoiding valleys and deep cleughs; the hazards and difficulties of swampy ground and peat hags having evidently been preferred to those of woods, screes, and torrents". Most of them are closely associated with hill settlements or forts of the pre-Roman or Roman period. The most that can be said with any certainty is that, the topography of the hills having remained the same, man and his animals must have followed the same routes with some variation on the open moorland but with a persistent concentration on the approach to river crossings, or ridges such as Windy Gyle and Cock Law Foot. Many of these must have been adapted for wheeled traffic at an early date, since the monks of Holy Island were granted passage for carts carrying peat over the Kyloe Hills in the thirteenth century. Others at that time were used for less reputable purposes; a 'thieves' road' in Cheviot was mentioned in 1255.[2]

Tracks forming a deep series of trenches in the heather abound on the Simonside hills in close proximity to the hill settlements of Lordenshaws and Witchy Neuk.[3] These were certainly used by eighteenth-century drovers, but this was the latest phase in their long history. These tracks are closely associated not only with prehistoric settlements but with

[2] Royal Commission on the Ancient Monuments of Scotland, *Roxburgh-shire*, Vol. I, p. 51.

[3] There is an interesting paper on these trackways by E. R. Newbigin, 'Notes on ancient trackways in the Rothbury District', *P.S.A.*, 4th series, Vol. IV (1929–30).

the fords over the Coquet and with a series of trackways running north into the moorlands above Holystone and Harbottle. The settlements and hill forts of Celtic times and earlier required some system of communications; the Salter's Road and Clennell Street both enter the hills under hill forts above Alnham and Alwinton. The chain of hill forts near Wooler, Humbleton, Harehope and Yeavering Bell, is linked by a line of trackways to the south between the Humbleton and College Burns. Under the Shaftoe Crags, in central Northumberland, also an area of ancient settlement, the Salter's Nick is a later name for the track passing under the hill fort.

The Roman road system constructed in the first century A.D. provided the only properly surveyed highways in Northumberland until the military road from Newcastle to Carlisle was constructed in 1752. The Normans added the North Road from Newcastle to Berwick but for most of its history this was no more than a series of minor ways linking a chain of fortresses. In the Middle Ages bridges were constructed at the river crossings, at Newcastle, Morpeth, Felton, Alnwick and Berwick.

The first road ever to be constructed in Northumberland was the strategic Roman road between Corbridge and Carlisle, the Stanegate, or Carelgate of later times, built in about A.D. 80 and taking its final form some twenty years later. The Stanegate originally began at *Corstopitum*, where the Romans reached the Tyne. The finest length in use today is the straight stretch of road from Settlingstones along the ridge above Grindon Lough with its wide view of the Wall on the crest of the Whin Sill to the northward above Housesteads.

The main line of communications between *Corstopitum* and the south was the road which the Saxons called Dere Street, the 'Deira road', to York. This crossed the Derwent at Ebchester and the modern motor road follows the greater part of its length from Ebchester through Apperley Dene.

Between Riding Mill and Corbridge the modern road diverges slightly from the line of Dere Street, which crossed Dilston Haughs near the modern cemetery and so made for the bridge across the river west of Corbridge.

Campaigns in Scotland, and the military supervision of tribal territory, required the extension of Dere Street northwards. Modern traffic today follows the Roman road from about half a mile north of Corbridge on the A68 up Stagshaw Bank to the Portgate and on to the crossing of the Rede at Elishaw north of Otterburn. The only important deviation is where the modern road turns over Elishaw Common to avoid the direct Roman descent down to the Rede below West Woodburn. Portgate is 'the gate' *par excellence*. The name is derived from the Latin *porta* with the Old English suffix *geata* added to duplicate the original meaning. The modern crossroad,[4] where Dere Street meets General Wade's road by the Errington Arms on Stagshaw Bank, has a long history. Here troops, officials and convoys set out from the gate in the Wall on their journey through the wild frontier hills to the Tweed and the Clyde; and here the shaggy Highland cattle with their Gaelic-speaking drovers came to the stances of Stagshaw. The site still preserves the atmosphere of a frontier. Here the Tyne valley and the distant fells of Cumberland and Durham disappear after the ascent from Corbridge; ahead lie the broad moorlands and hill pastures of central Northumberland.

The modern A68 leaves Dere Street in the Rede valley north of Otterburn to cross the Border at the Carter. This route was opened in 1776. Until then maps marked as the Jedburgh Road[5] the track which leaves the North Tyne at Falstone over Hawkhope Hill. Much of it is now used as a forestry service road, and much is obscured by plantations. The last section can be followed as a track across Kielder

---

[4] Recently much altered by the construction of a roundabout.
[5] e.g. Armstrong's map of 1768.

Moor to the Border at Knox Knowe, one of the recognised walks in Kielder Forest.

North of the Portgate the second of the two major lines of Roman communications with the north, the so-called Devil's Causeway, branched off from Dere Street in a north-easterly direction at Beukley to cross the central Northumbrian highlands, a straight line on the map with no significant deviation from the neighbourhood of Great Whittington to the Coquet below Brinkburn. The road turned north at the Coquet to cross the Aln below Whittingham. North of Glanton it followed the valley of the Breamish, to cross the Till below Horton and continue north through Lowick, making for the Tweed below Berwick. The greater part of the Devil's Causeway today is invisible except from the air but the road from East Horton to Lowick follows the Roman line.

Dere Street and the Devil's Causeway ran through the main areas of settlement in Celtic Northumberland. Lateral communication between the two was maintained by the subsidiary road which left Dere Street at High Rochester, crossed the Coquet between Holystone and Sharperton, and joined the Devil's Causeway at Low Learchild, near Whittingham. It is interesting, though the possibilities are speculative, that two of the ancient holy wells of Northumberland, at Holystone and Whittingham, are both in close proximity to the lateral road through the heart of the Celtic highlands. St Ninian's well, at Whittingham, now protected by corrugated iron, is situated in a field near Whittingham Lane Farm close to the line of the Devil's Causeway. At Holystone, where the Roman road descends from the moorlands of Redesdale to the Coquet, St Ninian's Well, also called Lady Well, is situated close to the line of the road which was probably used by St Ninian in the fifth century.[6]

Communications between villages and hamlets usually

[6] The possibility is suggested in *N.C.H.,* Vol. XV, p. 455.

Plate 33 The Quay, Berwick
Eighteenth-century houses built at a time when Berwick had become a quiet
provincial town with an important export trade in salmon.

Plate 34 Border tracks

This photograph shows the line of The Street, an ancient Border track and drove road, which runs along the ridge in the centre and climbs Black Braes on the left. The far ridge in the centre is Windy Gyle, a medieval Border meeting-place.

Plate 35 Corbridge bridge
Built in 1674, it was the only bridge on the Tyne to withstand the great flood of 1771. It replaced a medieval bridge. The Saxon tower of Corbridge church is just visible.

Plate 36 Chollerford bridge, North Tyne
Built by Robert Mylne in 1775 and one of the several fine bridges of the second half of the eighteenth century.

Plate 37 Kielder viaduct

This fine viaduct carried the Hexham to Riccarton section of the Border Counties Railway which was opened to traffic in 1862. The line, now closed, followed the North Tyne valley, crossing the Border at the Deadwater.

Plate 38 Longwitton station

Longwitton station was originally on the Northumberland Central Railway opened in 1870 and absorbed by the North British in 1872. Now one of the many disused stations on the closed branch-lines of Northumberland.

evolved piecemeal as rough tracks. Many have reverted to their former condition, or have become public footpaths often difficult to follow. The lane leading off the B1341 through Bamburgh Fields, between Bamburgh and Glororum, was once a medieval road.[7] So probably was an equally overgrown lane between Lucker and Ratchwood. Both are clearly marked as bridle tracks on Greenwood's map of 1827–8. This map also shows as a bridle track the line of grassy lanes and footpaths, which can still be followed with some difficulty, south of Warkworth, and which lead to Broomhill and Widdrington.

The monks of Newminster must have followed well-marked tracks in the course of business with their granges. One such track is now the ridge road over Duddo Hill to Horton Grange, near Prestwick Carr, which crosses the upper reaches of the Blyth by the eighteenth-century Bellasis Bridge.

Until the eighteenth century the sands and links provided the easiest means of communications along much of the coast. These provided a route between Beadnell and Alnwick until 1759[8] and part of it can be seen today as a track behind the links between Beadnell and Newton-by-the-Sea.

Before the construction of turnpikes began, in the second half of the eighteenth century, Dere Street was the main route into Northumberland from the north. This was usually the route followed by the Scots in the Middle Ages because Newcastle barred the passage of the Tyne along the coastal route; for the drovers Dere Street avoided the cultivated lands of Tweedside and Glendale. The Roman road gave access southwards to Corbridge by High Rochester or along the easy ridgeway between Rede and Coquet to Elsdon. Elsdon itself, and the prominent landmark of Steng

[7] *N.C.H.*, Vol. I, p. 289.

[8] Sir J. Craster, 'Beadnell in the eighteenth century', *A.A.,* 4th series, Vol. XXXIV (1956), p. 164.

Cross to the south, were ancient track junctions communicating with Rothbury and Morpeth along the line of the eighteenth-century turn-pike, the modern motor road, and with Coquetdale by the track across the moors to Holystone. From the moors of the south-west a drove road crossed the Ottercaps Burn and climbed under Tod Crag through the heather on its way to Steng Cross. This route was marked as a drove road in the first edition of the Ordnance Survey and still appears as a footpath, though part is blocked by the fir plantation under Tod Crag.

North of the Coquet, Alnham and Alwinton have been gateways into the Cheviots since the hill forts were raised on the hills above the sites of the later Anglian settlements. At Alnham the grassy track of the Salter's Road climbs into the hills past the church built on the site of a pre-Conquest church and aligned on the Salter's Road itself. The name, Salter's Road, recalls the valuable medieval salt traffic from the pans on the coast, as do the Salter's Nick in the Shaftoe Crags and the Salter's Bridge over the Ouseburn at Jesmond. Above Alnham it passes under the hill fort on High Knowes, occupied in pre-Roman and Roman times, making for Ewartly Shank and the crossing of the Breamish at Bleakhope. Avoiding the eroded moss-hags on the heights of Bloodybush Edge the track keeps to the lower slopes to the north before descending by the Clay Burn to join Clennell Street in its ascent to the Border. South of Alnham the ancient route to Rothbury is represented by a series of lanes and footpaths along the ridges to Lorbottle and Cartington and thence into Rothbury, probably by the footpath representing the old track to the medieval chapel of St Helen near South Cartington.

Alwinton was a junction of two important trackways, Clennell Street, and the series of routes called The Street which followed the Coquet and branched off to the Border by a series of convenient ridges. Clennell Street today is perhaps the easiest route for the exploration of Border tracks. Starting from Alwinton, from a point determined by the ford over the Housedon Burn, it passes as a grassy track close to the hill fort on Castle Hill and follows the ridge above the Alwin and the Kidland Burn to the derelict cottage at Wholehope. Beyond this point it becomes a forestry track for the new plantations before emerging onto the heights of Yarnspath and slanting down the fell to the important track-junction above the Usway under Hazely Law. North of the Usway Clennell Street is still an easy and well-defined track, the medieval Hexpethgate, joined by the Salter's Road and climbing to the ridge above Outer Cock Law. Outer Cock Law itself is a short distance on the Scottish side of the Border where traffic over the centuries has left well-marked gulleys and tracks. On Black Braes, just south of the Border, the course of The Street is also well-defined (Plate 34).

Exploration of these tracks, and especially a walk along the Border ridge between Cock Law and Black Braes, at a height of between 1600 and 1800 feet, is an exhilarating experience. The ridge itself offers a platform of firm heathery ground, broadest at Windy Gyle, poised high above England and Scotland, where the view ranges from the hills of Dumfries and the Pentlands far across the rolling Northumbrian moors beyond the Coquet. Here Bronze Age man erected his barrows; horsemen and drovers have travelled here since time immemorial.

This line of fells was once one of the great highways of the north (Fig. 19). It is crossed by four ancient routes climbing north from the Coquet and its tributaries: Roman Dere Street, The Street, Clennell Street and, easternmost, the Salter's Road. Northwards they descend to the Tweed, to Hawick, Selkirk and Kelso. Southwards they generally follow the higher ground above the burns which join the Coquet and the Rede.

These tracks were at their busiest during the eighteenth century, from the days of Andrew Fairservice and Rob Roy

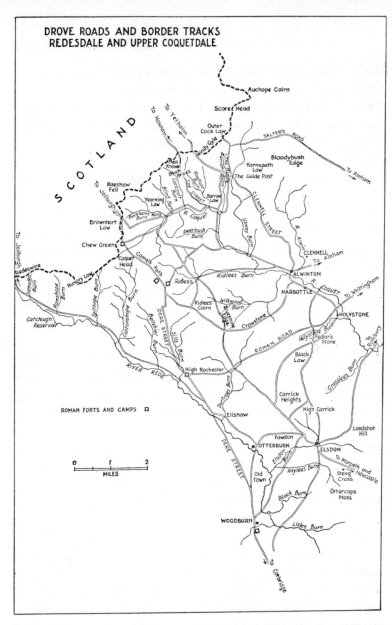

Fig. 19. Since ancient times the moorlands between the Rede and Upper Coquetdale have provided a relatively easy system of communications between the Tweed valley and the heart of Northumberland. The tracks were used by raiding parties from both sides of the Border and later, until the Railway Age, by the Highland cattle driven down to the markets of the south. Roman Dere Street became an important medieval route and then a major drove road with numerous feeder tracks. The modern road to Jedburgh, the A68, follows substantially the line of the medieval track through Redesdale, which crossed the Border at the Redeswire, now known as the Carter Bar. Elsdon was the heart of this track system. Otterburn is the creation of the turnpikes constructed in the late eighteenth and early nineteenth centuries.

Macgregor to the coming of the railways. There was an eighteenth-century inn for drovers on the Slyme Foot below the ridge followed by The Street from the Coquet to the Border. This inn was once "the resort of all the neighbouring sheep farmers, who used to spend their time drinking and gambling".[9]

Eastwards the ridge called the Middle Hill, between the Usway and the Barrow Burns, was one of the most important track-junctions of the Border fells, known to medieval Wardens of the Marches and to the later drovers and smugglers. At this point Clennell Street dips to the Usway between Yarnspath and the Border ridge. Down the centre of the ridge a track runs south towards the Coquet, and ultimately to Dere Street and Elsdon. Westerly another track gives access to what were once the medieval holdings now represented by the farms of Trows and Rowhope.

In medieval times the Middle was also a separate holding. It was mentioned in the report on the killing of Lord Francis Russell at the Border Tryst of 1585 on Windy Gyle, when it was called Oswold Myddle (i.e. Usway Middle).[10] Here there was once a drovers' inn, and a rectangular excavation still visible in the grass is reputed to have been a cockpit. Rory's Still, a fine illicit whisky still higher up the Usway near Davidson's Linn and close to the Salter's Road, was well situated to do business with the drovers, pedlars, smugglers and shepherds who followed the tracks over the Border hills in the early nineteenth century.

These tracks converged on Dere Street, one of the main routes for Scottish armies in the Middle Ages and for the cattle driven south through Jedburgh and Kelso in droving days. For the drovers the moorlands between the Rede and Coquet provided a choice of easy routes, many of which exist today as farm tracks and military roads. Roman camps

[9] D. D. Dixon, *Upper Coquetdale* (1904), p 18.
[10] *Calendar of Border Papers,* Vol. I, p. 189, 'Statement as to Lord Russell's Death'.

and forts provided convenient cattle stances, as at Chew Green and High Rochester and the Roman staging camp near the medieval boundary stone known as the Middle Golden Pot where Dere Street begins the descent to the Rede.

The Elsdon route followed the high ground by Bluestone Edge and Davyshield Common. It is now monopolised by military vehicles, but to the south of Leighton Hill the modern tarred road forms a narrow strip between the turf walls which once confined the herds in their approach to Elsdon. The Pedlar's Stone, a landmark visible for miles under Black Law above Holystone, marks an important track junction between Coquetdale and Redesdale. The approaches to Holystone and the Coquet fords to the east were at one time guarded by the earthwork still to be seen across the ridge between Dove Crag and the Holystone Burn. The earthwork was probably Tudor, but the original sanctity of the sacred well at Holystone, where the clear water flows between the *mimulus*, probably extends far back beyond the Christian era and suggests a similar antiquity for some of the tracks on the neighbouring moors.

South of the Tyne the old droving route has been obscured by later developments in forestry and agriculture. There was a concentration of droving traffic at Corbridge and Riding Mill. At Corbridge the old approach to the ford over the Tyne is marked by the narrow passage between walls which leads down to the river at the east end of the town. The forestry road through the middle of Slaley Forest was a drove road, which also survives as a track through the heather of Blanchland Common to what was once the drovers inn at Pennypie, and so west of Blanchland to the Durham border.

In Hexhamshire and Allendale the moorlands are threaded by the old pack-horse routes from the lead mines, used by the galloway ponies moving in file behind their leader. The track known as the Broad Way, from Allenheads, can still be followed over Byerhope and Lilswood Moor, where it becomes an enclosed lane before joining the secondary road which descends under Whitley Chapel to Devil's Water and the Dukesfield smelt-mill. North-east of Allendale town there are several carrier routes which begin as lanes between stone walls before crossing the open moors north of Spital-shields on their way to Hexham.

By the early eighteenth century the Northumbrian road system was so bad that there was probably less wheeled traffic than at any time since the thirteenth century. "On the North Road rich men's coaches and carriers' wagons lumbered along at three miles an hour, but elsewhere men and goods went on horseback or not at all."[11] Many of the tracks along the moorland ridges and over the Cheviots must have provided much better going than inter-village routes.

In 1745 Field-Marshal Wade found it impossible to move his artillery westwards from Hexham to Carlisle. Four years later, therefore, the line of a new road from the Westgate of Newcastle was surveyed. This was completed in 1752–3, the first scientifically constructed road in Northumberland since Agricola's road and with the same strategic object. Wade's[12] road is the modern A69 from Newcastle to Heddon on the Wall, and then becomes the B6318, with its famous view of the Wall along the Whin Sill in the neighbourhood of Housesteads and Thirlwall. Most of the eastern section of the road used the Wall itself as a foundation between the Westgate and the North Tyne. The completion of the military road was followed by intensive road construction throughout the county. This lasted for about a century and created the modern road system of Northumberland characterised by long stretches of straight roads, wide verges between walls or hedges, and the effective use of trees. The old coach road from Morpeth to Rothbury over

[11] R. C. Bosanquet, 'John Horsley and his Times', *A.A.*, 4th series, Vol. X (1933), p. 59.

[12] Wade died in 1748 but the term 'Wade's road' has long been used for this military road and distinguishes it from the Roman military road.

the heights of Harelaw and through Todburn is a good example of one of these improved roads, though the difficult country inhibits straight stretches for any considerable distance. More characteristic are the straight late eighteenth-century roads west of Hexham, from Low Gate to Haydon Bridge by Lowe's Fell, and the ridge road of Yarridge.

The country gentlemen busy making huge capital investments in the improvement of their estates took the lead in promoting new roads. Lancelot Allgood of Nunwick was prominent in promoting the Corn Road from Hexham to Alnmouth across the central highlands of Northumberland. The Corn Road, constructed in the 1750s, was the first of the new roads for purely economic purposes. Its line was from Chollerford by Little Bavington, Kirkharle, Wallington and Cambo to Rothbury and Alnwick across the Rimside Moors and thence to Alnmouth through Lesbury. This road is now represented by the modern A6709, B6342 and B6341; the long stretches on the uplands between Little Bavington and Kirkharle remain a good example of a planned eighteenth-century road through the country of improving landlords, such as Swinburnes and Blacketts. At Hexham the Alemouth Road between the station and Hallstile Bank still recalls this new road across the county, as well as the old pronunciation of Alnmouth. In the same period Elsdon was connected with Morpeth by the turnpike through Scots Gap and across the Harwood Moors past Steng Cross.

The Northumberland section of the London to Edinburgh coach road through Newcastle, Wooler and Kelso was completed in 1763, passing through Whittingham and Glanton to the west of the modern road. The construction of this road was followed by the rebuilding of Glanton in the early nineteenth century before the road was diverted to the east, leaving Glanton an excellent specimen of rural architecture of its period. Part of the original route exists as a lane forming the eastern boundary of Thrunton Wood.

Near Whittingham Lane Farm the lane becomes a wide grassy track between crumbling walls to confine the stock passing through the cultivated fields between Whittingham and the moors. In the neighbourhood of Alnwick the modern road to Eglingham was constructed in the 1820s, on a new alignment west of the Aln and the Eglingham Burn to replace the ancient track through Brizelee and across the moorland above Kemmer Lough. This new road made it possible to close the traditional routes through Hulne Park, and to build the great wall which encloses the park along the new road. Eglingham itself was reorientated by the new road and spread southwards along the road in the vicinity of the Tankerville Arms.

Apart from the main turnpikes, landowners were constructing their own roads as outlets for their estates. In North Tynedale Sir John Swinburne co-operated with landowners north of the Border to construct a road from his new village of Mounces along the Lewisburn and Akenshaw Burn into Liddesdale. The route followed had once been used by the moss troopers of Liddesdale, and later by the drovers on their way to Bellingham and Dere Street. This road now exists as a forestry service track through Kielder Forest. It becomes a track across the Larriston Fells from the point where an inscribed pillar, on the edge of the moorland at Bloodybush, sets out the tolls to be paid at Akenshaw Bridge for horses, cattle and sheep, and the coal from the North Tyne collieries.

The new roads and the increase in traffic led to the development of the famous inns of coaching days. At Belford the Blue Bell became a noted coaching inn in 1812 under the management of Elizabeth Macdonald. The construction of the Kelso route in the 1760s was followed by development of the fine early nineteenth-century Castle Inn. The Bridge of Allen Hotel at Weldon Bridge on the North Road also dates from this period.

Road construction and wheeled traffic were accompanied

by an equally vigorous period of bridge building. In the early eighteenth century there were practically no bridges at all in central and western Northumberland. On the Tweed there was no bridge above Berwick until the Coldstream Bridge was completed by Smeaton in 1766. Fords across the normally shallow rivers were numerous; the measures taken by the Tudors for the security of the Border include long lists of fords to be watched by the representatives of neighbouring townships. Occasionally there were ferries, as at Hexham and Prudhoe. The ferry across the North Tyne at Humshaugh, above the late eighteenth-century paper mill, was mentioned in the thirteenth century and was subject to an agreement in 1788 when the paper mill was built.[13] It is still in use.

The Romans had bridged the Tyne at Newcastle and Corbridge, and the North Tyne at Chesters, where the remains of the Roman bridge of the third century provide some of the most impressive Roman stonework in the county. All three fell into ruin during the Dark Ages but the Normans used the piers of *Pons Aelius* to carry a wooden superstructure soon after the foundation of Newcastle. This was replaced by a stone bridge in the middle of the thirteenth century on the line of the nineteenth-century swing bridge. At Corbridge the first medieval bridge was constructed in 1325 by agreement with the lord of Dilston on the site of the present bridge (Plate 35), one of the finest bridges in Northumberland, built in 1674. It was the only bridge on the Tyne to withstand the great flood of 1771, which destroyed the newly completed bridge at Hexham as well as the medieval structure at Newcastle.

The important line of communications between Newcastle and Berwick was carried across the rivers by some of the earliest medieval bridges in Northumberland. Of the bridge at Morpeth nothing remains but the piers incorporated in the modern footbridge across the Wansbeck. At

[13] *N.C.H.,* Vol. XV, p. 205, footnote.

Felton the now disused bridge over the Coquet was built in the thirteenth century and its existence may have contributed to the abandonment of Old Felton in favour of the site of the present village. The late fourteenth-century bridge over the Coquet at Warkworth is one of the finest fortified bridges in England and was used for twentieth-century tourist traffic until its closure in 1961. Berwick had a bridge in the days of its thirteenth-century prosperity; a bridge at Berwick was reported as decayed in 1513, like so much in the north at that time. The existing Old Bridge at Berwick was completed in 1624 to take the North Road into the commercial centre of the city and is still the best vantage point from which to study Berwick rising on the steep slope above the Tweed. The North Road itself has been diverted to the Royal Tweed Bridge of 1928.

Twizel Bridge over the Till, perhaps the best known of the old bridges of Northumberland, was probably constructed in the fifteenth century, over a river which markedly lacks the shallow reaches characteristic of Northumbrian rivers. It played an important part in the battle of Flodden, when it was used by the earl of Surrey to transport his artillery across the river. A beautiful bridge in its construction and setting, the bridge spans the Till in a single arch taking flight across the water. The design reappears in cruder form in the attractive high-arched bridge over the upper Till below Weetwood Hall, in Glendale, which was probably originally constructed in the sixteenth century and was certainly reconstructed in the early nineteenth. There is a similar high-arched bridge across the South Tyne at Featherstone dating from the second quarter of the eighteenth century.

Two attractive pack-horse bridges are the Linnels Bridge over the Devil's Water near Hexham and the bridge over the burn at Riding Mill. Both are seventeenth-century in origin, though the Linnels Bridge, which is the older of the two, may have had a medieval predecessor.

In the eighteenth century bridge-building was actively encouraged and financed by the leading landowners as part of the vigorous programme of agricultural improvement, and pains were often taken to ensure that they conformed with what Lancelot Brown termed the 'capability' of the landscape. The bridge which carries the modern road over the Wansbeck through Wallington park was built in 1760, at the time when Sir Walter Blackett was transforming the moorlands by improved agriculture, enclosure and road construction. In the tamed landscape where the Wansbeck flows quietly under the trees Wallingford Bridge carries a public road, but it is a park bridge, a fit setting for a portrait by Gainsborough. At Alnwick the famous Lion Bridge with its Percy Lion, which takes the North Road across the Aln, was built in 1773 above the old medieval bridge in order to conform with the new lay-out of the castle grounds.

Out of sight of the great country houses landlords built simpler, though still attractive, structures for the new roads, such as the bridge across the Rede above Redesmouth, and Sir John Swinburne's bridge across the Akenshaw Burn for his new road into Scotland. These bridges supplemented the major structures erected during the third quarter of the eighteenth century at the time the new turnpikes were under construction. The fine bridge over the North Tyne at Chollerford (Plate 36) was completed by Robert Mylne in 1775. Hexham Bridge was completed by Mylne in 1788 after earlier disasters in bridging the river. West of Hexham the attractive Cupola Bridge across the Allen was completed in the same period. The last of the major bridges in Northumberland to be built in the great century of bridge building was the Duchess's Bridge at Alnmouth, built at the expense of the duchess of Northumberland in 1864.

In the nineteenth century the bridges and viaducts required for the new railways provide some of the finest examples of the alliance between engineering and architecture in the country. Coal was originally transported by pack-horse. When the great expansion of coal exports began, in the seventeenth century, production was based on the pits near the Tyne, as at Blaydon, Winlaton and Stella on the Durham side, at Newburn, Wylam, Elswick and Walker on the Northumbrian side, or near the sea at Cowpen and Seaton Delaval. The first known waggonway to the Tyne was constructed about 1530 from Ravensworth, south-west of Gateshead in County Durham, to the river. By the second half of the seventeenth century waggonways, or railways as they were also called, were being extensively used. "Some time before this conveyance," wrote counsel in 1672, "a new method was invented for carrying coals to the river in large machines called waggons made to run on frames of timber fixed to the ground for this purpose, and since called a waggon-way, which frames must of necessity be very near if not altogether from the colliery to the river."[14]

From these waggonways there was a straight line of evolution to the railways. For the most part they have disappeared under modern developments but the line of one of the oldest is still visible. This is the famous Plessey waggonway constructed in the first decade of the eighteenth century to carry coal from the pits south of the Blyth near Hartford Bridge to the staithes at the emerging coal port of Blyth Snook. The Plessey waggonway was constructed of a double line of beech rails on oak sleepers.[15] East of Horton Bridge, on the A192, the line of the waggonway exists as a footpath between banks, a narrow grassy lane between hawthorn and elder. East of the motor road it is continued as a footpath across the fields of Low Horton Farm to New Delaval. Here the Plessey road continues the line of the waggonway into Blyth and to the site of the vanished staithes below the Oddfellows Arms.

[14] C. E. Lee, 'The Waggonways of Tyneside', *A.A.*, 4th series, Vol. XXIX (1951), p. 141.
[15] J. Wallace, *History of Blyth* (1869), p. 157.

North of the Blyth the line of the old Sleekburn waggon-way is clearly defined in part as a public footpath, across the fields of Sleekburn Grange Farm: a raised track above old ridge-and-furrow between scattered hawthorns, ending at the ruined staithe among the rushes at the mouth of the Sleek Burn under the power station of Cambois. The waggonway from the Holywell pits to the Delavals' port at Seaton Sluice similarly survives as a footpath.

In the course of the eighteenth century iron was used for colliery rails. The Bedlington Iron Works, which had begun using coal for the smelting of pig iron in 1736, was noted for its iron rails by the end of the century. In 1829 George Stephenson (1781–1848), who had experimented with steam traction on the waggonways of Killingworth, triumphed with his locomotive in the famous trials for the Liverpool and Manchester Railway at Rainshill. The Railway Age had begun.

Tentative plans for the construction of a canal from Newcastle to Carlisle and Maryport on the Cumberland coast, a distance of ninety-three miles, had been made at the end of the eighteenth century. In 1825, the year of the opening of the Darlington and Stockport Railway, notice was given of the intention to construct a railway from Newcastle to Carlisle through the Tyne Gap. Construction from the Close, in Newcastle, was authorised by Act of Parliament in 1829, subject to the impossible condition that no moveable steam engine was to be used within sight of certain country houses. This restriction was removed later. In May, 1835, Blaydon and Hexham were joined by rail along the south bank of the Tyne. The line between Blaydon and Carlisle was completed in 1838 and the final link with Newcastle was completed with the construction of the Scotswood Bridge in 1839.

The main engineering achievements of the Newcastle and Carlisle Railway, amalgamated with the North Eastern in 1862, lay across the county boundary, in Cumberland. The cutting through Farnley Scar, opposite Corbridge, was impressive by contemporary standards, and the line was noted for its attractive stations at Stocksfield, Riding Mill and Hexham.

The through rail link between Newcastle and Edinburgh, part of George Hudson's empire, was completed by the construction of the High Level Bridge at Newcastle in September, 1849, and of the Royal Border Bridge at Berwick, in 1850. Both were the work of Robert Stephenson and are superb examples of the self-confident architectural engineering of the early Railway Age. Stephenson had originally advised that the new line to Berwick should follow the coast through Warkworth, and also through the grounds of Howick, one of the outstanding examples of landscaping in the age of Capability Brown. This disaster was prevented by the opposition of Earl Grey of the Reform Bill.

The line from Newcastle to North Shields was completed in 1839, a month after the completion of the Newcastle to Carlisle line. It involved the construction of the imposing viaduct across Dean Street, and also the Ouseburn and Willingdon viaducts, all three demonstrations of the sudden flowering of new technical ability.

The railway network of Northumberland was the object of fierce competition between the North Eastern and the North British, personified in those pioneering days by able and aggressive characters such as George Hudson and Robert Hodgson, the squire of Carham Hall. On the coast the lines were constructed for the transport of coal and in due course were absorbed by the North Eastern. The Blyth and Tyne began with the construction of a line from the pits at Seghill across the Shire Moor to the Tyne at Hay Hole close to the future site of the Northumberland dock. This line was linked with the colliery railway from the Hartley pits to Blyth. A further extension took the line from Newsham to Bedlington. In 1852 the line became incorporated as a public railway and was later extended from

Bedlington to Morpeth, thus providing a line through the heart of the Northumbrian coalfield to the staithes at Blyth and on the Tyne. The termination of the colliery lines on the river was the area between Howdon Pans and North Shields which was transformed by the construction of the Northumberland Dock, where the staithes of the Blyth and Tyne were situated, in 1857.

The potential mineral resources of North Tynedale, especially the coal of Plashetts, were the lure which led the construction of the Border Counties Railway up the North Tyne valley from Warden in the 1850s. The line was completed with the help of the North British into which it was absorbed. Penetrating into the heart of the old Border country, the line wound its way up the full length of the North Tyne valley between the river and the hills, over the fine Kielder viaduct (Plate 37) and the Deadwater, to the new village across the Border created by the North British in a roadless wilderness at Riccarton Junction.

In central Northumberland the Wansbeck Valley line reached Scots Gap in 1862. The line was absorbed by the North British and carried on to Redesmouth on the North Tyne in 1865. The Northumberland Central Railway originally planned a line from Scots Gap to Cornhill, and thereby met opposition from Alnwick fearing the diversion of business. The new line stopped at Rothbury in 1870 and was also taken over by the North British. The Cornhill line was the last important local line to be constructed in Northumberland, when the N.E.R. built the railway from Alnwick through Glendale over the viaduct at Edlingham. Completed in 1887 it was closed in 1965.

In the south-west of Northumberland coal and lead provided the incentive for the construction of railways through the fells hard on the heels of stagecoaches. The Haltwhistle to Alston line was completed in 1852, only twenty-six years after the inhabitants of Alston had turned out to cheer the arrival of the first stagecoach. The work included the construction of the great viaduct spanning the South Tyne at a height of 110 feet at Lambley, perhaps the most impressive monument of railway enterprise and optimism in the branch lines of Northumberland, where the fells surge up from the river towards the 2000-foot plateau of Cold Fell. This line was a contemporary of the last of the great enclosures, on Knarsdale Common, and of the drift roads descending towards the railway. The thirteen miles of the Allendale line from Hexham through Langley and Catton were completed in 1869 in the last years of the old lead industry. It was closed in 1950.

The Railway Age in Northumberland overlapped with the century of road construction which lasted for almost exactly a century, from 1750 to 1850. Within another 100 years many of the railways themselves had become obsolete. The country was opened up for cheap travel to an unprecedented extent but life was drained from the smaller towns, towns, such as Belford which had prospered briefly as a coaching town. Droving ended, since stock could be moved more easily by rail. Morpeth, "the great Northern mart for cattle", had shown some prescience in its vigorous protest against the railway in 1837.[16] Rothbury, on the other hand, developed as a tourist centre; the rebuilding of the old town dates from the arrival of the railway in 1870. Seaside resorts such as Alnmouth, and especially Cullercoats, Whitley Bay and Tynemouth, entered a period of vigorous growth. The stations at Riding Mill and Hexham led to the development of both places as residential areas for men with business in Newcastle. Memorials of the capital, energy and optimism poured into the country railways are the impressive viaducts at Kielder, Lambley, Edlingham and Langley; the disused tracks and cuttings, half-blocked by brambles and wild roses, such as those along the North Tyne and above the Rede; the sad stations, in railway Gothic above the Coquet at Warkworth (opened in 1847 and closed

[16] Quoted in *P.S.A.*, 4th series, Vol. IX (1939–41), p. 104.

by 1962), more unassuming at Plashetts, Falstone and Longwitton (Plate 38); the utilitarian buildings at Blyth (opened in 1847 and closed by 1964), terminus of the Blyth–Tyne line which had never failed to pay a high dividend and had had no fatal accident when it was incorporated in the North Eastern in 1874. The last branch line to be constructed was the Newcastle to Ponteland line, opened in 1905, which made Ponteland a suburb of Newcastle. By then the age of the internal combustion engine had begun. The line was closed in 1967, its short life an indication of the pace of technological change.

SELECT BIBLIOGRAPHY

Dixon, D. D. *Upper Coquetdale* (1904).

Haldane, A. R. B. *The Drove Roads of Scotland* (1968).

Jervoise, E. *The Ancient Bridges of the North of England* (1931).

Margary, I. D. *Roman Roads in Britain*; Vol. ii. 'North of the Fosse Way' (1957).

Northumberland County History Committee. *A History of Northumberland* (N.C.H.), 15 volumes (1893–1940).

Tomlinson, W. W. *The North Eastern Railway, its Rise and Development,* new ed. (1967).

Society of Antiquaries of Newcastle upon Tyne. *Archaeologia Aeliana* (A.A.), 1st to 3rd series, 50 volumes (1822–1924); 4th series from 1925 to date.

Proceedings of the Society of Antiquaries of Newcastle Upon Tyne. (P.S.A.), 5th series, 32 volumes (1855–1956).

5. The modern landscape

ONE OF THE most impressive and significant scenes in Northumberland today is the huge pit made by open-cast mining on the coast north of Ellington. At the bottom 'Big Geordie', the largest dragline excavator in Europe, crawls like some vast prehistoric saurian at the rate of 300 yards an hour. 'Big Geordie' can move 100 tons of material at a time. It works in an open-cast mining area planned to produce one and a quarter million tons of coal annually. Of the same species is the cutter-suction dredger with fifteen-ton drill bits used to deepen the port of Blyth for the ore-carriers of Alcan Ltd. Smaller relations of these machines crawl elsewhere over the Northumbrian landscape driving dual carriageways round Morpeth, and across the pleasant fields of Alnwick in the landscape modelled by Capability Brown.

Northumberland today is experiencing change at a greater pace and with more unpredictable consequences than at any previous period in its history, not excluding the Railway Age. Modern developments are impressive in scale and express in their own way the energy with which the waste was colonised and new towns founded in the Middle Ages. They continue the transformation of the landscape effected by eighteenth-century landlords and, later, by the Stephensons and their peers of the railways. They presage the final subordination of the countryside to the needs of Urban Man and raise the question whether, even in the wide landscape of Northumberland, the distinction between town and country can retain any validity.

New towns, new roads, new industries, new forests, new housing estates and new facilities for holidays and tourism are being created for a growing and increasingly mobile population; hence the trampled peat of Cheviot and the brilliant cartons and wrapping papers among the grey rocks of Dunstanburgh. Picnic parties oust the grey wagtails and sandpipers from their nesting sites by Coquet and Breamish. Much of the south-east between the Tyne and the Blyth is becoming neither town nor country, but a standardised suburbia.

The largest and most striking feature of the modern landscape is the transformation of the bent and heather moorlands into forest. Already twelve per cent of the total area of Northumberland is managed woodland. The Forestry Commission now own over 152,000 acres of land. Kielder Forest alone, with some 48,000 acres under trees, is two thirds the size of the New Forest, and the area under trees is substantially larger. With the 14,000 acres of Redesdale Forest and the 36,000 acres of Wark Forest, a huge area of trees covering some 123,000 acres is coming into existence, forming an almost continuous forest from Greenlee Lough under the Wall to Raven's Knowe on the Border.

The great sweep of Kielder Forest over the fells of North Tynedale, as seen from the crest of the Larriston Fells or the heights of Peel Fell, is an impressive achievement. Fell-top, burn and forest, the green haughs of the North Tyne, blend harmoniously into a scene which, with some qualifications, is not more artificial than the hill-pastures created over the centuries by man and his animals which the trees have replaced. With the trees the roe have returned. These entrancing little deer are more likely to be seen in the neighbourhood of the Akenshaw or Blakehope Burns than at any time since Leland, in the sixteenth century, recorded of the Cheviots "There is plenty of . . . Roe Bukkes."[1]

Conifers form geometrical patterns on Haughton Common, obscuring old drove roads and the line of the Black Dyke. They line the old raiding track south of Steng Cross above Elsdon and stand close to the enclosure of the Celtic settlement of Manside; as Slaley Forest they look down on

[1] *Itinerary*, Vol. V, p. 67.

the Devil's Water and enclose the drove road from Corbridge to Blanchland.

Forestry is doing something to replace the lost population
of the Border. New villages such as Kielder and Byrness are
but the latest form of settlement in the waste. The deserted
medieval village of Ray, near Kirkwhelpington, has been
revived for forestry workers.

New methods of agriculture, rising costs and labour
problems, have added to the latest chapter in the long story
of the amalgamation of farms, which began in the sixteenth
century. Between 1956 and 1966 there was a marked decrease
in the number of holdings below 300 acres. Holdings of
between 500 and 1000 acres increased in number by over
ten per cent; holdings of 1000 acres and over by almost
twenty-six per cent. In the same period there was a fall of
thirty per cent in the full-time agricultural labour force.[2]
Farm buildings and equipment have been modernised. The
silo is a prominent feature of the rural landscape. Lonely
shepherd's cottages stand tenantless, their crofts reverting
to the moorland. In North Tynedale the cottages once
occupied by miners, railwaymen and farm-workers are in
demand as weekend cottages near the site of the proposed
reservoir.

Lack of adequate public transport has added to the
difficulties in obtaining, or keeping, labour. All the railways
which opened up rural Northumberland in the nineteenth
century have been closed with the exception of the line from
Haltwhistle to Alston; and the closure of this line is under
discussion (Fig. 20). The little stations of the countryside,
Coanwood, Plashetts, Glanton and the rest, are derelict.
Tynemouth station, once noted for its flowers, is a shabby
memory of its past.

The growing pressure of urban demands on the countryside has led to other changes comparable in scale with the

---

[2] These statistics are obtained from the Northern Economic Planning
Council's *Challenge of the Changing North* (1967).

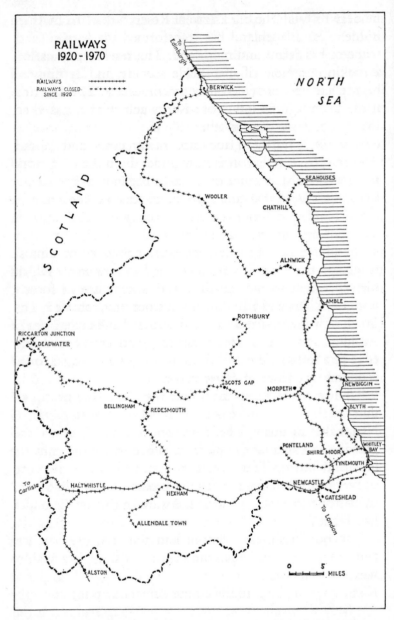

Fig. 20. The map shows the railway system at its height and after the closure of lines in modern times. The numerous small colliery lines have been omitted.

modern forests. The big Derwent Reservoir on the Durham border near Blanchland has transformed the former landscape of hill farms and moorland. The reservoir in itself is a striking example of man-made scenery. It is a thing of beauty and has provided new amenities. At the same time it has increased the influx of visitors and their cars and so, inevitably, it has been another step in the transformation of even the wide northern landscape into an urban playground. An even larger reservoir is now under discussion. This will require the submergence of much of the North Tyne valley from Kielder to Falstone, the large-scale construction of access roads, and hence the revolutionary transformation of the landscape and its way of life.

Urban needs, and the understandable need for urban man to escape from the environment he has created, have laid the coast under siege. Much of the Northumbrian coast is protected, albeit with difficulty, from modern demands. Much of it is studded with caravan parks and collections of seaside shacks, which are an affront to the landscape, on the edge of a sea where the bird-life is being slaughtered by the economic activities of *Homo sapiens*.

To meet urban needs in another form close on 400 square miles of the county have been declared the Northumberland National Park under a head warden based on Ingram, and provide an essential escape from office or factory into the hills and burns. Thus, on a fine summer weekend, cars converge onto the haughs of the Breamish and Coquet and transistor-noise mingles with the water-music of the Grasslees Burn.

The Border Forests, destined in time to cover an area almost one and a half times the size of Rutland,[3] are provided with well-designed camping and picnic sites, and car parks. Kielder Castle, built in the eighteenth century as a shooting

---

[3] Area now under trees: 125,907 acres; to be planted: 16,020 acres; agricultural and other uses 29,241 acres. See Forestry Commission, *Fiftieth Annual Report 1969–70*, pp. 47–8.

lodge for the dukes of Northumberland, and now occupied by the Forestry Commission, is a particularly attractive centre, with facilities for visitors and their litter unobtrusive against the magnificent backcloth provided by the Tynedale forests and fells. Under discussion is a park of a different type to replace in due course the open-cast mining behind Druridge Bay and to offer in the more austere coastal landscape of Northumberland some of the amenities of Battersea or the Ruislip Lido.

The energetic encouragement of modern tourism includes the Christian heritage as one of its principal attractions. To supplement the unique associations of Holy Island suggestions have appeared in the press that Bingo halls and other amusements should be provided by the daughter of that other island which established Christianity in Northumbria and gained Dr Johnson's famous tribute: "That man is little to be envied, whose patriotism would not gain force upon the plains of Marathon, or whose piety would not grow warmer among the ruins of Iona."[4]

Modern needs and conditions, which necessarily bring car parks, litter baskets and lavatories to the landscape, have changed the role of many of the great country houses. Northumberland is still distinguished by the activities in public life of those whose ancestors did so much to mould the modern county. It is still a land of large, well-maintained estates. Inevitably, in modern circumstances, some historic buildings have to serve new purposes. Ford Castle is now a teachers' training college; Wallington, the former home of Fenwicks, Blacketts and Trevelyans, belongs to the National Trust; Haggerston Castle is the centre of a caravan park; Kirkley Hall, the old seat of the Ogles, is occupied by the Northumberland College of Agriculture; and the sign of Welwyn Electric Ltd. is the modern equivalent of the medieval banner over Bothal Castle. Alnwick Castle is in part a college of education. Restrictions imposed by the

4 Since this was written these proposals have been rejected.

old-time gamekeeper appear in new guise for defence purposes on the moorlands of Redesdale and the wastes of the upper Irthing.

The great triumvirate of coal, shipbuilding and heavy engineering, together the power-house of nineteenth-century Northumberland, is now dissolved, with still incalculable consequences for the landscape. The decline of coal-mining has been more dramatic than its rise; it has been compressed within a few years. Between 1959 and 1969 employment in the coal industry was reduced from about 38,000 to about 16,500. The closing of pits all over the county has involved a new migration of population. Pitmen from Haltwhistle and Scremerston inhabit the new colliery village of Shilbottle Woodhouse. Amble and Blyth have ceased to be coal ports and have joined in the search for new industries. Even Ashington is destined to be superseded, as a coal town, by Ellington and Lynemouth, which are planned to produce four million tons of coal annually by the late 1970s. Changing sources of power and new developments have brought the power station of Cambois, which commands the coast no less impressively than Bamburgh and Dunstanburgh, and the installations of Alcan Ltd. dominating Newbiggin Moor.

The great slag heaps, such as those near Seghill and Ashington, are destined to disappear. The new landscape of the coastal plain is a landscape of overhead wires and pylons, and the wide new roads which are eating up the fields.

To those who knew the older Northumberland much of the transformation of the older landscape is not only progress but also improvement; in particular the contrast between some of the nineteenth-century coal towns and villages and the modern housing estates, such as those ringing Blyth or looking down on the Wansbeck from Ashington and Guide Post. But the improvement in material welfare is also the conversion of the distinctive Northumbrian landscape into a section of cosmopolitan suburbia reflecting the standardisation of twentieth-century culture. Newbiggin is once more a new town equipped with sailing dinghies and caravan parks, its decorative touches reminiscent of Jacksonville, Florida, or Tel Aviv. The thirteenth-century church on the headland, though still in use, discourages the casual visitor with locked doors. The Methodist chapel in Vernon Place, built for a small community of fishermen, is now decaying quietly, withdrawn from the modern environment.

A people cannot live on historical memories though people are inescapably the product of their history. Northumberland's population cannot live by evoking "the old song of Douglas and Percy", or the legionary trumpets on the Wall. The incidence of unemployment is high. The energy and planning which are manifest in the modern county are required to achieve a new industrial revolution to replace the debris of the old and will bring equally far-reaching changes.

The new towns of Cramlington and Killingworth are to provide new means of livelihood and prosperity in an area where, some twenty years ago, about three quarters of employment was in coal. Cramlington is designed as a town for over 62,000 inhabitants "in a country and rural setting", and "to obtain all the advantages of village life with the wealth of service obtainable in a very large town".[5] Killingworth is to accommodate 20,000 people, with town facilities for a further 30,000. Both are stimulating exercises in twentieth-century architectural design. Both are large-scale invasions of the countryside by the town, despite the nostalgic references to a 'rural setting' and 'village life' which suggest once again that modern man is an unwilling prisoner of his own environment. In conception and appearance both reflect the cosmopolitanism of modern technology. They are designed for 'successful living', a term,

[5] D. C. Slater, *Cramlington for Successful Living*, pp. 1–2.

much in vogue in modern advertisement, which invites a whole book for its analysis.

From Newcastle to Tynemouth an almost continuous belt of industrial and residential estates has been created since the 1939–45 war and linked with the commuters' belt on the coast by new roads. The rural landscape, which survived side-by-side with the collieries, is reduced to a vestige. Marden House and its farm survive from that older Northumberland, though now embedded in the bright houses and tidy gardens of the Marden Road.

The future of the Tyne as a port is in question. Lloyd's signal station is symbolically closed. The great iron-ore quay is silent. One of the most interesting experiences in modern Northumberland is to walk from North Shields to Newcastle close to the Tyne. Here were concentrated many of the achievements of nineteenth-century Northumberland as well as the problems bequeathed to the twentieth century. Both are recorded by the landscape in all its variety: the old Bible School in the Albion Road, North Shields, built in 1809, and the smoke-blackened stone and slate, of 1878, of the boys' school in Murray Road, Howdon; the shipyards of Swan Hunter, the tall cranes towering over rows of brick cottages and the derelict houses of Edward Terrace in Walker; Wincomblee Bridge, of 1865, and behind, on the bluff, the huge towers of Wardroper House, Hunter House and Merlay Hall, at their feet sad little trees with the tops pulled off; the red roofs of Beverley Terrace and Royston Terrace with their bright, well-tended gardens; Pottery Banks and the dreariness of the Walker Road; the Civic Centre and the tower-flats seen from under the railway bridge below Byker; the green, irridescent mud of the Ouseburn at low tide; the Tyne bridges under All Saints and St Nicholas.

No part of the Northumbrian landscape is changing more rapidly or more dramatically than the urban landscape of Newcastle itself. The process is as fundamental as in the days of Grainger and Dobson. The pace is such that written comment is soon outdated. Not only are new architectural styles involved but the more subtle question of the relationship of man to his urban environment.

The new Newcastle is the city of Swan House, a fine technical achievement without soul on a difficult but commanding site, which has wrested from castle and cathedral the primacy as the main architectural feature of the city when approached from the south. Justly described as "big and brutal in scale",[6] above the new wide and windy road system at the approaches to the Tyne Bridge, Swan House and its environs bludgeon the individual into insignificance in the face of technical and corporative power. It is the peer of the tower-flats of Shieldfield Green where the wind blows waste paper at their feet among the notices prohibiting football and other ball-games.

Above Quayside the eighteenth-century church of All Saints has been deconsecrated, preparatory to becoming part of a new entertainment centre amid office blocks. To the north, Eldon Square, one of the finest creations of urban architecture in England, is being converted into a hotel and shopping centre, a prime example of the difficulty of reconciling progress and improvement.

At Barras Bridge the new Civic Centre successfully and imaginatively creates a new focal point for the city and bringing into one harmonious whole the buildings of the nineteenth-century, such as the houses fringing the Great North Road and Jesmond Road, St Thomas's Church and the Hancock Museum. Here Newcastle has come to terms with new conditions by means of evolutionary growth.

Modern motor traffic has enforced a new road system upon Newcastle and on much of the coastal plain. Its consequences cannot yet be reckoned. That Jesmond is under sentence from a new motorway has been admitted in the reported statement of an official: "it was considered that

6 *The Journal* (Newcastle), 16.9.69.

some damage to the existing environment, some interference with customary routine, some inconvenience, and
some losses of amenity, were inseparable from schemes of
this kind."[7] The destructive aspects of modern technology,
and of the palliatives designed as a remedy, are self-evident
throughout much of the wide Northumbrian landscape
today. Corbridge Bridge and its approaches reek and shake
with traffic on a summer day. The unique walls of Berwick
have been challenged by the A1.

The demand for new roads, with all their direct and indirect consequences for the landscape and its inhabitants, is
intensified by economic development which, in its turn, is
spurred on by a high level of unemployment in the North-
East. Projects under discussion at the time of writing
include the construction of one of the largest paper-mills
in the country at Prudhoe, the removal of over three million
tons of gravel from Millfield Plain, in Glendale, and of some
600,000 tons of coal, by means of open-cast mining, at
Whittonstall near the Durham boundary.

The landscape is the work of man using the materials
provided by geology and climate and the instruments
created by intelligence. In Northumberland it has taken
some 6000 years to reach its present form since small groups
of Mesolithic people wandered near Bamburgh and
Budle Bay. Change was in progress when the grey stones on
the moors were first carved with the enigmatic rings and
cup-marks of a lost culture. It was intensified by the Anglian
farmers with axe and plough, by the introduction of the
stone castles and town life of Norman rule, by the sheep of
medieval monks. The eviction of sixteenth-century villagers
from Outchester and Hartley caused as much inconvenience
and interference with customary routine as are likely to be
experienced by the inhabitants of Jesmond. Eighteenth-
century improvers remodelled their rural heritage and
demolished villages; and judging by contemporary comment

[7] *The Journal*, 28.7.69.

no modern invention has aroused the same degree of awe and wonder as greeted the replacement of horse-power by steam.

What is new today is the pace and ubiquity of change, the all-enveloping shock of urban needs and values, in one form or another, over the county as a whole from the South Tyne under the Pennine fells to the crest of the Border ridge. It is these new factors which demand analysis of the term 'successful living' so casually used today.

Trevelyan's moving interpretation of the Border country, *The Middle Marches,* was written seventy years ago. Northumberland is still rich in the peace and beauty which he found on the Usway and Alwin. Newcastle is still rich in the monuments of an age which did not find economic growth incompatible with urbane architecture. But the whole landscape today, urban and rural, faces change more momentous for good or ill, and surely more fateful for successful living, than at any previous period of its age-long habitation by man.

SELECT BIBLIOGRAPHY

Burns, W. *Newcastle, a Study in Replanning at Newcastle upon Tyne* (1967).
Northern Economic Planning Council. *Challenge of the Changing North* (1967).
Northumberland County Council. *Northumberland; the County Handbook.*
Northumberland County Council. *Cramlington* (1963).
Northumberland County Council. *Killingworth* (1964).

Index

Acklington, 68; deer park, 116–17
Ad Gefrin, see Yeavering
Ad Murum, 145
afforestation, 37, 123, 236–7
agriculture, *A General View of the Ag. of Northumberland,* 123; modern, 25, 237
agricultural labourers, cottages of, 136, 140–1, 237; employment of, 138, 237
Akeld, 70
Akenshaw Bridge, 228; burn and toll road, 174, 228
Aldenscheles, medieval settlement, 89, 104
Alemouth Road, *see* Corn Road
Allendale Town, 172, 174; Common, 127; parish, 83
Allendales (East and West), 72, 81–82, 92, 172–3
Allenheads, 142, 173; church, 201
Alnmouth, 41, 89, 154–5; St John's church, 202
Alnham, church, 86, 200–1; and Salter's Road, 218
Alnwick, 56, 148–51, 205–6; castle, 100, 114–15, 205–6; church, 86; Lion Bridge, 150, 228; park, 117–18
Alston, 172, 232
Alwinton, 38, 56, 138, 218; church, 86; cultivation terraces, 93; hill fort, 47
Amble, 41, 182–3, 187
Anglians, Conquest by, 30–31, 52; place-names, 32, 55–58; settlements of, 31–32, 52–60; sites favoured by, 52–53; in western Northumberland, 55, 64

arable farming, 25, 40, 106; conversion to pasture, 109, 110, 111; frontier of, 38, 56
Armstrong, William George, 1st baron, 125, 198, 199, 208
Ashington, 174, 176–7, 241
Auchope Cairn, 212
Aydon Castle, 112

Backworth, 42, 109
Baliol barony, 86
Bamburgh, 30, 53, 155–8; castle, 27, 30, 53, 71, 88, 145; parish, 83; Newtown, 91–92, 107
Bamburghshire, 71, 83, 102, 138, 139, 217
Barrow Law, medieval boundary on, 96, 142
bastles, 101
Batailshiel Haugh, 38, 104
Beadnell, 41, 71, 126, 180, 217
Beal, stone houses, 137
Beaufront Castle, 115
Bede, The Ven. 145, 150
Bedington Iron Works, 230
Belford, 124, 225
Bellingham, 32, 36–37, 52, 55, 175; chapel, 87, 88
Bell's Kirk, 87
Belsay, castle and hall, 113
Benwell wood, emparked, 116
Bernicia, 30
Berwick, 23, 40, 54, 56, 146, 205; castle, 98, 146; bridges, 227, 231
Biddlestone, 107, 115, 118
'Big Geordie', excavator, 235
Birling, 32, 53, 92
Birtley, 93

247

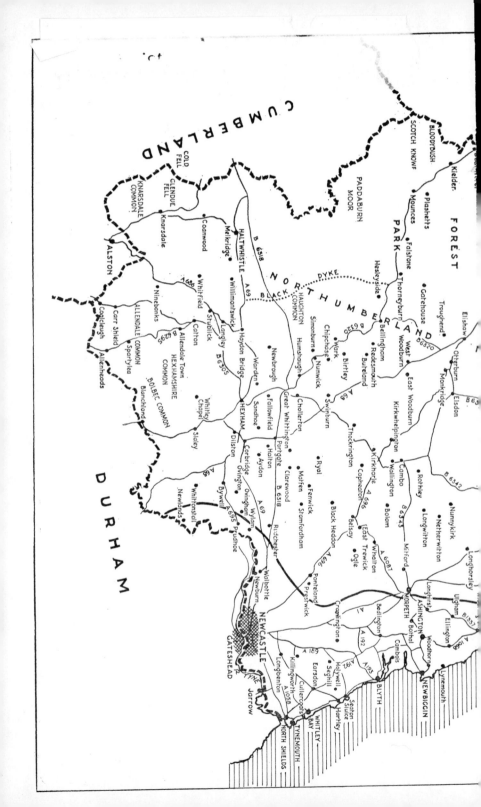